ACCLAIM FOR *SOUL-SICK NATION: AN ASTROLOGER'S VIEW OF AMERICA*

"…A rigorous eye-opener for anyone looking for a contemporary view [of] the U.S. chart. …In the current rage of interest in mundane astrology which includes Richard Tarnas and many more, this is undoubtedly a must-read and an enjoyable and entertaining experience throughout."

–Reviewed by John Townley, *AstroCocktail.com*

"Richard Tarnas's *Cosmos and Psyche* and Murray's *Soul-Sick Nation* are the two most important evolutionary astrology books written since Rhudyar issued his works – Tarnas's for describing individual and collective worldwide *histories*; Murray's for solving individual and collective American *mysteries*."

–Sao, Shamanic Astrologer

"This is not a dry, academic book for astrologers but rather a must-read for anyone with the slightest social conscience. Jessica has also provided hope, with the concept that each and every one of us can make a difference by gaining more understanding of ourselves, our lives and therefore our place in humanity as a whole."

–Sue Thompson, reviewed in *AstrologyHome.com*

"Jessica Murray's *Soul-Sick Nation* raises the symbol system of astrology to the level of a finely-honed tool for the critical work of social insight and commentary. …Just breathtaking!"

–Raye Robertson, author of *Culture, Media* and *the Collective Mind*

"Murray does not stop with her vast breadth of understanding and analysis of the dire troubles we face as a nation and as a planet today…. [She explains] what can be done by each of us as individuals to help alter the course of world disaster…."

–Vidya Frazier, author of *The Art of Letting Go*

"Jessica Murray has done the impossible: used astrology to explain America's current state of affairs. And she's done it with wisdom, wit, insight, and intelligence… This is a must-read book for anyone who cares about America."

–Paula Grace, consultant and writer

"The clarity and transparency of Ms. Murray's writing style allows the issues she illuminates to be explained in real terms in real-time. *Soul-Sick Nation* is that rare specimen of astrological writing which effectively transcends astrological myopia. This is a book for every intelligent and discerning bookshelf: Ms. Murray is able to shine a brilliant, yet nuanced light on our beloved country's paradoxical 'sickness' and its many opportunities to transform and heal itself."

–Adam Gainsburg, Soulsign Founder, author of *Chiron: The Wisdom of a Deeply Open Heart* and *The Soul's Desire & the Evolution of Identity*

"There is something – dare I call it fierce? – in Jessica Murray's tone as an author that is very powerful, cutting through the usual tentativeness about asserting astrological insights, as it relates to political trends. It spoke to something within me that said: Have courage, take a stand, trust in what you know."

–Molly Hall, *About.com:Astrology*

"Murray explores all of our goodies including: media, collective attitudes and justifications, even our democratic ideals.... With exceptional writing, this book is an absolute MUST for anyone concerned about the state of America's soul."

–Eric Meyers, *Astrologysight.com*

"Considering all the problems, issues and complexities of current national and global situations, many readers would likely rush to explore any book that could shed some light, reason and clarification on such issues. *Sick Nation* does just that for me. I was glued to its pages, rushing from page to page to discover insights and interpretations the news media never explains.

–Gayl Woityra, reviewed in *Booktalk phenomNEWS.com*

"This is a thorough investigation that leaves no stone unturned.... You don't need to know very much astrology to appreciate the points being made.... You will appreciate ...[Murray's] passionate desire to wake people up, make them aware, goad them out of apathy and into active participation in the new era."

–Sue Lewis, reviewed for *The Astrological Psychology Institute*, UK

"Her depth of psychological understanding, combined with an astute awareness of current social and cultural events, makes it relevant; and her wry sense of humor and scathing critical eye make it an energizing read. Pluto and Saturn have never made more sense!"

–Vicki Noble, author of Motherpeace, *Shakti Woman,* and *The Double Goddess*

"Jessica wrote the book for non-astrologers and astrologers alike, and she succeeded in making the book accessible to both. ...Suitable for everyone, interest in politics not required."

–Anne Massey, President of the Fraser Valley Astrological Guild and author of *Venus, Her Cycles, Symbols and Myths*

"*Soul-Sick Nation* is a truly remarkable book which will reward any reader who takes the time to read (and reread) it... I loved this book."

–Andrew Palmer, *Psychic* and *Spirit Magazine*

"...The book that can provide both an intellectual and emotional growth experience is rare. Such a book exists in Jessica Murray's *Soul-Sick Nation*, a trenchant yet ultimately loving indictment of the United States of America at the beginning of the 21st century. ...Murray clearly keeps her fingers on the pulse of current events and writes intelligently about how to view these events with astrological eyes... For the interested literate citizen of the world, Murray offers unique ideas and incentives to examine the self and mature toward one's potential as a way to heal the soul of the nation...and fulfill what Murray believes to be the U.S.A.'s highest calling: the responsible use of power."

–Natori Moore, C.A. NCGR reviewed in *SoulFoodAstrology.com*

"[Murray's] ability to See the Big Picture and to relate so many things to it is a beautiful process to behold, and [her] appreciation of the tiny pictures is as dear as a bug. [Her] Skywatches are beautiful and real and soaring with sense."

–Christine Helbling, writer, Tiburon

SOUL-SICK NATION

SOUL-SICK NATION

An Astrologer's View of America

Jessica Murray

Jessica Murray MotherSky Press
San Francicso

For information about special discounts for bulk purchases for educational, business, or sales promotional use, contact MotherSkyPress@gmail.com

First Jessica Murray MotherSky Press Printing, February 2008

Library of Congress Control Number: 2008900474

Cover design by Dee Turman
Author Photograph by Jason Langer

ISBN-13: 978-0-9814875-0-2
ISBN-10: 0-9814875-0-5

Printed in the United States of America on acid-free paper
10 9 8 7 6 5 4 3 2

Dedication

To meaning-seekers everywhere

Acknowledgment

Portions of this book first appeared, in altered form, in
THE MOUNTAIN ASTROLOGER MAGAZINE.

CONTENTS

PREFACE

Politics and astrology might at first seem strange bedfellows. Folks of a metaphysical persuasion tend not to resonate to the "political" label, and political thinkers tend not to give astrology the time of day. But it is time to shake off the constraints of both labels.

In its popular usage *politics* connotes something far narrower than its dictionary meaning, which is the study of systems of power. For many Americans the term evokes no more than the national infighting between two grotesquely stage-managed political parties. Why take it seriously, if it's just about a bunch of corrupt rich guys posing for photo ops? Meanwhile, the media hypes "politics" at the same time that it oversimplifies and compartmentalizes it, like a promoter putting on a big, meaningless show.

Thus do many Americans justify ignoring the most pressing questions that exist in the world today. Many who would self-describe as "apolitical" seem to believe that the fouling of the Earth's waterways or their government's use of torture or child soldiers in the Congo are of interest only to those who are *"into politics."* This marginalization of political awareness has resulted in America's failure to face the rest of the planet—and even its own struggling citizens—with empathy, a cornerstone of spiritual health. Neither a person nor a group can opt out of empathy without becoming soul-sick. To begin healing as a collective we must first of all recognize that what is being dismissed here is the arena where critical humanitarian, moral and spiritual dramas are being played out in the world. This isn't "politics"; it's real life. To shrug it off is to turn one's back on this moment in history.

It is time to consider astrology, too, in a larger way. The stakes are too high at this point in human evolution to keep the great truths of the ancients in a stuffy old library, or pursue them as a mere hobby. We need to pull out all the stops right now to see what is really going on in the world, and ancient wisdom confers the perspective without which such seeing is impossible. This book will seek to shed light on difficult and confusing global issues by looking at them from a celestial distance: a point of view that is vastly higher up and farther away than sociopolitical viewpoints alone can offer.

Astrology is a system of symbols that confers meaning on other kinds of systems, and as such it appeals to those whose primary drive is the search for meaning (a search which is, according to the positive psychology movement, far more predictive of life satisfaction than the pursuit of pleasure). More a spiritual language than a science, astrology requires a leap of faith—something astrologers ought not to be shy about asserting. It is an act of trust to believe that our birth-day means something—something very particular and very important—about who we are. It takes unconditional confidence in the cosmos to believe that we were put on the Earth in a specific location for a reason. Astrology is a very useful tool—not the only one, of course; it is one of a multitude—that can steer us back to this meaning, once our leap of faith has been taken.

A deep faith in cosmic appropriateness does not preclude skepticism; quite the contrary. A distinction needs to be drawn between our confidence in human beings and their societies, which are by definition flawed and often undeserving of our trust, and our confidence in that which is eternal and essential—let us call it Natural Law—in which our trust is always rewarded. "Trust in God," says an old proverb, "but tie up your camel." Our belief in the workings of the universe can be quite literally unconditional at the same time that our awareness of the imperfections of human agencies can be, and should be, sharp as a tack.

This book will look at the entity that is the USA as a collective soul whose high and noble potential has become dangerously distorted, to the point where the nation is in desperate need of the clear, critical vision of its citizens to turn it around. The airwaves and cyber-sphere are buzzing with critiques already, of course—some creative and some not so creative. Citizen criticism of an ailing society is crucial, but cataloguing flaws without perspective is destructive; and the last thing we need in this fraught scenario is more destructiveness. We need criticism that is intelligent, imaginative and healing.

Astrology is an ideal way to approach issues that are rancorous and frightening, because it is a way of perceiving that is exceptionally pure and abstract. When the state of the world is described in the language of cosmic principles, it helps us remember that the strivings and errors of human beings, as immense and all-involving as they are, are still just components of an immeasurably larger whole. And when we remember this, the folly we see around us takes on a cosmic sense. We start to glimpse the meaning in it, and the meaning of our presence in it.

San Francisco, California
September 2006

ONE

SOUL-SICK

AMERICA IN CRISIS

Our world is in crisis.

There have been natural disasters throughout the ages, as FEMA officials are quick to remind us. But it is not the natural disasters that concern us here. Any earthquakes or tsunamis the current epoch may have in store are dwarfed by the horrors wreaked upon the planet by humanity itself.

Over the last hundred years the proud human mind has developed the technology to mechanize war; to the point where we are capable of destroying everything alive; and after a brief hiatus, the nuclear arms race is once again in full swing. Business cabals have grown more soulless as they have grown more powerful, taking over government and civic life in the First World and wiping out local economies in the Third World. Western science, once heralded as the balm of all ills, has been harnessed by profiteers to create drugs which do not heal, seeds which do not regenerate, plastics which do not decompose and fuels whose poisons undermine the very geological cycles upon which human, plant and animal life depend.

Humanity has set itself up either to break down or break through.

Moreover, it has become impossible to ignore the fact that the entity at the lead of this perilous trajectory is the USA. Right now, for better or for worse, as America goes—so goes the world. This means that America is where we must look for both a diagnosis and a cure.

It is time to acknowledge that the USA is suffering from a profound soul-sickness. I mean this neither as rhetoric nor as mere metaphor. We must accept that America is gravely and epically ill if we are to begin the only possible treatment: a shift in consciousness.

America's Crisis of Maturity

America is a country barely out of diapers, historically speaking, that has ended up basically in charge of the fate of the Earth. What does this mean, in the big picture?

On the level of cultural personality, it means that in the USA, youth is king; juvenility is cool. Much has been written about the adolescent quality of American society, a feature that foreign observers tend to regard with dismay but which Americans themselves seem to accept with a kind of swaggering pride—which is, of course, what teenagers do. When the satirical German magazine *Der Spiegel* portrayed the American president as a comic-book superhero on its cover a few years ago, the man was not offended. He was flattered.

With the USA behind the wheel and the rest of the world in the backseat, it becomes critical to understand the nature of this immaturity. The nation's obsession with physical youthfulness has been widely noted; the very word "mature" has become a euphemism for *no longer young and beautiful* (e.g. *mature* skin; *mature* actresses[1]). But America's chronological immaturity is not the problem. The problem is spiritual immaturity, which is far more insidious. It is upon the non-physical aspects of its citizens that America's cult of immaturity has inflicted its most deadly damage. The USA lacks a maturity of mind and soul.

Maturity is not the same thing as intelligence. Americans suffer no lack of intelligence, if only in the classical sense of the word: access to education and information, of which they have a surfeit. But if we do not read deeply enough in the newspaper, behind the puff pieces and beyond the enormously distracting game-playing of national politics; and if we do not listen between the lines of the blaring television lead stories to see patterns of meaning, all that information serves us not at all. The failure of Americans to process the information they have is a problem of maturity.

Virtually every aspect of American culture betrays the fact that the American mind suffers from a deadening superficiality. The country's religious institutions have calcified into bureaucratic dogmatism, as institutions will, and have lost their ability to engage the numinous imagination. Church theologies do not help to form the questions that would lead parishioners deeper into their soul-lives; instead they offer pat answers to only those questions church fathers say should be asked. Religious seekers are not encouraged to seek at all; one is supposed to learn one's answers by rote, as children recite the ABCs.

Theology in its most simplified form is fundamentalism, which one can find everywhere except in a social context informed by spiritual maturity. Were we encouraged from childhood to develop our spiritual selves—to cultivate our own unique cosmological understanding with increasing artistry as we aged—the notion of a literal, static Paradise would find no takers. Such a reductionist picture of the infinite inter-

---

[1] The word's other prevalent usage, to signal pornography ("*mature* audiences"), distorts the concept of maturity into a virtual oxymoron.

cyclic universe would be viewed as a bizarre attempt by clerics to keep people in arrested development spiritually.

If philosophical maturity were valued in America, a policymaker would be hired for the subtlety of his or her ideas. An elected official would be laughed off the podium if he came out with the kind of absurd black-and-white pronouncements that we have recently been hearing under the auspices of authoritative decree. Bad-guy/good-guy characterizations would be confined to kindergarten discussions, just as stick-figure drawings are appropriate at only the very beginning levels of making art. For a leader to declare that the rest of the world is "either with us or against us," or that his enemies "hate freedom" would be considered insulting to the intelligence of his listeners. That such phrases are currently being voiced by a regime that topples self-determined governments worldwide and spies on its own citizens bespeaks a hypocrisy too obvious to belabor.

Were political maturity valued in our civilization, pundits would be judged on the basis of their critical thinking. Government spokesmen would not dare to tell journalists to "watch what they say," as if they were naughty children at a dinner party. Were ideological maturity the goal in public discourse, sound bites would be relegated to selling chewing gum, not used to sum up world affairs. Historical complexity would inform what was written on the Op Ed page. It is doubtful whether the public would have gone along with the invasion of Iraq, for example, had American newspapers accompanied their reporting of Saddam Hussein's weapons capabilities with at least a fleeting mention of the fact that Washington helped him attack Iran with chemical weapons in the '80s. As it is, information-vendors blatantly indulge the public's alarmingly short attention span, instead of expanding its understanding by providing intelligent context.

It is no accident, of course, that television does almost nothing to challenge the public's ignorance. The American telecommunications industry has fundamentally changed over the past few years, as we will see in Chapter Seven. A few immensely powerful conglomerates now control all the major media outlets, and the industry's ties to Washington have never been tighter. Consumers of the evening news who imagine that this will not skew the information they are receiving have not heard the tale of the fox guarding the hen house.

And what about consumer maturity? In a capitalistic society, free thinkers are a liability because they are less likely to follow orders as to what to consume. Fashion, whether in clothes, tech toys or foreign policy, depends upon suggestibility and conformity; and both are more likely when the self is insecure or undeveloped. Blue jeans manufacturers may insist that by buying their jeans, purchasers are making a wild and crazy statement of uniqueness; but the truth is that self-aware individuals are unlikely to throng into Macy's to take up the latest sartorial trend.

Youth is by definition a phase of life with a shaky ego-structure, and it is to youth that most of the advertising in America is directed. As teenagers, instead of a solid identity we have a yearning to fit in with our peers; which makes us a Madison Avenue gold mine. By the time we reach chronological adulthood, we have theoretically developed the requisite ego cohesion to be able to say, "That may be a nice pair of jeans, but I do not need it in order to have a self-image." It is the mature buyer who is more likely to beware. But in a cultural milieu where chronological age does not guarantee true maturity—indeed, where most forms of maturity are suspect at best and despised at worst—such discernment is not encouraged to fully develop. Without discernment, we are left with insecurity; and we buy whatever the cleverest advertisement is selling.

As I write these words, the clique of oilmen who run this country are trying to bully the nation into yet another war, a plan whose obvious moral, financial, geopolitical and even military indications feel to many Americans like a nightmarish déjà vu. The prototype for the current saber-rattling against Iran is, of course, the invasion of Iraq, for which the president's viziers began their big media push the day after September 11, 2002. They made no bones, then, about trying to *sell* the war, publicly admitting that their timing was "a centerpiece of the strategy"—that is, the strategy to exploit the fear and grief of the citizenry on the anniversary of the World Trade Center attacks. Indeed, they went so far as to make mention of the conventional marketing wisdom to delay the introduction of a new product until after Labor Day.

Being targeted, pitched at, and gulled is so much a part of the life of the average American consumer that as one hears these businessmen-cum-politicians smugly discussing the details of their plans to sell campaigns of massive death and suffering, one is almost numb enough to accept it. The movie "Wag the Dog," which presented as laughable just a few years ago a situation very similar to what is happening now, would fail as satire today because the scenario has lost its giggle of implausibility. The darkly ridiculous has become the darkly unremarkable.

The antidote to this lethal folly is for the US public to reclaim its moral adulthood. An emergency dose of intellectual maturity must be summoned up, in order to expose and denounce the appalling onslaught of propaganda polluting the mass media. Americans must begin to inform themselves through alternative means—for example, the international press—as to what is really going on in the world. Emotional maturity is needed, too, an example of which would be for Americans to modify their 9/11 mourning rituals to reflect a sense of proportion: the reality is that since 2001, killings in Afghanistan, Iraq, Palestine, Lebanon and other places in the world—bought and paid for by American taxpayers—have surpassed by many, many times the number of Americans killed that dreadful day.

Spiritual maturity would mean refusing to be infantilized by morally bankrupt leaders, no matter what ideology or political party they belong to. It would mean trying, like big girls and boys, to rein in fear and reactivity, and opt instead to follow a planetary vision bolstered by a genuine curiosity about what is going on outside the country's borders. Such maturity would mean citizens rousing themselves out of denial and credulity, and taking stock of what one's government is doing in one's name. It would mean using the thinking mind independently, grounding the self in the facts while centering the self in the heart.

It's time to grow up now. I propose in this book that within every one of us is a magnificent potential maturity, designed to be grown into, to be lovingly cultivated as we age. We must take another look at our particular version of adulthood, re-interpret it, embrace it and put it into action. If we do not, we will suffer, and cause suffering, like lost and dangerous children.

The Way Back to Sanity

Let us cut to the punch, because the situation is urgent. Every one of us with a social conscience and an affection for this small, blue planet has been casting about for a way to address the insanity of our times, and the unique role the USA plays in them. From podiums across the land, from pulpits, lecterns and blogs, we get a raucous cacophony of points of view; there is certainly no lack of opinion out there. But how does a conscientious person approach a state of affairs so immense and complex without being overwhelmed? How do we avoid being just one more futile cry amidst the culture wars?

I propose that before we commit ourselves to action, we must commit to understanding. And for this understanding we need a conceptual model that is sufficiently vast and deep to provide a real perspective, the kind of perspective that is woefully lacking in so many of the social analyses being attempted. Astrology, a symbolic system that has been around since the beginning of time, elucidates the essential purpose of living beings: both individuals and group entities. When subjected to astrological study, the chart of a person—or a country—

reveals core values, inclinations, motivations, blind spots and soul lessons that help explain otherwise incomprehensible patterns of behavior. And the same chart contains clues that point the way towards healing.

This is the kind of insight we need right now. We need a way of seeing that reaches beyond cultural assumptions, while making sense of those very assumptions. This kind of insight can be found from a study of the birth chart of the USA (the entity born July 4, 1776 in Philadelphia, Pennsylvania[2]) and from certain astrological patterns (*transits*) that offer time-specific teachings for humanity. In the following chapter, we will begin our exploration of this chart by a means that is perhaps the most familiar: through studying its Sun, Moon and Rising Sign (also known as *the Ascendant*). After that, we will look at other of its key planets and aspects in order to get a fuller perspective on what is making America soul-sick.

The final chapters of this book will invite the reader to consider how each of us might come up with creative responses to the acute distress our epoch is in. This study will make the case that the only way to effectively heal our collective sickness is by dedicating ourselves to bold, clear understanding of the situation. Can the quality of our individual consciousness really make a difference? I will argue that it is the only thing that makes a difference. Living mindfully is not just a spiritual hobby, nor merely a personal matter at all. As the great teachers have told us throughout the ages, a mindful human being becomes the agent through which consciousness comes into the world.

---

[2] See Page 203 in Appendix I for a discussion of the astrological theory behind national birth charts.

TWO

THE CHART OF THE USA
SUN, MOON AND RISING SIGN

Before we launch into our study of the US chart (see Page 220), a few words need to be said about the approach to astrology used in this book, especially for those who have not studied the subject in depth. For those readers who are completely new to astrology, please refer to the user-friendly Astrological Appendix I on Page 196, for further explanations of basic principles and definitions of terms.

Astrology: Maligned, Misrepresented and Misunderstood
The bad press astrology gets is really a shame, and more than enough to make a reader of a book like this wary. Somewhere along the line astrology got misconstrued as a caricatural personality identification game that seeks to stereotype people one way or another. A person visiting an astrologer for the first time might even wonder whether he'll have to defend his view of himself against that of a stranger who claims to have an inside scoop—reductionistic but somehow magically authoritative—on who he is.

Moreover, most people are under the unshakable impression that modern astrology exists to make predictions. Certainly, centuries ago this was true, and many astrologers still make predictions, especially in those societies such as India where the predominating worldview follows a more fatalistic bent. It is spiritual psychology, however, rather than divination, that underlies much contemporary astrology in the West.

These days, aficionados of Western astrology tend to use the rudimentary question "What's your sign?" to sum up the infinite complexity of a person's astrological profile. Its answer provides, at best, a thumbnail sketch; referring as it does only to the Sun sign in the natal chart[1]—whereas there are nine other planets[2] (all in various signs with various geometrical interrelationships) that together constitute the

---

[1] Also known as the *birth chart*. For further description, see Page 203.

[2] Astrologers include the Sun and the Moon among the planets when interpreting a chart. As for Pluto, see the footnote on Page 13.

horoscope's basic data. To know only our Sun sign is to know something about our core life purpose, to be sure, but it is only the beginning. As is often pointed out (especially by those who know nothing about astrology except that they don't believe in it), everyone born within the same roughly thirty-day period will have the same Sun sign; how much meaning could be expected from a category that general? Astrologers realize only too well that knowing just this one piece of the chart doesn't go very far to explain human individuality.

Then there is the slightly more meaningful opening gambit to the chart—not sophisticated enough to keep astrologers from wincing, but better than "What's your sign?"—that includes not only the Sun but the Moon and the Rising Sign too, combining them into a handy shorthand astro-ID. These are the three bits of data one might be asked at a cocktail party (at least in San Francisco). They give us just enough information to begin to understand a chart, as a smiley-face drawing would to represent a human being. So though it may make the serious astrologers shudder, this might be the easiest way to begin our study of the chart of the USA.

The USA's Sun in Cancer

As explained on Page 204 of the Astrological Appendix at the back of this book, the Sun sign expresses the basic life force of the native[3]. It sums up the core reasons he, she or it is alive. In an individual natal chart, the Sun sign conveys in very general terms the main plot of the story that is their life; and in a country's chart, the essential meaning is the same. The fact that the USA was born with its Sun in Cancer[4] means that throughout its lifetime the nation will be grappling with the three core issues of Cancer: security, nourishment and shelter.

There is an uncomplicated innocence to Cancer; its imagery is that of family picnics and apple pies. But as an unconscious water sign, its central impulses are also darkly primitive, fed by the Mother/Child archetype. This suggests that the world's great superpower is actually driven by the fears and yearnings of an ingenuous child, one who is all bound up in its own safety and comfort. (In this instance astrologers cast their lots with the Freudians in finding significance in the American obsession with women's breasts.)

There is a higher potential to the Cancer archetype, too—clues to which we can see in the country's sometime need to take care of the world like an epic Mother. This is the sign of the protective home, a

---

[3] The *native* is the entity the chart describes.

[4] The Sun is not the only planet in Cancer in the US chart: Jupiter, Venus and Mercury are there too; and this cluster operates as a whole, strengthening the Cancer effect.

theme poignantly expressed in the famous lines inscribed on the Statue of Liberty that welcomed so many thousands of the world's "tired and poor" to New York Harbor. Cancer also governs food, as is signified by the country's immense agricultural capacity—vividly symbolized by the bushels of foreign aid the country was once known for giving away—as well as by the psychological emphasis Americans give to eating, and its inverse, dieting.

The nuclear family strikes a distinctly sentimental chord in American political and popular discourse, but actual families receive relatively little logistical and economic support. This irony is easier to understand when we remember that water signs like Cancer are fueled by emotional energy, not practical or intellectual energy. Cancer's meaning encompasses all aspects of the hearth-and-home archetype, from real estate to native land; which explains the peculiar primacy of home ownership in the highly charged notion of "The American Dream." It also explains the nation's historic isolationism and distrust of foreigners. In a Herculean effort to keep outsiders out, at this writing there is a plan afoot to construct a 700-mile-long steel wall at the Mexican border: sort of a white picket fence on steroids. These are story lines in the national saga to which we will return.

The next step in our interpretation is to factor in the meaning of the seventh house, where the US Sun resides. As explained in Appendix I (see Page 206), astrological *houses* provide another layer of meaning to planetary placements; and in the case of the US Sun it is a critical layer. The seventh house is that of friends and foes, and the agreements we make with them—or fail to make. This placement intensifies all of the country's relationship issues: alliances and enmities, business and legal partnerships—and marriage, an institution which has become ground zero of the country's culture wars, as recent transits attest. The following chapters will look at these issues in depth.

The USA's Moon in Aquarius

The Moon in this chart is in Aquarius, a sign associated with information (especially in the third house of communication and media, where it falls[5]) and advanced technology. The USA is a breeding ground for inventive opinions, scientific innovations and futuristic ideas, whether or not they are implemented or even widely understood.

---

[5] There are schools of thought which place this chart's planets in different houses, based on varying ideas about the nation's moment of "first breath." In this book we refer to the most widely used version of the US natal chart—the *Sibly chart*—which derives from the most likely signing time of the Declaration of Independence in Philadelphia, Pennsylvania on July 4th, 1776. See Page 203 of Appendix I.

Aquarius is a mental sign and the Moon is an emotional planet. This suggests that although the country's self-image as a "land of the free" is based on fine, high ideas, they are held with such subjective feeling that it is difficult for Americans to perceive the issue with clarity. Without a doubt, the right of every citizen to express his or her uniqueness (Aquarius) is more than an opinion in the American mind: it is a dyed-in-the-wool emotional conviction (Moon). But these impulses are no guarantee of freedom reaching the level of practical policy; the Moon is an instinctive, fluctuating body, not known for consistency.

This fluctuation is about to increase exponentially, as the US Moon is hit by the oceanic planet Neptune (peaking 2008-9). The national self-image is due for a sea change. This period suggests confusion and disillusion on a massive scale, as well as the potential for a collective spiritual breakthrough. It is one of several planetary patterns over the next few years—as we will see in Chapter Twelve—that signal a confrontation between the nation's traditional ideals, its unconscious fears and the unprecedented requirements of the epoch itself.

The USA's Sagittarius Rising

The Rising Sign in any chart expresses the *persona* of the native—the entity's outward form—and in this regard America is a veritable Sagittarian poster child[6]. This sign is known for its enthusiasm, optimism and relentless excess. Sagittarius is blusteringly proud, bold, open-minded and self-righteous at once. The symbol of Sagittarius is an arrow flying forth from a bow; it governs exploration (*Go West, young man*) and foreign travel, personified by the waves of immigration that settled this vast land. In popular astrology, Sagittarius is associated with cowboys, proselytizers and naifs—all stereotypical of the American personality in the eyes of the rest of the world. In Chapter Six we will go into this archetype in more detail, discussing the overriding natal theme of which it is a part.

The USA's Sun, Moon and Rising Sign give us the barest glimpse of what might be called *the American personality*. The more of the chart we explore, the fuller a picture we will get of the nation whose soul path we seek to understand.

Groups and individuals

Let us take a moment at this juncture to state the obvious: countries, like all other groups, are made up of individuals. For Americans, in particular, to come to grips with the meaning of the USA's

---

[6] See footnote, Page 203. The Sibly chart features Sagittarius rising.

fundamental soul character and its ailments is not merely an abstract conceptual exercise. In astrology it is axiomatic that individuals reside where they do for a reason.

Popular astrology places so much emphasis upon the personality characteristics of the natal chart that we tend to forget this basic metaphysical dictum: that our individual reality and our collective reality are two sides of the same coin. Every culture is blessed and benighted with its own peculiarities, each of which is tailor-made for every individual who chose to belong to that group. No matter how much we may prefer to see our own opinions as distinct from those of the mass mind, if we are brought up amidst painfully skewed financial values, for example, they will have an inescapable effect on our personal value system. Thus does astrology presuppose that there is a psychic give-and-take between Americans and America. A concrete expression of this give-and-take is the paying of taxes. In San Francisco, for example, last year both pro-war and anti-war households alike paid five out of thirteen thousand of their tax dollars, on the average, to fund the military.

Conscious Choice vs. Super-Conscious Choice

I have said that we each "chose" our own group, but the word needs clarification: it implies conscious volition, so our impulse is to balk at its use in this context. It suggests that ego desires are responsible for our being born in a certain location, or ending up somewhere even in the case of forced immigration or hardship. In order to believe we "choose" such things, one has to presume the existence of a soul that masterminds these choices. Most astrologers maintain that each of us has a soul identity, which, for its own mysterious cosmic purposes, does choose everything that happens to us, including our birthplace and time.

It follows that, as surely as one is indelibly bonded with the parents one was born to–not just actually, but psychologically—one is a part of one's country for better or worse; and this bonding has a psycho-spiritual meaning. In a karmic sense, if not in an electoral sense, we each have a relationship with our country's soul path as surely as we do with its popular culture and climate. This is so whether that relationship is enthusiastic, antagonistic or completely unconscious. And as with all relationships, this one can be used to burn off karma—both our own karma and that of the group.

Many of us have tried over the years to understand the blind spots in our family of origin, so as to keep them from becoming our own blind spots. The same process must be undergone with national blind spots if we want to live free of them.

The US Pluto

The next step in our analysis of the US chart will be to look at its Pluto. This is the planet of regeneration, and we must know how it works if we want to plumb the deeper meaning of America's identity crisis and its impact on the world. Pluto allows us to hold our gaze at that which is otherwise frightening and taboo; it lets us look at horrors without being horrified. It holds the secret to integrating whatever has been hidden and unnamed—within an entity's consciousness and without, in the global situation. Pluto, the planet of secrets, will give us the vocabulary to look at what is making America sick.

THREE

God of Secrets
The Planet Pluto

Pop astrology has saddled Pluto with an aura of lugubrious intrigue. Its lore is so loaded with superstition that serious students soon find the gulf between *sort of* understanding Pluto and truly understanding it to be wide indeed. But this tiny little planet[1] is what put the *power* in *superpower*; and we need to know what it is really about.

Mundane Rulerships of Pluto
We will begin our study of Pluto in the way most textbooks do, by citing some of its *mundane rulerships*[2], which range from the ridiculous to the sublime: sex and death; recycling; lost objects; mines and caves; detectives, spies and powerbrokers, the occult; the atom bomb; snakes, vultures and bats.

Okay, good: vultures and bats. But what does it mean that a planet can "govern" *sex* and *death*? At this point the student may ask himself, Does it also govern drugs and rock & roll, for heaven's sake? No matter where Pluto is placed in our natal chart, we've probably

---

[1] Though a committee of international astronomers declared Pluto no longer technically a *planet* as of August 24, 2006, we will use the term *unamended* for the time being (the word's literal meaning is simply *wanderer*; and Pluto's wanderings persist despite its size). Since Pluto's "discovery" in 1930 astronomers have been debating its classification, and astrologers take even longer to render judgment. Readers of archetypes rely on a gradual buildup of associations over time before making definitive statements about celestial developments. We wait for world events to suggest correlations, and we allow impressions to coalesce in the collective mind; all the while taking into consideration that Plutonian events, in particular, are never as they first appear. At this point the only layer of meaning we can be sure of about Pluto's official change in status, and about the nature and systemic relevance of the Kuiper Belt of which it is a part, is the most obvious one: that modern science has refined its technology to the point where more and more bodies are being discovered up there in the sky, more details about them are becoming known and humanity's impressions of them are changing faster and faster. The job of astrologers is to apply Hermetic Law – As Above, So Below – to this new information: to de-code these developments as their meaning becomes apparent.

[2] Mundane rulerships are compiled lists of everyday phenomena that have been assigned to each planet by astrologers over the centuries. See Page 200.

experienced sex, and most assuredly we will experience death. Clearly Pluto's mundane rulerships, though they give us a place to start, do not tell us what the planet means. We need to read between the lines— between the spaces of the various entries on the list—to discover their common themes.

Endings and Beginnings

The most profound of these themes is that of endings and beginnings, and the mysterious processes that link the two.

Beginnings constitute one side of the Plutonian coin, and in this category astrology places procreation, sexuality and childbirth. Sex belongs to Pluto, whether we're talking about the hormones of orgasm, the abortion debate, the practice of tantra, or the porn industry.

The *endings* side of the Plutonian coin is represented by breakdowns of all kinds, including the death of the human body. All the ceremonies and trappings of death belong to Pluto: from the solemn sanctifications of funerary ritual to the necrophilic titillations of horror movies. Pluto also governs the process of decomposition: corruption, putrefaction, toxicity and pollution. This includes both literal dirt and figurative "dirt" (tabloid scandals).

Though it may strike the modern thinker as odd that astrology considers birth and death to be dual aspects of the same symbol, we have a law of physics that sums up the same idea: energy is neither created nor destroyed, it just changes form. Astrologically speaking, that change is governed by Pluto, whose laws preside over the netherworld between death and rebirth[3]. Pluto governs the "death" of not just living things but of objects, and their subsequent reassembly into new objects. Recycling and sewage plants are expressions of Pluto; as is the fascination with *Extreme Makeovers*.

So *rebirths* of every stripe belong to Pluto. The scientific and cultural flowering in Europe that we call the Renaissance was a Plutonian phenomenon. So is the born-again Christian, the transgender faction of the gay rights movement, and the rehab industry. These are governed by Pluto because they feature a person dying to her old self and starting over with a new identity[4].

---

[3] It is a peculiarity of the current era that this realm has lost all intellectual legitimacy, and has become the niche interest of spiritualists and purgatory theorists.

[4] It could be argued that the whole point of Pluto is rebirth, which a precedent death simply supports: there can be no resurrection without a corpse. In Western culture, of course, it is death that gets all the attention, with rebirth relegated to a conceptual sub-category if considered at all. It is easy to see why the death part of the equation has come

In the process of breaking something down and renewing it, tremendous power[5] is released. Plutonian power is neither fast nor flashy; it is intense and thorough, for it has built-up slowly from invisible depths, like fossil fuel. In the chart of a country, this takes the form of formidable forces that operate below the surface of collective consciousness, accumulating their power slowly enough to occupy an entrenched and relatively unquestioned position...like Congressional lobbies; and, as we will see, literal fossil fuel.

Pluto and Power

In the chart of an individual, Pluto is the source of the greatest power available to the native. When it is fueling the ego, it often shows up as behavior that feels "driven." When it is fueling a collective entity, it shows up as institutional forces that have insidious and pervasive impact. Lifestyles, work choices and relationship decisions informed by natal Pluto are possessed of a certain *you-can't-go-home-again* finality. If a person has Pluto strongly influencing Mercury (opinions) in his chart, for example, he may change his mind with drastic, mortal decisiveness. Such is the power of the clean break. We see in Pluto's group function that whole sectors of society sometimes have to break down in order to change at all (e.g. American economic policies before and after the Great Depression).

Plutonian power is primitive and sub-rational, and it must be mitigated by the rest of the chart in order to be applied in a healthy way. All by itself, Pluto is unapologetically amoral, leaving such niceties as social considerations and moral responsibility to the other planets. Plutonian impulses are too raw to be expressed on their own. Unless softened by Venus and Jupiter (personal and ethical values) and boundaried by Saturn (civil law), our Plutos wouldn't be allowed out in polite society. Unalloyed, the planet would get us locked up, or impeached for war crimes (that is, they would in a working democracy).

Pluto makes whatever house it's in a magnet for make-or-break experience. Even ordinary functions of the house in question have a non-ordinary feeling about them; a larger-than-life quality. As we will see, the activities suggested by Pluto's natal house possess an intensity that

---

to get all the press. Where there is collective disbelief in the existence of the soul, death is seen *not* as a phase in an irreducible cycle, but as an isolated event—and an uncommonly baffling one. But in Plutonian terms, dying has no meaning except as a precursor to rebirth. There is huge diversity in the ways the death/rebirth cycle is viewed from culture to culture and from individual to individual, and Pluto governs them all.

[5] The word *power* as used here is to be distinguished from *force*, which is more superficial and does not involve irreversible change.

eludes simple explanations or even psychological analyses; and the people, places and institutions belonging to that house may seem as if they are charged with supernatural power.

Underground and Undercover

Pluto is also the governor of secrets: students of classical mythology will remember that this god wore a helmet of invisibility. Astrological tradition links Pluto with anything kept underground, literally (bunkers, caves, oil) and figuratively (spies, heretical thinkers, terrorists). Its mundane associations include objects that are out-of-sight (classified documents, microscopic particles) as well as psychological complexes that are out-of-sight (suppressed memory syndrome; "blind spots", cultural taboos). In the natal chart, Pluto governs those energies that we keep under wraps because we would be embarrassed to publicly proclaim them, like sexual urges and private compulsions. Whether we see these feelings and habits as valuable or shameful does not change their peculiar power.

Modern astrology has given Pluto rulership over psychology, the study of the secrets of the human mind, as well as over the occult traditions that predated psychology: those of the shamans who went between the worlds, and of the alchemists whose inquiries took them into the Dark Mysteries, as they were once called. To the Greeks and Romans, Hades/Pluto was the god of underground riches: jewels and precious ores whose extreme value is partly a function of how difficult they are to unearth. In a country's chart, Pluto gives clues to the national psychology—the meanings of its crazes, obsessions and collective shames—as well as its hidden resources, both literal and figurative.

As the governor of hidden things, Pluto is associated with those social interchanges which exist *under the radar*: black markets, secret police, clandestine affairs, covert conflict. It governs off-the-books government policies (e.g. the high-level leaking of classified information; rendition; the outsourcing of illegal incarceration techniques) as well as international smuggling networks and saboteurs. Whether conducted by elected officials or enemies of the state, Pluto governs activities that are indirect by design. To the extent that such behaviors succeed, it is by undermining extant systems, not by confronting them in open conflict.

Whatever house Pluto is in natally shows us where we have been operating undercover. The act of hiding may be enforced and deliberate, as when we swear to secrecy; or it may be inadvertent, as when we repress desires that would humiliate us were they made public. Thus the placement of Pluto in our natal chart provides clues about the secrets we keep from ourselves. Pluto's shadow holds our repressions, both individual and collective. Any study of Pluto must include a look at the mechanics of secret-keeping, which has a logic to it—a logic which, considered astrologically, can be understood without making a pathology out of it.

Taboo

This is a key point, because these explorations involve broaching issues that are usually shuttered with extravagantly negative judgments. One of the reasons a study of Pluto is so necessary is that dispassionate thinking about taboo topics, whether in the personal or collective sphere, is rarely done.

In American society, sex, death and the occult are the three big taboos. Indeed, a good indication of their Plutonian rulership is the fact that there are libraries in existence in this country today that would ban books about them.

When Pluto Work is done within the self—a process we will look at in depth in Chapter Thirteen—it involves the examination of energies unobserved and un-debated by the self. When expressed socially, Pluto Work may involve research into topics undiscussed by polite society—as it did for Oscar Wilde, who brought not only himself but a whole cultural reality out of the closet; for Elizabeth Kubler-Ross, who wrote about death without sentiment or fear; and for Jessica Mitford, whose muckraking blew the cover off the American funeral industry.

Pluto in the Houses

The next step in understanding Pluto is to see how it impacts whichever one of the twelve houses it resides in. To factor in the houses is like ushering an actor—in this case a very powerful actor—onto a certain stage and letting him go to work: the setting, the props and the lighting will determine the nature of his performance. The reader is encouraged to download a natal chart if she does not already have one (see Page 210), and then to use the delineations in Appendix II to look up her natal Pluto house placement. The USA chart features Pluto in the second house of money and material possessions, which we will examine in Chapter Four.

In general, a Pluto residency imbues the circumstances of whatever house it's in with an aura of incipient power: the relevant activities bear the stamp of nothing less than the destruction-and-rebirth cycle. A person born with Pluto in the sixth house of work will tend to be impacted by a job change as if it were a death leading to a new beginning. The most everyday experiences may feel as if they are mortal dramas. Whereas the eleventh house of friends might denote a casual and ordinary department of life for the native who has Venus there, for example, the native who has Pluto there may see friendships and the drives they inspire as nothing less than transformative, though fraught with peril.

As always, we will get more out of these astrological shorthand delineations if we look at them metaphorically rather than literally. For instance, we might read in an old astrology book that Pluto in the seventh house means "the death of a spouse"; and while we might find the suggestion ethically irresponsible (not to mention unlikely), we will still find it useful if we read it as a metaphor. For the native with this Pluto position the departure of a partner is likely to be so thorough that the person may as well have literally died. Such placements do not tell us whether the "death" will be external or internal. Pluto's manifestations are often not outwardly visible at all, except as an intense energy surrounding the topic at hand.

Pluto in Our Times

The sign that Pluto appears in has a significance different from its house position. Pluto's erratic orbit results in its spending from about twelve years in some signs to as long as thirty years in others. Its slow movement (it takes 250 years on average to go around the Sun) creates a long tenure in each sign, making it an indicator of a whole generation's issues. Thus its sign placement sets the tone for broad collective themes. We look at Pluto's sign when we want to get a sense of the vast changes humanity goes through, epoch by epoch.

Putting together Pluto's function as the governor of breakdown and renewal with what we know of the essential energy of the sign Pluto is in, we can get clues about where the most profound disturbances to the *status quo* will be percolating. Let us glance briefly here at Pluto's previous tenure in Scorpio, its current tenure in Sagittarius and its upcoming tenure in Capricorn:

Pluto's entry into **Scorpio** (1984–1995), the sign of its rulership, corresponded with the eruption of AIDS into public consciousness. Much has been written about the fact that this period presented us with an astounding fusion of the two big issues with which Pluto is most commonly identified: sex and death. This transit also saw a resurgence of books and seminars about the occult, angels and the existence of the soul, as curiosity about hidden things in general flooded into popular culture.

Pluto in **Sagittarius** (1994–2009) is key to our understanding of what's going on in the world right now, so it will get its own chapter further on in the book. By way of introduction, let us say that this transit has exposed the decay within extant systems of belief, education, international relations and travel. Holy wars and the breakdown of once-sacrosanct cultural mores give new meaning to the question *Is nothing sacred?* During this period the reigning sky-god religions—Judaism, Christianity and Islam—are each being held up to mass scrutiny and reacting with extreme excess, which is what tends to happen when entities go through mortal purging.

Pluto in **Capricorn** (2008–2024) will put together the planet of transformation with the sign of government, economics and corporations. Long-unquestioned truisms about business leadership, statesmanship and fatherhood will be challenged one way or another, for Pluto is fated to root out the dysfunction within all Capricornian systems: those structured on a hierarchical and/or patriarchal model. The shifting of national boundaries and the impact of globalization on the integrity of discrete cultures will beg questions about what actually constitutes a nation-state. Because Capricorn is an earth sign, it is likely that the Earth will be viewed as a physical entity first and foremost, with inter-related biological and geological systems. Global warming and environmental degradations may trigger a brand new (and very old) definition of *conservatism*: the responsible stewardship of a limited material world.

Pluto in Action

Now that we have a sense of Pluto's function and style of operation, in the next two chapters we will look at what this planet is up to in the chart of the USA. It is easy to freak out about the destructive power of Pluto when it manifests in a group chart; and it is easy, when interpreting America's Pluto, to focus only on its destructive potential. But seeing Pluto as merely dominance and destruction isn't the deeper truth, and freaking out is not the deeper response.

Once we have a sense of Pluto's linkage to Natural Law, we should be able to look at the phenomenon of national power with sufficient distance to ask the pertinent questions. What does it mean to be a global power? How is a power that is fundamentally about invisible forces made manifest? And how do individual members of the group respond to this power?

FOUR

Money Neurosis

Pluto in the Second House

Every feature of the chart needs to be taken into consideration, of course, in order to understand the karma and dharma[1] of the entity that is the United States of America; but our focus here is upon Pluto, because it is the key to the country's issues with power.

In the chart of the USA, we find Pluto in the second house, which intensifies all dealings with finances and resources, and bestows the potential to go to neurotic extremes. Any group or individual with its Pluto so positioned might be expected to claim an unusually strong territorial prerogative. We wouldn't be surprised to see a tendency towards power plays where ownership is concerned. We might see radical makeovers through the transformation of attitudes towards money and wealth. The entity may have to "go through hell and back" in its approach to material security.

These would be the classic astrological expectations of this signature in any chart. The next step is to apply what we know of both planet and house to the USA's chart, to see where the nation's essential drives are encoded.

The Second House

But before we do that we need take closer look at this house of the chart, which is often underestimated. Of the twelve, the second house seems to be the one most often described in simplistic terms: some astrology books link it to *wealth and possessions* and let it go at that. If we didn't know any better, we might take this to mean that astrology views the material world as superficially as contemporary American culture itself does. But like every other house, the second has layers of meaning of which the familiar literalisms are just the tip of the iceberg.

The first inference we need to draw from this idea of "possessions" is that the things we own are symbolic of our *values*.

---

[1] In this context, *karma* refers to the cosmic lessons the chart says must be learned by this collective consciousness. *Dharma* refers to its fundamental purpose. See Dane Rudhyar's *The Astrology of America's Destiny*.

Astrology posits that our attitudes towards the whole material plane are reflected in our approach to the things we own. So it is not the *thing* that has the charge; it's the value attached to it. It is our values that determine what we buy at the store or want to write our initials on. It is our values that determine how we feel about that thing and what opinions we hold about it. It is our values that prompt us to use it—or not use it—in a certain way.

In a group chart, the second house is the indicator of collective values, symbolized by certain resources that are prized above all others. These vary from era to era; but whatever a society's treasures are at a given time—be they diamonds or dot.com stock—they are as characteristic of that culture as language and native dress. And they all belong to the second house.

Unless we're doing a study like this, we don't usually think about how relative the idea of *worth* is. But consider how peculiar to a given culture are the things it holds dear—how descriptive of its place in the world and its moment in history. Recall that *spice* was once the premier symbol of worth throughout the civilized world. Later, it was gold; and if you had told the miners in the hills of California, a century and a half ago, how low gold would sink in the stock market of the late twentieth century, they would have looked at you as if you were insane, not believing it possible.

Now it's oil. And soon it's going to be water[2].

Slavery

This placement of Pluto is also the key to the meaning of the darkest chapter in American history—the Civil War. Though generally talked about in purely moral terms, this war was essentially about the nature of ownership: a second-house (economic) issue. With slavery, Pluto took the idea of territorial control to its most literal and absolute extreme—one group of humans made possessions of another group for material gain. We have seen that Pluto is an amoral planet—that it has nothing to do with good or bad, right or wrong—and when unintegrated with the other planets, its raw power takes over, unabated and undistracted by ethical considerations.

Though the abomination of slavery has been practiced by many cultures worldwide, past and present, black and white, America's interlude with slavery was paradigmatic. It was not a historical deviation or afterthought in the nation's history—it was there from the start, firmly

---

[2] Outside of the USA, the shift of meaning that water has undergone—from unquestioned given of Nature into endangered resource—has already begun. Worldwide, more than a billion people don't have access to clean water.

in place when the colonies were transforming into a nation—which gives it a distinct astrological significance. Slavery was woven into the fabric of American culture from the birth moment, giving it a karmic resonance that must be worked through and transcended. Racial oppression and the genocide of its indigenous tribes are America's great original sins.

These must be expiated if they are to be healed, and before they can be expiated they must be fully addressed. But instead of addressing them, America as a whole pretends it's acceptable that one in four black men is unemployed across the fifty states; that there are more black men languishing in prison than enrolled in college; that black youth die by gunfire by the hundreds in ghettos where hopelessness is not aberrant but normative. Though laws have been passed to right some of the surface wrongs and every once in a while a symposium on race relations is held, there continues to be a terrible insufficiency to these efforts that those on all sides of the issue cannot fail but see.

Haphazard remedies will not heal this second-house wound. Until the abomination of slavery is returned to the forefront of American consciousness in a spirit of genuine collective redemption[3], the country will stay the way it is, with the wound intact; like an old Confederate soldier who never submitted to having his shrapnel dug out and just hobbles along anyway, accustomed to the pain.

Greed

American slavery was only the most graphic example of the act of *possessing* gone horribly awry. The nation struggles with unhealthy impulses towards all forms of ownership, which have skewed the group's experience of material to such a degree that the distortion has become routine.

Ubiquity has made American materialism unremarkable; indeed, greed has become legitimized as a function of social success. The bizarre manipulations of advertising are utterly taken for granted at this point in US culture—even admired as an art form. Shopping is seen as a form of self-expression. Most Americans have come to see themselves just as the corporations see them: as consumers first and citizens second. This mentality keeps the individuals' material values stuck at a very low frequency, which exerts a deadening pull in the opposite direction from self-actualization.

---

[3] Pluto transits often coincide with events that offer clear opportunities to heal this and other cultural taboos, as we will see in Chapter Twelve.

Disparities

With Pluto in the USA chart's house of money, America is destined to explore the most extreme reaches of the wealth/poverty polarity. In the USA the richest citizens are very, very rich indeed; and at the other end of the spectrum, folks are hurting. While the nation's inflation-adjusted gross domestic product has virtually tripled since 1973, the poverty rate has hardly budged. Yet America remains obsessed by the fiction of its own classlessness. Recall the general public's flat-out incredulity after Hurricane Katrina (*"But this only happens in Third World countries!"*).

It would come as a surprise to many Americans to hear that thirteen million children in the US are malnourished, or that the infant mortality rate is the highest in the developed world. What do the staunch supporters of the American Way of Life (whatever they think that means) make of the studies showing that nearly forty percent of single mothers with young children live in poverty in this land of unprecedented wealth? The fact that so few Americans make much of it at all indicates that these realities fly in the face of the collective self-image.

After the 2005 hurricane, it was reported that all those Louisiana levees could have been repaired for *one day's worth* of Iraq war expenses ($200 million). But somehow the two contexts—money for war, money for public safety—are kept oddly compartmentalized in the American mind. The madness of the incongruity fails to register. It fails to register because it is too grotesque to assimilate. I'll warrant that even those diehard patriots who claim that the war is worth any cost would have a hard time assimilating the fact that executives of the contracting firms doing "security" in Iraq–i.e. upscale mercenaries—make 30 to 175 times as much as a US army captain with twenty years' experience and 2,000 times the pay of entry-level soldiers.

The mind boggles. The natural urge is to shut down and look away.

Skewed Priorities

There is a money sickness here, and if we are not part of the healing, we are part of the disease. For the sake of ourselves as well as the group, we need to actively develop a perspective.

A random glance at some of the ways America spends its money reveals a system of priorities that is almost surreally counter-intuitive. The amount the federal government allots for smoking prevention, for instance, is outspent—by billions of dollars a year—by tobacco companies on legal fees and settlements. The lack of logic behind these spending patterns is matched only by the lack of empathy they express. Consider that the amount of grain fed to American livestock in a year is the same amount eaten by human beings in India and Africa. And what kind of priorities might we infer from the fact that the USA spent five hundred billion dollars on advertising and marketing in 2005—half the worldwide total—while donating the smallest amount of tsunami relief, proportionately, of any First World country? For that matter, the US charitable aid budget for the entire world just about equals the amount of money Mexican immigrants send home to their families.

And then there are the tax cuts. The most egregious of these ideas, the repeal of the estate tax, would effectively shovel a billion and a half dollars a week from the collective treasury into the accounts of the twenty thousand richest American families.

Revolutions have been fought against injustices far less blatant than these.

Privatization

Recall that Pluto governs the process of digging beneath the surface of things, down to their core definitions. Pluto's effect on a house of the chart is to reach under the hood of its most basic operations and tinker around. The field of activity in question is not just quantitatively but qualitatively altered. The most commonplace life experiences—like going to a baseball game—undergo a meaning shift below the surface. And especially in the case of a collective—where conformity immediately establishes a semblance of normalcy—the group may barely register that this change is happening. This is what has happened in America with the phenomenon of ownership.

Like a surgeon with a scalpel, Pluto has manipulated the fundamental premises of the concept of ownership so that many of the old verities no longer apply. A few years ago, nobody would have thought of water as something to buy in a plastic bottle. The concept of owning your own name (e.g. domain names; identity theft insurance) did not exist *per se*. The idea that the local city park could be sold to a business would have shocked people. What happens when the rules change about what can be possessed? What does this do to the notion of valuables and to the values of the people? It is said that the Native Americans stared in bewilderment when European settlers thrust in their faces pieces of paper ceding to white ownership plains and valleys which the indigenous residents saw as un-possessable: They belonged to the Great Spirit; how could they be owned?

America's governmental system has itself become commodified, though its citizens seem hardly to notice. So steeped are Americans in a culture of buying and selling that they have gotten to the point of shrugging off even the most cravenly greed-driven policies—like the tax cuts—because they recognize that their legislators' votes have themselves already become commodities, purchasable by lobbyists. On paper, "the American people" are supposed to be the whole *raison-d'être* for public policy; but in practice, they are treated as mere consumers of it. Business metaphors are showing up where they would once have been considered in very bad taste: politicians now speak of "selling" this or that policy. This is the not the language of a public servant but that of a salesman maneuvering a mark.

In the Plutonian epoch at hand—whose timeline we will discuss in upcoming chapters—America is commodifying everything in sight. It's as if the last few inhibitions against commercializing certain categories of social experience suddenly lapsed all at once, and a feeding frenzy has broken out among American business interests—each grabbing at whatever is not nailed down and rushing to trademark it before somebody else does. We have entered an era of mass privatization, whereby resources once thought to belong to the common weal are now auctioned off to the highest bidder. The profit motive is overpowering values that were once universally felt to be off-limits to personal gain. Some of us can remember when our hometown baseball game and parade down Main Street, though they may have had their merchant sponsors, were first and foremost expressions of community pride: their primary meaning was above and beyond the range of business. Now, virtually every corner of public space in every American city is stamped with a corporate moniker for the sake of signaling a financial purpose, from ads on park benches to billboard boats on the bay.

Privatization is not without its opponents. The public seems to be reacting with a mixture of distress and resignation as even public schools are falling here and there under corporate sponsorship, making one wonder whether the naming of hospitals and libraries after civic leaders may soon seem a quaint bit of nostalgia. There was quite a dust-up in San Francisco recently over the ignominious corporatization of the name of the baseball stadium. When the enormous letters affixed to its front wall were hoisted to read "Pac Bell Park", it seemed funny and shocking—a ridiculously corporate moniker for one of the folksiest institutions in American life. Then, as the telecommunications giants gobbled each other up, the name was stripped down to "SBC Park". Bloodied but unbowed, a small group of baseball fans have launched a valiant appeal to rename the park after Willy Mays; but last I heard the powers-that-be had settled on "AT&T Park" and there it stands: any last nod to aesthetic, historic or even human activity has been bleached out of the ballpark's name. But of course, it is not really a *name* anymore. It is an initialing of territory—the megabucks version of a graffiti artist's tag.

Capitalism: *Good*. Anything Else: *Bad*

The deeply unsettling effect this corporate encroachment is having upon America's quality of life has been widely noted by pundits from every corner of the political spectrum. Yet somehow any thoughtful analysis of the economic system that breeds it is nowhere to be seen.

The words "capitalism" and "communism" are so freighted with emotional charge in American parlance that a kind of pre-emptive hysteria seems to preclude any sober thinking about either one. One rarely hears intelligent discussion in the USA about the actual workings of its economic model of choice. No economist could get away with going on an American talk show, for instance, and suggesting that capitalism might have serious drawbacks. All hell would break loose. Sponsors would bail. His career would be toast.

Why do Americans take capitalism so personally? To make sense of it we must start by understanding that in the collective mind, *capitalism* has become fuzzily equated with *democracy*. The two have slid into an amorphous merger with the concept of *patriotism*; and the resulting thought-form is fraught with such a hair-trigger charge that it has been pushed out of the bounds of safe debate. It is even more rare to hear the word *communism* used as a neutral technical term: it has been reduced to a code word for *Everything "Un-American"*[4]. In the USA, questioning the official economic system seems to be utterly taboo.

The fact that parsing *capitalism* has become taboo seems obvious when stated, though it almost never *is* stated—perhaps because when it is framed this way, one can't help but see that there is something baldly irrational about it. Why would a society feel the need to declare its economic system off-limits even to intellectual inquiry?

But its irrationality isn't hard to understand when we look at it astrologically. Pluto governs taboos, as we know, and in the second house it makes changing one's financial status quo feel like a fate worse than death.

Just Like Fidel Castro

When it comes to mass irrational fears, we often see a culture lag between historical fact and collective myth. Certain economic myths

---

[4] This term, too—though its denotation describes nothing more than national status–has acquired a connotation that verges on the diabolical.

reign supreme in the American imagination despite all contravening evidence, and they hang in there because they remain undiscussed.

An example is the hardy American tradition of red-baiting, which—almost twenty years after the end of the Cold War—still works as a ploy in public discourse. When the good Reverend Jerry Falwell accused Country Joe McDonald in late 2005 of being "just like Fidel Castro," it was like pressing a button: the Right roused itself lustily to the battle cry; the Left decried the attack as evidence of Falwell's idiocy. But almost no one stopped to question why the charge is presumed to be a slur.

It is not as if most Americans had a clue about what Castro actually does or says, so as to formulate an educated opinion of him. Thanks to the extraordinarily intense propaganda campaign that has for decades choked off any real news about Cuba, the general public has no idea how much disinformation they are getting. Though Che Guevara charmed the pants off American audiences in 2004 (as played by Gael Garcia Bernal in "The Motorcycle Diaries"), most of his fans do not seem to have been troubled by the disparity between the historical Cuba of the film and the Evil Socialist Dictatorship they hear about from their government.

A few reports did manage to escape US censors after Hurricane Katrina, about the exemplary successes Cuba has had with its own massive hurricane evacuations and rescues. Especially ironic was the news that Castro had volunteered to send 1100 doctors to New Orleans but was given the cold shoulder by the Bush administration, which apparently did not even grace his offer with a reply.

Ever since Che kicked the American mobsters and their politician friends out of Havana, Cuba has been the target of a globally orchestrated war of attrition waged by Uncle Sam. It is more than noteworthy that this dinky little tropical isle seems to pose such a threat to the world's only hyper-power. Cuba has kept Washington spooks busy for years: blackmailing European countries that attempt to sell Cuba food and supplies, funding the violent campaigns of rightwing thugs in Florida, and plotting to assassinate the seemingly bulletproof Fidel—a guy Washington has been calling a "dictator" for so long you'd think it was his official title; though the man is, of course, elected. Indeed, the Cuban people keep electing him over and over again.

The American Dream

Somehow, Cuba has survived. Despite the blockade, Cuba manages to provide its people with free health care and education. It has no homelessness. Nobody goes hungry; they go to neighborhood warehouses to get rice and beans, sugar and oil. Old folks are taken care of as a matter of course. Those artists and peace activists who defy the travel ban to venture onto Cuba's verboten shores report that the cops there are humble and helpful; the people are well used to scarcity, yet seem happy and relaxed. Corporations do not own the utilities or the baseball stadiums. The people themselves own these things, as well as the factories, the universities, the hospitals, the museums and the beaches[5]. The most stunning irony of all is that most Cubans, poor as they are, own their own homes.

Home ownership, a goal ever more out of reach in the world's richest country[6], is the ultimate signature of "the American Dream:" that much-touted chimera which is now part of the global lexicon. The phrase is so steeped in mass yearning that it seduces us into ignoring what the words themselves admit: that it is an illusion. Those who aspire to wakefulness as a way of life will sooner or later dissociate from it, as we must from all illusions.

Healthy and Unhealthy Ownership

There is something very odd about the driving idea behind the *American Dream*: that home ownership is the ultimate human experience. How is it that owning an object–even a very big, expensive one—has become a benchmark of success and happiness? What is the nature, exactly, of the psychological forces behind the American experience of possessing?

In a society with Pluto in the second house, the act of valuing certain resources, from real estate to designer watches, can become hyped-up to the point of dysfunction. An object can take on an imagined worth all out of proportion to its use-value. It can be put up on a pedestal, where it becomes the focus of a kind of magical thinking. In the case of a paper lottery ticket that claims somebody's last dollar, valuing has become superstition. Superstition, as Stevie Wonder tells us, is a

---

[5] The Cuban people, citizens of the most stable regime in the hemisphere, are at this writing (September 2006) actively preparing for an American military invasion once Castro dies, an event they know Washington has been awaiting (not to mention trying to expedite) for fifty years. Just before Castro's hospitalization, the Bush Administration was paving the way for the return of public property in Cuba—including schools and clinics—to its pre-revolutionary private owners, via the characteristically misnamed *Commission for Assistance to a Free Cuba* (July 2006).

[6] One of the myths that comprise the American self-image is that the nation's wealth leads to *more* home ownership rather than *less*—a belief that fails to allow for the fact that this wealth is increasingly concentrated at the very top. In relatively well-to-do San Francisco, only twelve per cent of households earn enough to buy a median-priced house.

belief in things we don't understand. It isn't simply that we abstract the object from its practical or realistic use. It is that we do so without understanding.

By contrast, when we use a resource with awareness, it becomes a true talisman. The most commonplace object–a candlestick, an old shawl, a teddy bear—is made into a tool of spiritual practice when we deliberately put our energy into it and dignify it with our intention. It becomes the physicalization of an ideal. It is no longer "inanimate." Even a lottery ticket could conceivably be used this way, if its symbolism were mindfully integrated and pressed into ritualistic service.

Gold, Silver and the Lottery

The difference between healthy and unhealthy ownership depends upon the energy with which something is owned. It is this difference that is the moral of all those myths and legends about gold and silver, whose lore is filled with tales of abundance that turns ugly (e.g. King Midas, The Goose that Laid the Golden Egg, Judas' thirty pieces of silver). Gold and silver—symbolic of the light of the Sun and Moon, respectively—are not just metals but archetypes. In stories from around the world, they figure in the struggle between the enlightened and unenlightened approaches to wealth. The modern version of this parable is the lottery winner whose windfall, far from bestowing happiness, triggers identity crisis, altercations with loved ones, even suicide.

Pluto, The Button Pusher

Pluto's placement here tells us that issues of wealth arouse the darkest human drives that exist. Pluto's purpose is to push our buttons. And there can be little doubt that in America, money is the button-pusher.

Even the most mundane of second house activities in American culture has a compulsive quality. Consider the energy attached to asking for a raise; look at Christmas shopping. The charge around these activities defies superficial explanations. Without Pluto adding that peculiar intensity to the proceedings, it would be hard to explain why, when the conversation turns to money, utterly reasonable people tend to knit their brow, shorten their breath and assume a defensive posture. Even the most Zen-like folks—people who make a point of putting fear in its place in every other arena of life—will blithely open the door to fear where money is concerned, as if it had never crossed their minds to not do so.

Bigger is Better

One of the most striking features of America's money neurosis is the unassailable conviction that bigger-is-better, a value reflected in every aspect of the national lifestyle. This derives from an implicit choice made by second house planets, whether in a group chart or an individual chart, between two distinct means of assessing worth: *quantity* and *quality*. Americans have always come down solidly on the side of quantity, fetishizing *size* in everything from skyscrapers to genitalia.

However, it does seem that the issue is enjoying a robust debate. America is increasingly and bitterly divided about its preference for cars the size of army tanks. Letters-to-the-editor are being written about what a shame it is to bulldoze lovely old single-screen movie houses in order to replace them with ugly sprawling multiplexes where buckets of popcorn are sold that look like they're big enough to feed a Korean village. It is starting to occur to more and more people that there is something not quite right about the fact that the size of an American family's house, and the number of cars parked beside it, usually reflect increases in income rather than increases in need. As the first decade of the millennium enters its second half, America's lust for quantity at the expense of quality seems to be on the minds of many.

But it remains a topic of mass confusion, even as it elicits more and more public distress. It's a funny thing about Plutonian subject matter: we may find an intense self-scrutiny wherever the planet resides, but it is still often accompanied by stunted awareness. Attention gets riveted on a given topic without any understanding of what to do with it.

Consumerism

If there is a consciousness shift around the *quantity* issue, it has a darkly humorous twist: we are starting to see the American penchant for consumerism *itself* becoming the subject of a wide array of media entertainments and opinions. Consider the voyeuristic reality shows featuring rich girls on a farm; and the blockbuster diet books, which are themselves gobbled up as fast as they come off the press.

Grabbing the heart with particular poignancy is the recent epidemic of childhood obesity. This sad grotesquerie of modern American life seems a qualitatively different kind of wake-up call than any of the other symptoms, for here the pathos is much closer to home. The image is one of innocents falling victim to something in the collective unconscious that has turned the corner from mere peccadillo into abject pathology.

This and other distress calls are leading the way to a major self-image breakthrough on the part of the US populace. Now Americans are not merely out-of-control consumers, but *know* they are: it is a conscious part of the group portrait, with all the ambivalence that that implies. And inevitably, psychological theory has been pressed into service to shed light upon it. A therapist might use the word *compulsive,* for example, to describe ritualized behaviors that one knows to be bad for the well being, but one enacts them anyway.

An astrologer might use the word *Plutonian.* We *expect* there to be a self-destructive subtext wherever Pluto is involved; we don't see it as incongruous. Sometimes this undercurrent results in creative self-destruction, whereby a person or a group entity experiences nothing less than rebirth in the area in question. Otherwise, the self-destruction is blind.

Pluto in the second house tells us that America's cult of consumerism is symptomatic rather than causative. We won't get anywhere just cataloging its myriad expressions. We need to know what makes it tick.

America's Entitlement Complex

America's money neurosis is clearly also linked to what the psychologists might call an *entitlement complex,* a phenomenon astrologers usually chalk up to a prominent Jupiter. In the US chart, Jupiter—largest of the eight planets—is conjunct the Sun[7], so Jupiter is the obvious culprit: this is the governor of increase, exaggeration, abundance, opulence and waste. With the solar system's biggest gas ball (the Sun: planet of identity) merged with its second biggest gas ball (Jupiter: planet of expansion) it is easy to see how the bigger-is-better ethos came to be a central feature of American self-expression.

But the Jupiter-Sun conjunction cannot all by itself account for the intensity with which the United States' collective psyche engages with the material world. The highlighted Jupiter certainly explains why excess is a national theme, but it does not explain the compulsiveness about wealth that exists in this country. For that, we have Pluto to thank, and the second house.

---

[7] The US Jupiter, also discussed in Chapter Six, is itself tightly conjunct Venus, planet of enjoyment and luxury. As the planetary ruler of Taurus, the sign of money, Venus emphasizes the physical-comfort-seeking trajectory of America's entitlement complex, and gives the chart a particular fondness for pastimes and pleasures that are both showy (Jupiter) and security-conscious (Cancer). Venus' rulership over sugar and sweets, and its presence in Cancer (eating and food), also help explain America's tendency to express growth (Jupiter) through dietary indulgence.

The Metaphysics of Materialism

American greed has not gone unnoticed by social critics in every part of the world, with reactions ranging from the morally accusative to the fearfully dismayed. Let us back up from the subject of materialism for a moment, and look at the phenomenon through the dispassionate lens of metaphysics.

The second house is the one that most directly refers to life in the tangible realm. And here we immediately run into the limitations of cultural assumption. The unquestioned beliefs our society harbors about the nature of tangibility run so deep that we forget they exist. Unlike in philosophies like astrology—which divides all experience down into four utterly equal parts: matter, thought, emotion and spirit—in modern scientific thought it is axiomatic that the realm of matter has greater validity than the other three realms.

Modern thinkers presume that the nature of physical things is incontestably objective, whereas all other experience is more or less subjective. (Of course now we hear, from the New Physics, that even the scientists—at least the cutting-edge ones—are coming round to where the metaphysicians have always stood with this idea: quantum physics[8] has pretty much refuted old assumptions about the incontestable objectivity of the physical world. But consensus opinion has been slow to register the news.[9]) The language we use to speak about the material plane reveals the way most people think: that physical energies are *more real* than other energies. We say an opinion is "only an opinion," but an object "really exists."

Money is clearly thought to be the *sine-qua-non* of the material realm, as evidenced by the fact that the word *material* has become synonymous with the word *financial*. So it follows that money *issues*, too, are thought to originate and dwell exclusively in the external world. This makes it hard to own up to them, because we feel our money issues live *out there*; whereas *we* live *in here*, in our internal world—and the barrier between these worlds is seen as an absolute existential divide.

The skewed logic in this line of thinking goes like this: If the realm of matter has a monopoly on realness, and money is a concentrated symbol of matter, it must be that money is *über*-real. Ideas, by contrast, are given only qualified credence in this worldview (and usually only if they become marketable). Our poor feelings are seen as having very little

---

[8] For a brief discussion of the philosophical similarities between quantum physics and metaphysics, see *Physics and Metaphysics*, on the Writing page of my website, MotherSky.com.

[9] As usual. Consensus opinion is governed by Saturn, which is always slow.

credibility: here we have an entire arena of human experience pretty much dismissed as "a woman thing." And our intuitions? They get snubbed entirely.

If we're going to understand Pluto in the second house of America's chart, we have to look at it against the backdrop of a cultural bias that singles out the physical plane for selective interest. And then we have to look at how Pluto takes this interest to an extreme of slavish devotion. Attention is directed to the material world and kept there, holding us captive to the assumption that our survival as human beings depends upon material security exclusively.

Americans are explicitly and implicitly taught that a Rolex watch, or a paycheck, or a stock quote flitting across the computer screen is possessed of a deal-breaking kind of power: a power that can either ruin or transform a person. It is almost as if one's financial life is seen to be governed by a different set of laws than those that govern everything else. Quite simply, this line of reasoning doesn't make sense.

But it doesn't seem to matter. Pluto somehow gets away with it anyway. This is a significant feature of the planet's function. Pluto surrounds its issues with a kind of primal urgency that makes us feel we cannot afford to question even the most blatant theoretical inconsistencies.

Practicality Argument

Consider the much-touted *practicality* argument. This line of reasoning is often used as a last word when other justifications fail. We say: "Well, it's true that I hate the color and the feel and the look of this thing I'm considering buying, but it *is* practical." Pragmatism is used to justify all manner of activities in American society that are neither beneficial nor pleasurable, nor even, sometimes, cost-effective. Think about the billions of dollars spent on insurance: an utterly *non*-cost-effective purchase, which everyone knows full well to be so. Yet it's considered a veritable heresy of *impracticality* to opt out of buying it.

People describe the most wildly fear-driven scenarios, such as staying at a job they hate, as being dictated by practicality. In fact, the term seems to have no meaning at all except as a signal that we've entered Pluto territory: *Question no further.* The irony is that when we are using the "dollars-and-cents" rationale, this is precisely when we seem to be most bereft of common sense. And in no other realm of life do we so disrespect our inner promptings.

Abstract Finances

So the second house expresses the nature of our attachment to the Earth plane, the one to which the modern world has pledged a lopsided allegiance. And we have seen that in a collective chart, the symbols of the second house derive from consensus: that whether a group values chunks of matter gleaned straight from the Earth, like precious jewels or cowry shells—or more conceptual tokens like rectangles of green printed paper—its wealth is measured by an agreed-upon vocabulary of worth.

At this point in its history, America, whose house of money is occupied by a trans-Saturnine planet[10], has come up with a financial vocabulary so abstract it has no physicality at all: little electronic numbers on a computer screen. It is one of the mysteries of America's second-house Pluto that these weightless, formless flickers of light—no longer even commodities at all, but *representations* of commodities (and dubious ones, at that, if we consider the recent market manipulation scandals of energy utility brokers)—have come to be universally supposed, with a suspension of disbelief that is uniquely modern, to signify the presence or absence of solvency.

Like those indigenous Americans baffled by the white man's deeds, small stockholders stared dumbfoundedly at their Enron statements two hundred years later, wondering whether their disappeared savings ever belonged to them in the first place.

Middle-Class Bag Ladies

The deep sense of urgency that inflects the attitudes Americans hold about money—an otherwise innocuous, garden-variety topic, when you think about it—comes out in ways that are sometimes almost comically irrational. When we look at American materialism as a creature of Pluto, the planet of power and control, the peculiar strength of feeling attached to any and all subjects relating to material insecurity starts to make sense.

One of these is the trenchant middle-class fear currently reaching epidemic proportions among midlife Baby Boomers of becoming a bag lady. (Our parents might have expressed the same phobia with the quaint Dickensian phrase *"ending up in the poor house."*) The genuinely indigent do not buy into these pictures, of course; they have their own stories. But among those whose middle-class expectations are slipping—

---

[10] The three outer planets in the solar system occupy a special category: they orbit beyond Saturn, the planet of material limitation. Thus the trans-Saturnine planets represent levels of awareness that challenge (Uranus), negate (Neptune) and break down (Pluto) the verities of our everyday, physical existence.

as well as those who would, by any standard, be described as quite well-off—a peculiar strain of financial panic is on the rise that might be called *First-World poor-mouthing.*

To remember that we live in a world where slum populations are estimated to be growing by a phenomenal 25 million people a year is to find ourselves conceding that the Bourgeois Bag Lady Threat seems, well, perhaps less than dire. Indeed, in the spirit of overall ecological balance, for the American middle class to consider lowering its standard of living just a teensy little bit might not be an altogether inappropriate idea. But Plutonian fixations resist global or philosophical perspectives, as nightmares resist logic. Pluto is an all-or-nothing planet and its myths are the same way. The Bag Lady Scenario would have us believe that any lowering at all of our financial status quo will lead to starving in a gutter somewhere, and that's all there is to it.

This abject dread of insolvency deserves a closer look. We find it everywhere in America—in advertising, in conversations with our friends, in fear-mongering scenarios spun by the White House: *You will die poor if you don't sign up for this seminar. You'd better buy this insurance or God-only-knows what will happen. If you don't vote for my social security overhaul plan you'll end up a decrepit old beggar.* As terrors go, it is remarkably democratic: it is no less prevalent in Americans who by no stretch of the imagination could be considered impoverished. Not that this constitutes grounds to dismiss it; the phenomenon is viscerally and painfully real for millions of people of every socioeconomic class, which certainly goes to show that everything is relative. Of interest here is that tell-tale certitude of doom—our tip-off that Pluto is involved. Those in the grip of this fear will defend the probability of their imminent poverty with a fervency that rivals that of a trial lawyer in a capital case[11].

---

[11] But there may be a covert spiritual mechanism operating here as well. The bag lady obsession seems to involve a kind of reverse projection, by which the American middle class is inadvertently reflecting what is going on in the greater world. It may be that, rather than making it their business to address, in thought or deed, the literal destitution that exists almost everywhere *except* in their own tiny demographic minority, middle-class Americans are identifying with global poverty unconsciously. We are, after all, psychically connected. If one subscribes to the belief that all people everywhere are linked through the collective unconscious, it follows that we cannot help but pick up what is going on across the globe, at every moment, whether we realize it or not. Perhaps all this worrying about their own future "*in the poor house*" is the American way of feeling at one with the millions of victims of genocide, AIDS and war they hear about daily in the news.

Code of Silence

Our look at America's money issues has revealed a veritable hornet's nest of group psychology; it would be hard to find an area of societal endeavor that is more tortured with contradictions and unasked questions. One would think a cultural problem this knotty would inspire all manner of robust debate and juicy doctoral dissertations. But American materialism is rarely deeply explored by Americans. Why isn't such a compelling feature of their collective life delved into more than it is?

The answer lies with Pluto, governor of ideas that are pointedly un-discussed by polite society. Pluto's core precepts operate, by definition, under the radar of consensus opinion. Everything Pluto touches in the national chart represents an area where American society is unwittingly committed to a code of silence.

Worms in the Can

But Pluto is a cyclic planet; with each phase leading to the next, all heading towards inevitable change. We have seen that wherever Pluto resides in a chart, there are worms waiting to crawl out of a can. In America that can is business and finance.

An extraordinary number of white-collar money crimes have been exposed since this millennial period began. As we will see in Chapter Eleven, Pluto's opposition with Saturn across the axis of the USA chart marked the entry into an era of self-exposure from which there is no turning back.

Financial scandals have become a staple of the nightly news. It was when Pluto began to conjoin the US Ascendant that shady dealings in such heretofore-sacrosanct institutions as savings-and-loans, brokerage firms and energy utilities started showing up in the headlines. These were massive high-level malfeasances, and they were quickly earmarked to be bailed out—with crushing irony—by the defrauded taxpayers themselves; even as the rights of everyday citizens to declare bankruptcy were being watered down. More recently, the indictment in early 2006 of Jack Abramoff, K-Street lobbyist extraordinaire, sent politicians from both parties scurrying to distance themselves before the taint spread to them.

Issues like these have traditionally not been talked about. Monetary corruption is a longstanding feature of the American economy, but non-specialists didn't understand them and didn't want to think about them. Most of us still don't understand them and still don't want to think about them; but they are no longer in the closet. The fact that the little guy is getting fleeced is no longer a niche political opinion: it is a group assumption.

Ordinary taxpayers realize that they are losing ridiculous amounts of money because of the fraudulence of institutions like Pacific Gas and Electric. Viewers are seeing oil company spokesmen on TV twisting themselves into pretzels trying to explain how they can be making record-breaking profits at the same time that purportedly onerous operating costs force them to gouge us at the gas pump. The president of California's esteemed university system may be handed his walking papers because of the princely perks offered in secret to its top-level managers, while at the same time rising tuitions and disappearing aid have been squeezing students to the bone.

These are sources of national shame, and they are now in the public's face. These worms are not going back into the can.

Money is Power

In this chapter we have explored the ways in which Pluto's presence in the second house preternaturally intensifies America's attachment to material, an exploration which allows us to put into context the unboundaried consumerism and financial disparities that afflict this prodigiously wealthy land. We have said that souls who incarnated here did so in part to experience these lessons, and that they constitute an unavoidable feature of each citizen's karma. We have looked at some of the financial myths that prevail in the American mind, the consciousness shifts they are undergoing, and the effects they have on the cultural landscape. Our next step is to look beyond America's shores, at the impact the US Pluto has upon the world at large.

The astrological way of framing America's challenge is this: The most powerful planet in the sky has been trapped in an expression that binds it to the material plane, where it has nowhere to go. *Money is power* is too crude a battle cry to serve us any longer; it is a clumsy truism that humanity has outgrown. Not that it is untrue; with Pluto in the second house, it is all too true, and dangerously simplistic. The unenlightened use of Pluto in the American chart combines a skewed emphasis on worldly security with the shadow side of the darkest planet in the system, the result of which is a monstrous misuse of a sublime capacity. We need to reinterpret this part of America's potential with all the alertness we can muster, so as to bring intelligence back into the wielding of wealth.

FIVE

Power Madness

Pluto and American Hegemony

If there was ever a time to reconsider how America uses its power, it is now. The recent history of the world has seen America promoted from one of several super-powers to a single, untouchable *hyper-power*. There is something remarkably undemocratic about this, isn't there? They had to coin a whole new term to encompass the degree of power that the USA wields compared to the rest of the world.

There is not a corner of the globe where this power has not staked its claim. America has no peer in this epoch, and no oversight from the family of nations as a whole. Effectively immune to prosecution from the international bodies set up to supervise global issues like human rights and global warming, the US government strong-arms other countries into backing its aims and vetoes any accords it doesn't like—as if negotiation[1] were something only powerless nations engage in. The American military is bigger than that of the next fifteen biggest militaries combined, and the USA rattles its sword at any nation who takes a stand against it. It has the muscle to blockade (Cuba), to blackmail (Belgium, which quickly recanted its protest of the invasion of Iraq), and to bully the U.N. into backing its campaigns to starve upstart nations into submission (Iraq, Palestine, perhaps Iran). Civilian oversight of the Pentagon is nonexistent, with Congress in its thrall and presidents at its mercy[2].

Imperial Incursions

As of this writing (George W. Bush's second term) the current crew in Washington is being characterized by more and more citizens as the worst administration in American history. But it must be remembered that in the long view, this group is only a more extreme demonstration of dark leadership themes that have emanated from the American shadow

---

[1] This is a marked distortion of a key aspect of group karma—as indicated by Saturn's presence in Libra and the cluster of planets in the country's seventh house, to be discussed in Chapter Six.

[2] See *House of War*, James Carroll.

since the country's beginnings. There is nothing new about the US claiming the right to pre-emptively attack sovereign nations at will; either through explicit invasions justified by whatever political rationale seems to fit the occasion (Granada, Viet Nam, Yugoslavia, Iraq…since WWII there are have been hundreds of such incursions[3]) or through the underground instigation of coups (Haiti, Venezuela et al). More often, the USA funds puppet dictators (the Philippines et al) and maintains client states (Israel et al) wherever in the world there is a local populace too restless to control alone.

Globalization

Financially, the USA, through the World Bank, exerts de facto control over Third World nations by heaping crippling debt upon the very countries most in need of money to pay for food, medicine and infrastructure. The new mechanism for American power in the world economy is globalization, whereby *free trade agreements* devastate regional economies while enriching American companies and their largest shareholders.

Aimed at markets all over the world, globalization is America's new manifest destiny. Its "free trade agreements" are neither *free* nor *agreements* for the workers whom they directly affect: in Mexico, NAFTA is forcing the jobless multitudes north, into a transient labor force that further disempowers them through exploitation and criminalization once they get here. At this writing, 1.5 million Mexican corn farmers have been forced to choose between migrating and starvation; similar proposals are planned for Peru and Colombia.

The rationale behind globalization is certainly not economic fairness; it enables high-tech American farmers, for example, to take export market sales away from impoverished West African soybean farmers, by means of billions in federal supports. Nor does globalization seem to be motivated by whatever's-good-for-the-country pragmatism, for these are exorbitant sums for America to be paying out during a time when its own domestic infrastructure is crumbling.

As is always the case with Pluto, the impulses driving this campaign make little sense on the surface: they derive from deep within the collective unconscious, where themes of raw power originate. Globalization is not a model of economics that happens to be dominant, but a model of dominance that happens to be economic.

---

[3] See *Overthrow: America's Century of Regime Change From Hawaii to Iraq*, by Stephen Kinzer.

McDonald's and Britney Spears

And then there is the overpowering of global popular culture. The permeation of the world's airwaves with Hollywood and MTV imagery, the proliferation of US recreations and the Americanization of the world's eating habits have become a signpost of the modern age— with Burger Kings popping up in countries that don't even have their sewer systems together.

In our study of the second house we saw where this overpowering is rooted: in the drive to dominate through ownership and territory. When historians look back on all the various forms of territoriality America has wielded during this period, the most significant of all may turn out to be not regime change but Coca-Cola. This aesthetic hegemony, whereby American tastes are taking over the popular traditions of every culture where American products gain entry—an entry which is increasingly forced, in this era of oxymoronic free trade agreements—is more insidious than military conquest because it carries with it the illusion of desirability, like a lethal drug.

The anthropologically-minded will have noticed that the consumer choices of wealthy adolescents in Third World countries are a bellwether of this phenomenon. The fashions sported by revelers at a self-consciously American-style night club in Dubai or Palermo, for instance, offer testimony to which way the wind is blowing for their culture. And though American vacationers hoping to find exoticism in Thailand or Madrid are finding to their dismay that parts of these places are looking more and more like Indiana, the inevitable response is "But obviously they *want* these things." It is not without feelings of confusion and ambivalence that many hamburger-lovers—locals and tourists alike—walk into the McDonald's on the *Champs-Elysées* in Paris.

This form of American hegemony is far more complex than the political kind. We are seeing an all-out attack by the music, movie and snack food industries on the countries of Earth, launched under the innocuous banner of lifestyle choice.

Corruption

It is said that power corrupts, and absolute power corrupts absolutely. Astrological principles can help us make sense of this old truism, and enable us to consider dispassionately the squeamish issues of corruption and decay.

We have described Pluto as encompassing breakdown in all senses, from the organic to the moral. We have looked at how aptly corruption in the hallowed halls of finance fits the symbolism of America's Pluto in the second house: a decay that is as unsightly to look at—and as difficult to talk about—as fresh road kill on the highway. All Plutonian topics are difficult to even *think* about reasonably. Pluto governs things that are dirty or "dirty", which goes a long way in explaining the lugubriously complex feelings Americans have about money[4].

The notion of toxicity is a useful one in our effort to understand the further implications of Pluto in the USA chart. This planet presides over the reduction of obsolete material to its component parts: its job is to transform outworn things into detritus, whether biological or man-made. This includes garbage and trash. We have already looked at *waste* in the sense of profligacy and squandering (Jupiter). Factor in what we have learned about the second house and we get another meaning of *waste*, related but distinctly more Plutonian: debris that poses an elimination problem once its value has been used up.

Planned Obsolescence

The last few decades have seen a significant shift in American thinking about waste. As ecological values have moved gradually into the mainstream, there is a mass anxiety emerging about global desecration: part of the country's second-house shadow. Americans are starting to notice the connection between the fact that they heap more non-biodegradable trash upon landfills than can be absorbed and the fact that they heap humongous social debt upon future generations because they cannot pay for what they consume. The phrase *throwaway culture* was not even in the lexicon a generation ago; now someone can make reference to the forests cut down for the sake of the Sunday paper and everyone gets it.

As is usually the case with Plutonian subject matter, however, the most troubling features of the issue are the last to be talked about. Far more worrisome than barges of garbage carted out to sea are the tens of millions of American computers and cell phones piling up in dumps—in the Third World, where they are picked apart for reusable parts by, in many cases, the tiny fingers of children[5]. The peculiarly toxic nature of these consumer goods—compounded by the fact that their manufacturers build them to self-outmode at faster and faster intervals—raises the

---

[4] Pluto's association with uncleanness permeates American figures of speech about money. Note the locutions "filthy rich" and "dirt poor", which seem to indicate that the financial identity is unclean no matter where along the spectrum one falls.

[5] It is estimated that at least 90 per cent of the 315 million still-functional personal computers discarded in North America in 2004 were trashed; along with, the following year, 200,000 tons of cell phones—the electronic product with the shortest shelf life of all. See *Made to Break: Technology and Obsolescence in America*, by Giles Slade.

horrific issue of environmental injustice: the tendency of carcinogenic chemical refineries, nuclear plants and toxic dumps to be built either in impoverished foreign nations (Chernobyl is only the most notorious example) or in parts of the USA where the populace lacks the political and economic clout to stop them.

The idea of a throwaway culture is a deeply uncomfortable one. But the notion of a throwaway *world* is more than merely uncomfortable: it is apocalyptic. The twin issues of global warming[6] and peak oil have recently exploded into collective consciousness, taking the idea of misused wealth to a new level of relevance and urgency. Americans are beginning to realize that the way they use their resources is going to mark the difference between planetary health and ecocide.

A Long Shadow

It is clearer than ever that the USA's problems are the world's problems. No longer an isolationist fledgling state, content to focus on domestic production while nursing its inferiority complex to Europe and ignoring the rest of the world, America is reaching out. It no longer keeps its *values* (second house) to itself.

The ambition to Christianize the globe has not seen such zeal since Victorian missionaries set out for the jungles of Africa. From the narrow convictions of its government-backed religious minority to the eating habits of its overweight majority, American ideas and tastes are now exported as fast as they come off the pulpit and the assembly line. Just a few years ago only the most starry-eyed franchisers would have been able to imagine such a thing as a Disneyland in France, or a Starbucks in Oman, Austria and Peru.

Foreign policy-wise, American values are being extended far and wide, with many political and economic incentives in place to hasten the spread and nothing to stop them but people power[7]. Every country in which Washington desires a foothold is now invited to quickly install "democratic" regimes in the form of offers they can't refuse, a phenomenon we will examine in Chapter Eight.

---

[6] At this writing, the original phrase, "global warming", is vying for prominence with the oil industry's own coinage: the newer phrase, "climate change", which hints at the innocuous possibility of natural temperature shifts back and forth. "Climate change" is clearly an attempt to steer the public's attention away from the terrifying specter of a globe that is steadily heating up. The USA and Saudi Arabia fought for its adoption in international climate negotiations during the 1990s. See *Unspeak: How Words Become Weapons, How Weapons Become a Message, and How That Message Becomes Reality*, by Steven Poole.

[7] No small force, as we will discuss in Chapter Fifteen.

At this writing, there is a lot of talk in the US Congress about withdrawing troops from Iraq, but a look at the facts behind the rhetoric reveals the opposite. As untenable—politically and militarily—as a long-term occupation is looking to be, the truth is that an embassy is being built right now in Baghdad that will be staffed by more than a thousand workers (most embassies worldwide average thirty employees). While conversations about "self-determination for Iraq" circle round and round in Washington, no less than sixteen bases are under construction there amidst the chaos. One of them boasts its own video game arcades and fast food outlets: a little microcosm of America, hunkered down in the middle of the nightmare Iraq has become.

America's Pluto casts a long shadow. Whether by role-modeling or coercion, the rest of humanity is darkened by its umbra.

Obsession

In order to approach our study from another angle, let us leave the US chart for a moment and reconsider what we know about Pluto in the second house in personal astrology.

The second house encompasses our feelings about the contents of our drawers, pockets and shopping list, a rather ordinary department of life. But as we have seen, with Pluto, nothing is on the surface, and nothing is ordinary. Pluto in the second house can make a veritable totem out of anything the native has come to value; and the acquisition of it can become an obsession[8]. With Pluto, one always feels driven. The question is whether one understands what one is being driven toward.

We have seen that wherever it resides, Pluto gives us a sense of immense possibility, of making our lives over from scratch: a process triggered by instincts of regeneration that are inchoate and deeply internal. If we act upon these urges, we make them external. In the case of the second house, externalization is especially likely, for this is an earthy house prone to literalization. A possession may easily take on the Pluto projection; and if it does, it is not merely desired, it is coveted. If it

---

[8] Before we recoil at the word *obsession*, let's distance ourselves enough from the presumptions of modern psychology to remember that ancient mystery schools did not equate compulsion with pathology. It was believed that extremes of thought and behavior—when accompanied by awareness—confer a unique kind of wisdom that moderation cannot inspire. There are traditional cultures extant today whose shamans lead initiates into ritual fasting, enforced solitude under harsh conditions, vision quests with hallucinogenic plants and other drastic practices designed to lead the acolyte down into the depths of his being, there to find knowledge that cannot be found any other way. When the seeker emerges, it is as if he had surrendered to a death and come back to share its secrets.

loses value in the native's eyes, it is not just discarded—it is repudiated or destroyed.

As with all Plutonian urges, this one is neither pragmatic nor logical, although we may tell ourselves any number of earnest stories about why we must acquire that company or annex that property or buy that jacket with the fur collar... or we will *simply die.* Earning, envying, hoarding and spending may become life-altering dramas with Pluto in the second house. But if we approach them with enough self-honesty, we see that the intensity does not originate with the things we want to own but with the idea of ownership itself.

J. R. R. Tolkien's *Lord of the Rings* comes to mind here. The coveted ring in that story illustrates this principle like an arrow to the bull's eye. If you think about it, the narrative revolves *not* around the ring itself, but around who has it and when. The characters don't care about the ring; they care about *ownership* of the ring. Instead of paeans to its beauty or reports of its magical properties, most of what we hear, over and over again, are the words *"It's mine."*

Plutonian transformation begins with a craving. The craving may lead us through a tunnel of fanaticism, and then—if we are able to keep our eyes open in the dark—ends with a breakthrough into the light. If the learning process is halted halfway, we stay stuck in the tunnel. When expressed blindly, Pluto in the second house promotes an overweening fascination with the process of buying, selling and maintaining material possessions—but the part about dying and being reborn gets lost in the shuffle.

Where there is no self-discovery through money issues, there are just *money issues.* Where there is no consciousness with this placement, wealth—however it is defined—is not a means to an end; it becomes the end. It is not enough to acquire the coveted commodity: Pluto makes us feel we must control it; and in trying to control it, we give it our power.

In fairy tales, the treasure the hero seeks always has a dangerous aspect. The reason we desire the Plutonized valuable is not because it is good for us nor because it is pleasurable, any more than the Gollum wants the ring because it is pretty.

Black Gold

When we apply these ideas to the collective chart, we begin to understand the impulses behind America's devotion to a treasure that is becoming more and more dangerous with every month that passes: *oil.*

The placement of America's Pluto infuses whatever it values with a hybrid of control and desire. Since the country went off the gold standard, its symbols have become more and more estranged from their source meaning; but they are no less freighted with talismanic charge. It is easy to see how this would be the case, for Pluto governs the archetype of underground treasure: powerful secrets hidden within the psyche and raw mineral wealth hidden beneath the soil. Gold fever has been replaced in the history of America by oil fever, now ratcheted up to a fatal condition. Like any second-house resource, oil is, on one level, merely a useful commodity; but Pluto always hints at a darker significance. In the American imagination oil's meaning goes way beyond use-value.

It has become common knowledge that the USA's fossil fuel consumption in comparison to other countries is so disproportionate as to occupy a class by itself: Americans comprise five percent of the world population yet use a full quarter of the world's gas and oil. Much has been written about how the development of alternative energies has been stymied by decades of resistance from Big Oil[9], an industry whose role has changed from being merely influential in America's government to being actually personified by it[10].

America, obsessed with oil, has allowed its manufacturing base to fade out like a drunk who forgets to eat. If one were only using logic to understand it, it would be impossible to fathom the country's extreme dependence upon an energy source whose problems range from massive environmental abuse to the horrors of military occupation—when healthy alternatives have proven quite feasible (clean-fuel cars, solar heating[11]). But we are not dealing with logic here. We are dealing with Pluto.

Oil, an ancient black sludge, is at this writing in an archetypal transition period, oozing from one primary meaning to another in the collective imagination. Oil has been the modern world's premier symbol of empowerment; and, on the other side of the Plutonian coin, of

---

[9] Chevron, for example, spent $1.2 million in political contributions in 2005.

[10] But Bush and his crowd are just the most egregious example; the USA's oil addiction is utterly bipartisan in nature. While it is true that the Republican party has a higher profile of complicity with Big Oil than do the Democrats, the latter enjoy virtually identical industry ties and vote similarly for legislation that serves the industry—in the face of increasingly vocal popular opposition. In California, a state famous for the environmental consciousness of its citizenry, at this writing oil company lobbyists have helped tie up or kill almost a dozen state bills considered hostile to the industry—including a plan to tax windfall profits and a proposal to regulate refineries as public utilities. These never made it out of the Assembly—a body controlled by Democrats.

[11] Most estimates put the peak oil period from 2005-2010 (see *The Party's Over: Oil, War, and the Fate of Industrial Societies* by Richard Heinberg). The latter date corresponds to the much-heralded configurations accompanying Pluto's ingress into Capricorn (see Chapter Thirteen, *Grand Cross of 2010*).

destruction. (Perhaps one definition of a Plutonian resource is that it is coveted enough to shed blood to acquire.) It is now becoming the universal symbol of ecocidal madness.

Oil Wars

As we will see, astrologers credit the Pluto-Saturn opposition of 2001-03 with bringing to international attention the fact that covert (Pluto) American foreign policy has been largely dictated by subterranean wealth wherever in the world it is to be found—from Venezuela to Afghanistan. It was not politics, nor religion, but pipelines that were the subject of those discussions we are just now hearing about that were conducted in the late 90s between Texas businessmen and the Taliban—who were then just a random group of thugs that nobody but the oil men had ever heard of[12]. Had the general public known about these meetings, perhaps Washington's demonization of the Taliban after 9/11/01 would have seemed less random. As is so often the case with America's recent military adventures, things do start to make sense once we connect the dots back to Unocal.

All this has started to come out now, in books and blogs and documentary films that link up the energy industry with what the American government is up to around the world. But, significantly, this information is still not part of the collective consciousness—thanks mostly to a mass media controlled by plutocratic elements (indicated by the Mercury-Pluto opposition in the national chart, to be explored in the next chapter[13]). Despite the obvious connection between oil profiteering and the invasion of Iraq, there is an overriding desire on the part of the American public to avoid connecting the dots. And the true roots of these morbid campaigns retain their unadmitted status and their hush-hush quality.

---

[12] "Taleban [sic] in Texas for talks on gas pipeline", BBC News, December 4, 1997

[13] In the new era of oil wars, the CIA—which many of us thought had been disgraced and de-fanged by counterculture reforms in the 60s and 70s—has miraculously come back into full flower; and can be found all over the world where there is oil as yet uncontrolled by US interests (next stop: Sudan).

Though the tactics of America's ultimate undercover agency have not changed, the public perception of it has. CIA agents are showing up as the heroes in adventure movies. Gary Trudeau's cartoon-character protagonist has a son who joins the CIA as a postmodern career statement. The press now openly discusses CIA tactics like targeted assassinations and engineered coups in foreign governments as if they were the most natural things in the world.

Public in Denial

What is so Plutonian about the current American era is that despite the facts—e.g. that Big Oil is behind monstrously destructive government policies—the situation continues, business as usual. The marriage between the US government and a small group of the wealthiest humans on Earth is itself no longer literally a secret; but it is provoking as little outrage as if it were. The general public remains deeply in denial about the implications of the country's foreign and domestic policies, a denial that becomes more and more entrenched, it seems, with each new outrage its government commits.

Of interest here is the phenomenon of taboo and unmentionability that surrounds these subjects. We find with Pluto that the real secrets are always hidden in plain sight. The reader will recall that whatever house Pluto is in shows where we've been operating undercover: either literally, for example, in hidden love affairs and espionage; or figuratively—undercover of awareness. Here is where we have cultivated, over time, a set of obsessive habits. These take up residence in our unconscious, where they don't have to answer to criticism.

Psychology tells us that repressed material gains potency as a result of the energy invested in keeping it secret. Astrology tells us that Pluto governs power so acute that unless mindfully used, it waxes destructive. If the house of residence is the second, money is the agent of this potential misuse.

How America Spends its Money

Does America misuse the power of money? This country has more wealth at its disposal than any nation that has ever existed on Earth. Where does it go?

Many Americans don't like to think about how much money goes to the Pentagon, but let's look at it the way an accountant might for a moment. At this writing, summer of 2006, three hundred million dollars of American taxpayer money per day is spent on the war in Iraq. (We will leave aside for the moment the question of whether this money should, in any way, shape or form, have been disbursed for these purposes. We will even leave aside the lost and/or otherwise mysteriously disappeared portions of this money—such as the 28.8-billion dollar "accounting gap" recently reported by the Pentagon, and the billions paid to Halliburton et al that they say they *can't find*). Let us just try to wrap our minds around that number for a moment—three hundred million dollars per day. This amounts to twelve million dollars an hour of taxpayer money. We are talking about *ten thousand dollars a second*[14]. This is happening while national parks are being auctioned off to raise a few million dollars, and lunches for disabled seniors are being cut for lack of funds.

Meanwhile, America is in debt. Major debt. It is probably beyond the capability of most of us to conceptualize the several trillion dollars that America is in the red. And how are amends being made? By giving money away to those who need it least. In a world where four billion people earn less than four dollars a day, Washington policymakers are busy planning additional tax cuts for the already preposterously wealthy profiteers who put them into office. And so far, Congress and the public have been letting them do it.

Moreover, although we rarely hear about it, twenty billion a year is said to go into the "Black Budget"—a Pentagon fund so secret it doesn't even report its operations to Congress—and no one bats an eye. Whether those billions go to UFO research or fancy weird weapons, nobody knows. And upon whom are these luxury armaments meant to be unleashed? Osama bin Laden (still presumably Washington's most wanted criminal mastermind, though he is curiously mentioned less and less frequently in the media)? Does anyone really believe this is the way to fight the kind of criminals who pull off hijackings with box cutters? It is all so hideously and insanely wasteful, it hurts the brain and the heart to think about it.

It is time for America to raise its collective hand, as at a twelve-step meeting, and say: *"I have a problem with money."*

Pluto and Control

Just as individuals have all kinds of denial mechanisms operating to keep our addictions in place, so do group entities. The Plutonian level of the psyche is masterful at covering itself up. Its operations tend to take place in their own little world under their own separate laws, quite apart from our self-image and *its* laws.

In the personal chart, Pluto's placement by house and aspect indicates our personal myths. In the *national* chart, it points to our collective myths. It takes a special kind of awareness to see through our own myths; and it will take a sizeable consciousness growth spurt for the country as a whole to admit that as a nation comprising a mere five per cent of an increasingly impoverished world population, Americans

---

[14] For a stunning visual translation of this reality, see the running tally posted by the National Priorities Project, at
http://nationalpriorities.org/index.php?option=com_wrapper&Itemid=182.

harbor some rather incongruous beliefs about wealth, entitlement and power.

Astrology associates several planets with authority of one kind or another. Mars is the kind that expresses itself with assertion and threat; Saturn exerts a cool and trenchant leadership. Neptune overwhelms its target with a fog of confusion; Jupiter dominates with sweeping moral dogma.

Pluto's authority trumps them all, without striking a posture of any kind. It may not even show its face. When functioning without self-knowledge, the Plutonian dominator thinks absolute control is the only kind worth shooting for. From a hidden position, Pluto plans an invasion; and if it succeeds it will have no qualm about wiping out the landscape and walking away. There is no sleep lost over what others think about it; others don't factor into the equation at all, so long as they don't get in the way.

This kind of control is not for show. It's for power. Wherever Pluto is positioned in the chart, we want to dominate and manipulate some*thing* or some*one*. The positioning of America's Pluto tells us that in the mass mind, the sharing of resources is a strained and tortured concept. The second house has nothing to do with sharing. America's Pluto does not understand the concept.

We are talking about distorted Pluto here. Where Pluto is used with a high level of consciousness, anything and everything is possible. But in the absence of an integrated national consciousness, Pluto will take over whatever field of activity carries its projections. Attitudes and actions are compelled that fly in the face of the more refined values the society may harbor.

"The New American Century"

A consummate example of this drive at work is the "New American Century," the not-all-that-Secret Doctrine erected by several-administrations'-worth of Washington policymakers. This document outlines, quite specifically, a geopolitical and military action plan whereby an alliance of business and governmental elements would achieve control of the world's resources. Kind of exactly like the *I-want-to-rule-the-world-Bwa-ha-ha-ha* plotlines that supervillains are always hatching in comic books. One gets the same feeling from Donald Rumsfeld's pithy phrase, "Full Spectrum Dominance." It sounds like he dug it out of an old copy of *Superman*.

I submit that even if a foreign policy campaign like this didn't exist, a cursory reading of the US chart would have led us to predict it[15]. A second-house Pluto that is kept at a crude level of awareness will embark upon a laser-like trajectory to dominate whatever resources are there to be possessed.

Owning Life

In our discussion of privatization we saw this control in terms of American business' indefinite expansion of the range of saleable items that had been free before, and their identification as potential possessions natural experiences that had heretofore existed outside of human authority (e.g. frozen sperm and embryos, rainfall, the airwaves). As a corollary, if the item itself cannot be owned—*fun*, let's say—the context in which it is consumed must be owned. So we are at the point where sports stadium ads broadcast corporate control of games played by logo-bedecked athletes whose very bodies announce their patronage, like tattooed concubines in a harem.

In a move that would have struck ancient farmers as inconceivably perverse, even the capacity of a crop to reproduce is coming under Plutonian control. Companies like Monsanto have made bold to possess the "secret of the seed,"[16] designing grains that will not

---

[15] This astrologer is using the word "prediction" in a looser construction than is usually intended, which may need clarification. Pluto itself is not to blame for the *New American Century*; but absent a certain level of collective awareness, it would not be a surprising expression of this placement. Never forget that the wild card in astrology is the level of awareness of the native. This is why the only antidote to the dark use of this chart—or any other—is consciousness raising.

Whether interpreting the chart of a country or an individual, it is generally true that prediction is easier when the entity's level of awareness is low. Just as unimaginative people are sometimes referred to as "predictable," a native with little self-awareness tends to express its chart in a way that is relatively circumscribed and defined by its environment. By contrast, when a native's self-awareness is high it is harder to know what she is going to do.

We know from watching highly evolved individuals that they are open to an infinite range of potential expressions of the same impulse. If a native understands that he creates his own reality, he feels a responsibility for the way he acts out his chart. He does not have to confine himself to a reactive expression of Pluto or any other planet. In the case of a country, as Liz Greene writes in *The Outer Planets and Their Cycles*, consciousness raising is rather more difficult a proposition; this is where enlightened leaders often come in. But in their current vacuum of leadership, Americans are being tested to personify the Aquarian Age concept spelled out in their own Constitution: that every individual cultivate within himself the kind of vision heretofore expected of prophets and kings.

[16] The phrase derives from the Eleusinian rites, solemn celebrations of Nature's Mysteries that took place for thousands of years in the pre-classical Mediterranean. These

replicate; so that farmers are forced to buy them anew each season from the corporation that "owns" them[17].

Pluto governs the microscopic architecture by which an entity is broken down into its barest constituent parts: atoms, genetic blueprints. The idea of trying to control the genetic codes of not only plant life, but of animal and perhaps even human life, must strike every thoughtful person as a crossover into a qualitatively darker region of Pluto territory than has ever been breached.

Authority vs. Power

We know that Plutonian darkness can mutate, through awareness, from blind and destructive to wise and regenerative. We have seen that it is not the chart itself, but the native's awareness, that determines how Pluto's power will play out. But one thing we can be sure of: wherever along the consciousness spectrum it falls, Pluto is always authentic. It despises halfway measures and it will not pander for approval. An astrologer looking at Pluto in the natal chart may feel that she has just peeked beneath a polished veneer and glimpsed the hidden truth about a person. What becomes visible are the root causes beneath the native's operation. Pluto traffics in truth, warts and all.

Each of the pieces of a natal chart corresponds with a layer of the personality, and even the superficial ones have a role to play. But to focus on a chart's Pluto is to differentiate façade from essence. Pluto's placement enables us to separate the native's core rationale from her putative rationales. In fact, the native's hidden motives often blatantly contradict the persona she wishes to project to the world.

A case in point is the USA chart, with its strong and visible Saturn in the house of political authority (the tenth house), and in the sign of Libra—together representing the collective idealism of the great American experiment—which we will discuss in the next chapter. But we have seen that the planet of true power is that Pluto in the second. This suggests that, despite all the huffing and puffing in Washington about different types of governments—dictatorships vs. democracies, elections vs. tyranny—the real power comes from a house that doesn't

---

sacred exercises used grain as a talisman, honoring the Mother Goddess who gave humanity the gift of life—in the form of food that bore the promise of its own regeneration. When one considers Monsanto's machinations from the perspective of these ancients, it is hard to imagine an act of hubris more appalling.

[17] In a further revelation of the true motives behind Washington's intentions in Iraq, an order by Paul Bremer, administrator of the occupation until 2004, required farmers there to pay a licensing fee to an American corporation for patented seeds. His edict declared it illegal to grow harvested ones.

care a pin about all that. The second house tells us that the dominance America seeks has less to do with governments *per se* than it has to do with the control of resources.

In the civilized sign of Libra, the US Saturn symbolizes the ability of ordinary Americans to seek legal redress, for example, and to vote his or her conscience. This is the ideal. The reality, of course, is that Pluto in the second house is the engine behind American elections. In the current era of corporate-sponsored candidates, where the most compelling question in the news seems to be which candidate has spent more millions on his or her campaign, is there a voter so naïve as to believe that any politician, no matter how wildly popular, could spurn special interests and still win the White House?

Enlightened Use of Power

Now that we have parsed the symbolism of power and compared it with Pluto's location in the American chart, perhaps we can begin to glimpse the soul-purpose behind the placement's distortion.

On a metaphysical level, Pluto in the second house suggests a collective karma about *right use of resources*. This is a cosmic lesson about the difference between the enlightened use of material power and its shadow side. Wherever Pluto resides, there is a compelling shadow side. The entity is meant to face that shadow, enter into it and then transcend it, like an initiate in a shamanic rite.

In this chapter we have looked at the extraordinary power imbalance that prevails in the world today, noting the ways in which the USA throws its weight around through bombs, "sanctions," NAFTA, born-again Christianity, and Britney Spears. We have traced this global imbalance to a national tendency to obsessively go after whatever has been deemed valuable. We have seen how America's oil addiction illustrates a kind of magical thinking while promoting an entrenched collective denial that allows unspeakable injustice and human suffering worldwide. We have proposed that the Saturnine face the USA presents to the world—as a model of benevolent governance—bears little resemblance to the true motives expressed by its Pluto: a doctrinal plan to control the access to natural resources in whatever form and in whatever region of the world they are to be found.

The next chapters will address the other planets in the US chart that have particular bearing on these themes, the better to understand not only America's shadow side but its potential for redemption. Out of the entire web of the interconnected chart, a vision of unified meaning can arise: a sense of why this particular group of souls incarnated into this particular era.

As we continue our study let us begin to fashion an image of how the power of the American chart might be used with an integrity commensurate with its impact.

SIX

Big Daddy of the World

Saturn at the Top of the Chart

The next planet we will look at is Saturn: the planet of structure, tradition and high office. In the American chart it plays a critical role. As the signifier of the Father archetype, Saturn is the nominal face of government. Its posture in this chart tells a great deal about the institutions of leadership that the USA has come up with, and the individuals Americans choose to personify them.

But before we look at its role in the US chart, let us look first at some of the general meanings attached to Saturn, whose notoriety will have preceded it for those readers familiar with planetary lore.

The Greater Malefic[1]

Among the ten planets used in popular astrology, Saturn is far and away the most likely to get negative spin: in textbooks and interpretations it is all too often cast as the bad guy of the chart. This has less to do with the planet's essential meaning than with dusty old notions from the fatalistic Dark Ages, when Saturn acquired the cranky and

---

[1] Its medieval nickname signifies the dread and malevolence associated with Saturn in a harsher epoch. Since then, astrological symbolism has been informed by Enlightenment notions of individual choice as well as by psychological models of the unconscious (in particular, by Carl Jung's theory of *the shadow*), which offered new models with which to disabuse astrology of its old fatalisms and helped bring Saturn into the world of contemporary thought. The humanistic school of astrology introduced by Dane Rudhyar in the last century[*] takes the position that every symbol in the birth chart has both an ideal side and a shadow side; and whereas most modern astrologers would agree with this principle in theory (and apply it without hesitation to every other planet), with Saturn many seem to think of its shadow side as its primary meaning.

In any case, the deeper one gets into the study of astrology, the sillier it seems to project evaluations of any kind onto the archetypes. Eternal universal principles do not exist for the comfort and approval of human beings. As Rob Hand has said: " 'Good' means *I like it*; 'bad' means *I don't*. That's all there is to *good* and *bad*."[**]

[*] See especially *The Astrology of Personality: A Reinterpretation of Astrological Concepts and Ideals in Terms of Contemporary Psychology and Philosophy.*

[**]Remark in a lecture.

doomful pedigree with which it is still associated. Saturn has been connected to fear, pain, hardship and failure. Death itself was on the list before Pluto was discovered and took over that rulership. But when we look at its essential meaning we get a different picture of Saturn, a picture both more innocuous and more benevolent.

Saturn is the governor of nothing less than Time and Space. By this association it presides over the lessons of time—patience, integrity, maturity, effort—and the mastery of matter—construction, weight, density and solidity. Saturnine laws include contraction, limitation and boundary setting—functions that contain us, ground us, and bind us to the world of form. Among these is gravity, which is why we often find the planet strongly placed in the charts of people we think of as being *substantial,* of having *gravitas.*

Saturn in the US Chart

In the US chart, we find Saturn in the tenth house of public visibility. This planet is naturally[2] associated with this house, the house at the top of the wheel. Planets here are said to *crown* the chart, with all the connotations of royalty and statesmanship that that implies. A planet so positioned is "on top" literally as well as figuratively: the placement means it was located near the zenith of the sky at the time of birth, and by extension confers a relative societal prominence. Individuals whose charts feature Saturn near the zenith typically have a strong investment in their careers.

A group or person with Saturn here will tend to care very much what people think: the concept of *reputation* (whatever it means to them) is a highlight of both their self-image and their group purpose. Saturn in the tenth house bestows a heightened sense of accountability for one's public position, which, when expressed unconsciously, bestows an overarching ambition with fear of failure at its root. One feels deeply pressured to get to the top and to stay on top, whatever that means to the native.

But the ideal expression of Saturn in the tenth house is the ability to be a solid role model. This placement can indicate the achievement of a well-earned, managerial posture in some social hierarchy, a leadership role based on a genuine understanding of responsibility: a reliable employer, say, or a statesman who respects the laws of his office. When

---

[2] Every planet is associated with a certain sign and a certain house. In its *natural* house or sign, a given planet's qualities come out most prominently because the meanings of that sign and that house derive from the same archetype as the planet. It is like an actor being typecast in a role. So it is with Saturn and the tenth house.

in the tenth house, Saturn's true face—that of the Benevolent Father— has a chance of shining forth as a beacon to society.

In the US chart we find this crowning Saturn in Libra: the sign of justice, equanimity and the rule of law. Here Saturn indicates a need to *stand for something*: an ambivalent idealism about whatever notions of fairness and equality hold sway in the native's mind at a given time (ambivalent because Saturn always has a love-hate relationship with whatever sign it's in. It makes us doubt our abilities in the very area where we feel pressured to accomplish great things). The Libran goals of everybody-being-equal and everybody-getting-along become directives to be pronounced publicly, and to be submitted to judgment.

The glyph for Libra is a pictogram of a scales for weighing, suggesting a constant balancing of opposing forces—such as we find in binary systems, one-on-one debates and two-party governments. This is a conceptual air sign, concerned with ideas, not necessarily with application (that part would be up to the other planets in the chart). Saturn in Libra is always embroiling itself in ideological issues of negotiation, mediation, and the search for equitable solutions.

Air signs in general are concerned with ideals, not behaviors. It is earth signs that are concerned with practical application; water signs with empathic connections, and fire signs with spirited activity. By contrast, air signs are about the creation of mental stances. And Saturn, being the planet of structure, takes that mental stance and tries to consolidate it into a tract or policy. Or a constitution.

On Top of the World

In Chapter Four we discussed the distinction between Saturnine *authority* and Plutonian *power*. We said the USA's outer face is Saturnine—that of a righteous world cop—while its inner face is Plutonian—that of a control freak with its sights set on global resources. Though the rest of the world seems to harbor few illusions about the situation, in the American mind there remains a remarkable disconnect between these two faces.

Many Americans clearly identify with the prestige and authority signified by this chart's Saturn. They seem to view their country as a model of old-fashioned decency that has earned its global reputation (tenth house) as being tough (Saturn) but fair (Libra). Consciously used, a Saturn in this placement would rightfully lead a people to tout the rule of law (Saturn in Libra) as a proud justification for their country's top-dog status (tenth house). But it is becoming more and more difficult to ignore that it is Pluto—power, not law—that dictates actual procedure.

When it chooses, Washington flouts not only international laws[3] but its own constitutional laws—such as protections of civil liberties—at the drop of a hat.

Increase: *Good*. Decrease: *Bad*

Also very telling is Saturn's uncomfortable relationship with the Sun and Jupiter. On July 4, 1776 Saturn was roughly a quarter-circle of sky away from where the Sun and Jupiter were. This arc of separation is known as a *square*[4], and it can indicate that the planets in question operate at cross-purposes.

As we saw in Chapter Four, the Sun and Jupiter are themselves *conjunct*. This means the two were very close to each other in the zodiac the day the USA was born; from Earth's point of view they were overlapping in the sky. When planets are conjunct their astrological meanings are fused together, so the Sun and Jupiter operate more or less as one body in the US chart[5]. This makes *expansion* (Jupiter) the guiding principle of the national temperament (Sun). What does it mean for a chart to feature such a prominent placement of the planet of growth and expansion? And to feature Saturn (*lessening, selectivity, contraction*) linked to it by a stressful square? It means that rules and regulations are felt to be at cross-purposes with growth, rather than supporting growth. It means that America as a whole has real trouble understanding the interplay between *expansion* and *contraction*.

To have Jupiter conjunct the Sun is deemed very nice— "lucky"—in facile interpretations of a birth chart. Just as Saturn—the so-called *greater malefic*—has been stereotyped as a negative planet,

---

[3] An example getting a lot of attention at this writing is the Bush administration's abrogation of traditional protections against torture; but the USA has committed innumerable international crimes that receive far less press. A particularly egregious example, virtually ignored by the American public, was the 1998 bombing by the Clinton administration of that Sudanese "nerve-gas lab"—actually a pharmaceutical assembly plant whose medicines had supplied the entire region of East Africa, as the CIA knew quite well. Despite civilian casualties, the Sudanese were barred from suing in international court (as were the Libyans, who tried to go through the same legal channels after the American strike in 1986 that killed, among others, Khadafy's baby daughter. One winces to imagine the screams of "terrorism" that would have ensued had an incident even remotely similar occurred to the child of an American president). Reparations were never made.

[4] See Appendix I for definitions of astrological terms such as these.

[5] Venus closely conjuncts Jupiter, adding weight to the Jupiterian side of the contest (see footnote, Page 31). This exaggerates the chart's identification with pleasure and ease, and strengthens the tendency to hold Saturn's sober values at arm's length.

Jupiter, whose nickname is the *greater benefic*, has been given a pass in the other direction. But these connotations don't tell us much about either planet. Repeating the old saw that Jupiter is inherently desirable and Saturn inherently undesirable will not help us understand the highly charged duet these two play out in the US chart.

Growth as Default Reality

The Jupiter conjunction with the US Sun certainly implies a group celebration of increase, abundance and ambition, but this is just the tip of the iceberg. There is something more fundamental, and irrational, at work. The truth is that in the American mind, aggrandizement is seen as the natural state of things, and decline is seen as aberrant.

When Americans make more money than they made last month, it's the way it should be. But when they make less than they made last month, it's alarming; it's not supposed to happen; the wolf is at the door. There is a profound imbalance here between the concepts of *upturn* (Jupiter) and *downturn* (Saturn): an imbalance that informs every level of American society. At the level of official policy, this imbalance has inspired a coinage that speaks volumes: Wall Street has officially replaced the word *recession*—a Saturnine concept, taboo in Jupiter Land—with the phrase *negative growth*.

Most Americans would agree that periodic decreases must be part of human activity as much as they are a part of biological activity. Surely it would be absurd to curse the fact that the tide must go out as well as in. We have all learned that—at least in the rest of the universe—what comes up must go down. But in America, it's never supposed to go down. In general, when the Sun is conjunct another planet, the conjoining planet is seen *not* as one-reality-among-many, but as the default reality. (If you know your own chart to feature a solar conjunction, ask yourself whether this postulate applies.)

When seen from a purely conceptual point of view, inflation and deflation are two sides of the same coin. But this configuration in the US chart suggests that the *increase* side of the polarity has been subsumed into the national identity, and *decrease* has been rejected. America as a group entity identifies with the waxing phase—half of the cycle–and dis-identifies with the waning phase. The ego-self (the Sun) is considered to be the agent of increase (Jupiter), while malevolent external forces (Saturn) are considered to be the agents of decrease.

In Chapter One we talked about the adolescent quality of the American psyche, of which this conjunction is the astrological signature[6]. It is a worldview which unconsciously assumes that growth is a goal never to be interrupted by its opposite. Life is one long dot-com boom that never has to go bust. (To be fair, Americans don't ignore the dualism factor entirely: they seem okay with the dichotomy between *gain* and *more gain*.)

Putting a Positive Face on It

Seen through an archetypal lens, the belief in never-ending expansion is an oddly counter-intuitive one. When its advocates are confronted with historical and scientific facts—for example, when believers in a ceiling-free housing market are faced with the statistical verities of economic cycles—they will probably acknowledge that their expectations do not derive from logic *per se*. But at this point, instead of looking further into the matter, Jupiter apologists—whether countries or individuals—tend to quickly reframe their position as a matter of philosophical temperament: they'll shrug it off as jolly old positivism. Certainly this is the primary way the tendency is viewed in the case of the national chart—"optimism" being one of those benign traits by which the American character is known and admired (these days, it might be stretching it to say "loved").

Free Lunch in America

It stands to reason that if a people favor their Jupiter over their Saturn, they will try to find ways around working for what they get. Getting a free lunch (Jupiter) is the opposite of earning something (Saturn). Saturn's way involves a slow application of effort—that is, *slow* relative to getting-rich-quick; and *effort* relative to starting-out-privileged or tricking and wheedling oneself into a favored position[7]. Despite the homilies of American folklore, to look around at the cultural landscape is to realize that earning is not really how one *makes it big* (notice that the phrase celebrates Jupiter, not Saturn) in the USA.

Saturn functions to draw into the self certain experiences over time, where they deepen self-understanding and competence. The solar square in the US chart indicates that this approach clashes brutally with

---

[6] Strengthening this signature is the US Ascendant in Sagittarius—the sign ruled by Jupiter—described in Chapter Two. Jupiter is associated with the phase of life between puberty and age 28.

[7] There is no clearer testament to the Jupiter-instead-of-Saturn approach than the fact that America twice accepted as its chief executive an unclever scion like George W. Bush, who as a young man sailed into Yale, failed at every patronage business in which he was set up and went AWOL from the cushiest imaginable military duty in 1972 without penalty then or now.

the collective self-image as a nation of carefree young adventurers (Sagittarius rising) galloping headlong towards a destiny of wealth and comfort, which collective picture holds sway not only within the USA itself but is being exported at breakneck speed to all corners of the world. Underlying this picture is the assumption that if life isn't abundant and easy, something must be wrong[8].

Horatio Alger

Working one's way up the ladder is the much-touted morale of the Horatio Alger story, an exemplary legend that has been disingenuously used to cajole decades'-worth of American schoolchildren—all the while being significantly distorted in the re-telling. In fact, the story's original plot features a distinctly Jupiterian scenario, not Saturnine at all. It teaches that rich uncles[9] and lucky breaks lead to fame and fortune, thus laying out the quintessentially American doctrine of manifest destiny as it applies to personal success.

When you think about it, this is a bizarrely puerile—if cheerfully upbeat—approach to one's work of the world. The message is that with fortune (/God) on one's side, all one needs is an unshakable desire for the brass ring—a philosophy that relies upon what is essentially a religious suspension of disbelief (Jupiter). It is this childlike notion that renders young Horatio's mischaracterized achievements more apt than his proponents realize. With his self-aggrandizing positivism (Jupiter) far more developed than his dedication to work (Saturn), Horatio Alger is more Arnold Schwarzenegger than Abe Lincoln. And in identifying this story as the prototypical hero's tale, America implicitly teaches its children that *earning* is only for fools.

Fifteen Minutes of Fame

Getting attention, like earning money, means one thing from Jupiter's point of view and another from Saturn's. Jupiter is linked to the kind of attention that arrives unbidden, whereas Saturn expects no recognition without hard-won experience and a tangible product to show for it. In the surreal world of American celebrity, a lifetime of steady achievement (Saturn) has less appeal than a brief, incandescent moment

---

[8] Saturn also governs *saving*, as Jupiter governs *spending*. As individuals, Americans currently spend five to six per cent more annually than they earn. As a collective, their government would need $27,500. at this writing from each American man, woman and child to clear the national debt. See Juan Enriquez, *The Untied States of America*.

[9] Jupiter governs not only wealth but the actual Uncle archetype. Saturn governs the Father and the Moon governs the Mother.

of fame (Jupiter). Indeed, the veteran expert who has honed his craft over long decades is more likely to be dismissed than revered for the years he's put in; for time itself is seen as something to battle, abbreviate and out-maneuver.

There is something dismally inevitable about the ascendancy in American public life of Paris Hilton Syndrome: the state of being celebrated for being a celebrity. Andy Warhol's aphorism "In the future everybody will be famous for fifteen minutes" has proven more prescient than anyone could have imagined at the time he said it. The fact that his observation is now more likely to elicit resigned eye-rolling than derision or dissent tells us that it has shifted from barely credible satire to mere exaggeration. The phenomenon it describes illustrates the extreme of silliness that is reached when Saturn is not integrated.

Common Sense

How does a person, or a group, integrate Saturn? One begins by refamiliarizing oneself with its core principles. To be used properly, Saturn should express consistency, practicality and preservation: this is the archetype in its pure form. But much has gotten lost in the translation from archetype to societal expression, which raises some interesting questions about this aspect of the American psyche.

The most salient feature of a truly Saturnine viewpoint is *common sense* (though this phrase needs to be used with caution, as it has so many wildly divergent champions as to render its meaning very slippery). For example, Saturn has long been associated with risk-averse economics and the politics of pragmatism. As the most nuts-and-bolts of the ten planets, Saturn is supposed to make the trains run on time. That said, where do we find Saturn in America today?

Faux-Conservatism

The answer is everywhere and nowhere. Saturnine language fills America's airwaves and bellows from its pulpits, but the planet's true voice is all but drowned out amid the din. This is the planet that governs conservation, but it is by no means clear that its rulership extends to "conservatism" in its popularly understood political meaning. In fact, it is not clear *what* "conservative" means; but we need to be clear what planetary archetypes mean, for we are taking them out of the textbook and using them to provide clarity in social experience.

If we agree that Saturn's key features include keeping a cool head, making systems work efficiently, and securing the viability of the future, how *conservative* are the National Rifle Association and Rush Limbaugh?

62

If we could ask Saturn, the planet of rigor and clarity, what he thought of the matter, he would first of all have us define our terms[10]—for the principle of *definition* itself falls under Saturn's rulership. That pundits from all over the political spectrum would see fit to label "conservative" such alarmingly immoderate, precedent-breaking and choleric positions as Ann Coulter's, for example, is itself evidence of America's estrangement from the Saturn archetype. Here is where astrological vocabulary is exactly what we need to lend some coherence to the quagmire. Let us use the essential meanings of Saturn to cut through the babble of buzzword parlance and give us an understanding of what's really going on.

We might begin with what is sometimes called the *conservative agenda*, and ask ourselves what is actually being conserved and how effectively it is being done. The word *conservative* is often used, for example, to characterize the various religious sects that attempt through legal means to ban birth control and sex education. Do these attempts meet the criteria of the dry-eyed god of functionality? If we know nothing else about Saturn, it is this: if a proposition veers off the trajectory of its own stated goal, Saturn will not endorse it. Programs to keep teenagers from having sex have just about the lowest rate of empirical success of any social experiment that exists; there is no way they pass muster. Moreover, Saturn in and of itself has no time for emotion, and no interest in moral posturing one way or the other. Family-values crusades, with their penchant for histrionics and righteous denunciations, do not belong to Saturn.

The same critique could be made of what is called, officially but ambiguously, the "war on drugs." Self-professed conservatives tend to endorse this campaign (which spends a highly unconservative amount of money: more than fifty billion tax dollars annually), but how *conservative* are its key tenets? If we were to measure it against the yardstick of Saturn, we would first of all have trouble with the jarring inconsistency at its base: the core advocates of this domestic policy tend to favor foreign policies which finance regimes worldwide that make their money selling drugs (via networks so entrenched and so lucrative

---

[10] The American public has fallen into a lazy acceptance of a form of sloganism that serves, like mental pablum, to cover up inconsistent and simplistic thinking. If Saturn were consulted, he would particularly disdain the misuse of the anachronistic labels *right* and *left*—terms originating from the seating arrangement in the French National Assembly after the revolution of 1789, for heaven's sake. These words are currently tossed around in American English to refer to anything that could be construed as a partisan stance, as if everyone who hears them is in complete agreement as to what they mean, and as if everyone who uses them means the same thing by them. But in fact *right* and *left* as political and cultural identifiers are as expandable as latex.

that the US government itself has exploited them, in Latin America and elsewhere, to finance its covert operations). Moreover, if wagers of this "war" imagine the goal to be stamping out drug use, they lack the barest shred of evidence upon which to support their intention[11]. And if we were really thinking conservatively, Saturnine logic would lead us to conclude that long prison sentences to punish the use of certain—but not all—drugs (and not even the most dangerous of drugs) make no economic sense to anyone but the prison industry[12]. A *cui bono* inquiry would lead us to many strange-bedfellow interests that are handsomely served by these policies, and help us uncover the real impulses behind this doomed campaign. But it is a ludicrous misnomer to call them *conservative*.

Another group of self-described conservatives who seem to be blind to the law of conservation are the policymakers who react to budget crises by lopping off human service programs. Ethical considerations aside, are these decisions practical; do they conserve resources; are they driven by future considerations? A truly Saturnine approach would use demographic facts and figures to project what would be likely to happen, for example, to desperate public-assistance recipients when their small scraps of help dry up and disappear. It was Ronald Reagan, known as a conservative's conservative, whose public-funding-slashing approach to governance is identified as having launched the modern reality of mental patients fending for themselves on the mean urban streets.

Saturn's approach to harm is not to fight it, but to prevent it. Herein lies the genius of true conservatism. The Reagan paradigm could be called many things, but surely the one thing it was *not* was conservative.

True Conservatism

In its healthy expression, Saturn promotes survival into the future by faithfully preserving that which has proven worthy from the past. This is the planet that reminds us to conserve berries so there is something to eat in the winter, and to preserve the rainforest so the ecosystem may continue to thrive.

---

[11] In 1975, before the federal "war on drugs" got going in earnest, drug use among twelve-to-seventeen-year-olds was estimated to be just over fifty per cent. In 2006 the figure is almost exactly the same.

[12] Well over half of American federal inmates are in prison for drugs.

With Saturn as their muse, environmental scientists, engineers and ecologists are continually coming up with new ideas about how to safeguard the world's resources—techniques that cost little and have been shown to work very well. It is Saturn that is behind the rediscovery of pre-industrial methodologies like sustainable agriculture; and it is to programs like these that the word *traditional*[13] literally applies. Such efforts get at the very heart of what Saturn is about. But given the strained position Saturn holds in the US chart (square to the Sun and Jupiter), it comes as no surprise that these old, time-tested ideas are being pursued in spite of—rather than at the behest of—the institutions in America which hold worldly power.

Efficient transit systems, solar and wind energy, and local, organic agriculture would be the norm today if America had Saturn at the helm. Yet in the current era of ecological crisis, the genuinely conservative ideas are showing up at the fringes of consensus thinking.

Saturn Hunger

It may now be easier to see how Pluto was able to take over so completely from Saturn's leadership of the US chart. Though it identifies with the job description of Big Daddy of the World, America cannot truly inhabit the role of the benevolent patriarch because it rejects its own Saturn. For all the lip service it pays to family values, "traditional" marriage and old-time religion, America remains deeply estranged from Saturn's core principles. Maturity, sustainability and self-limitation are dismissed, mocked or espoused in an ersatz way.

Rules and those who uphold them are viewed with undisguised ambivalence in the USA. Hollywood heroes tend to be men who break rank and break rules: they're all loners, rogue cops and tough-guy underdogs—who, though they make a big show of fighting The Man, somehow manage to hold onto his patriarchal values, not to mention his material privileges. Rulers themselves are held with a strange fascination-repulsion in the American imagination (notice the fixation with British royalty[14]).

---

[13] Here is another term whose heedless ubiquity makes it seem as if it is meant to denote the same thing to every listener with every usage. But clearly what is called *traditional*— "traditional marriage," "traditional medicine," "traditional astrology"—depends upon which tradition one is referring to, and how far back historically one is willing to look.

[14] The Jungian astrologer Liz Greene has made bold to suggest that, in sharp contrast to its self-image, the United States—deep in its collective soul—yearns to return to a monarchy (an opinion perhaps only a British writer could get away with). Saturn's elevated placement in the tenth house bespeaks a strong-arm father figure shored up by long tradition; against which the Jupiter/Sun square with Saturn incessantly rebels—as

Shunned by the Sun-Jupiter-Venus conjunction, distorted and misapplied, America's Saturn nags and chides from beneath the national consciousness. And as is always true of unintegrated planets, the native smarts from the lack.

Though little understood, the harm caused by America's mass denial of Saturn is widely deplored. Parents, progressives, fundamentalists and Miss Manners all rail against the caving-in to the lowest common ethical denominator that has become the norm among our leaders, the blind conformity that numbs our social consciousness as citizens, the dearth of accountability in relationships, the absence in everyday encounters of little gestures of respect.

Father Wisdom

Popular imagery is always a good indicator of the attitude a culture has towards a planetary archetype, and we see in the case of US Saturn that benevolent father figures are in short supply. Households with actual fathers are on the decrease in American society. Buffoonish patriarchs on TV are the norm.

But in repudiating father-wisdom, America has become almost comically desperate for it. Where our environment shuns an aspect of human potential, it grows so precious to us that we glom onto whatever vestige of it we can find. Thus the rare instances of high-profile men who might qualify as a benevolent father are balm to the wound. Not terribly exceptional but idolized nonetheless, men like former newsman Walter Cronkite and actor-director Clint Eastwood are unlikely heroes who are seemingly cherished mostly for having aged with relative grace.

"Uncle" Cronkite, whom pollsters tell us was one of America's most trusted public figures during the divisive sixties and seventies, combined the paternal and avuncular energies of Saturn and Jupiter. His Saturn conjuncts Neptune, the planet that idealizes and mythologizes whatever it touches, enhancing Cronkite's ability to model the Father Archetype for millions of viewers. Eastwood's chart reveals a

---

the colonies did from the English king. Without a Big-Daddy form of government, Greene argues, the country does not know what to do with itself and founders like a teenager without parental guidance.

Further insight about the US Saturn dilemma can be gained from linguist George Lakoff's *Moral Politics: How Liberals and Conservatives Think,* which presents a model of the patriarchal dynamic between citizens and the state.

disproportionately strong Saturn in the sign of its rulership: no-nonsense, respect-worthy Capricorn[15].

And consider the case of John McCain, a politician who seems to be as esteemed as he is not so much for his actual policies as for satisfying America's Saturn yearnings. Like Cronkite, he has a Saturn-Neptune connection, giving his paternality a larger-than-life quality; like Eastwood, his Saturn is made extra appealing by Venus, to which it is opposed. McCain is widely perceived as having a hard-won integrity that makes him rise above his fellow congressmen—who, by contrast to him, come off as even more sordid and jaded than usual. McCain's Saturnine draw is so compelling that one is tempted to overlook his voting record and funding sources, which are basically no different than those of his far-less-popular colleagues. The secret to McCain's allure lies in his understanding, conscious or not, of America's Saturn hunger. In offering himself up as a personification of old-fashioned self-respect, he comes off as the exception that proves the rule.

The surprising thing is not that this tactic has worked so well to endear the man to an electorate numbed to despair by political cynicism, but that so few politicians have similarly recognized and exploited it. Indeed, the more common practice in campaigns for public office is to appeal to the nation's desire to get something for nothing (Jupiter). Promises of tax cuts and 100-dollar rebates are turning up in sober political speeches, reminding one of nothing so much as a desperate parent trying to bribe the toddler into the car seat.

Back to Basics

We have seen that Saturn is well placed by house in the American chart but weak by context. We have looked at the ways unconscious Pluto—the last planet you want to leave unconscious, because of the damage it can cause—has undermined the moral authority of Saturn, plundering its leadership potential in the process. We looked at how the Sun/Jupiter conjunction, all bombast and enterprise, has won out over Saturn's solemn dedication to impartiality and balance. We saw how the US Saturn has lost its authenticity but remains at the fore, like the cracked masthead of an aging ship.

We have considered how, in its collective unconscious, America pines for its banished Saturn. In human cultural life no less than in biological systems, Nature abhors a vacuum; the human heart knows very well what self-respect feels like, both on a personal and a group

---

[15] Although Saturn is not usually a planet associated with sexual charm, one is not surprised to see that in Eastwood's chart the Father Archetype carries the magnetism of Venus, which opposes his Saturn from the eighth house (sexuality).

level. Even the most defensive America-firster must surely cast a furtive glance, every now and again, over at Europe—with their universal healthcare and pleasant railway stations—and muse about what it would be like to live in a protective, good-parent state.

How might America's Saturn be turned around? As is always the case, the answer lies with consciousness change. To reclaim a planetary function we have to go back to basic astrology and see the planet in the raw—the only way to make sense of its various distorted manifestations. Then we consider how its current expressions diverge from what the planet really wants to express.

Like every other planetary archetype, Saturn represents a built-in spiritual constant; and the goal of this study is to get back in touch with those constants. We must look at the symbols as if we were seeing them for the first time, in order to reconnect with them at a level beneath wherever we were with them before. In so doing we begin to glimpse what the gods had in mind when they positioned these particular planets in these particular places at these particular angles.

In the case of the USA, the potential is there to be a stalwart supervisor of global justice: to be a nation that holds its eminence with the utmost seriousness; to be a nation that practices what it preaches. This is the potential America was born with—a potential that could, in theory, be stepped into at any time.

SEVEN

KILL YOUR TELEVISION
PLUTO OPPOSITE MERCURY

We will now consider a planetary dialogue that expresses one of the major plotlines in the American story.

Pluto is opposite Mercury in the US chart: the two bodies were positioned straight across the sky from each other that summer day in 1776. They form the spine of the chart and comprise its only opposition. This is a confrontation between the planet of *power* and the planet of *communication.*

Mercury is a mental planet, associated with cognitive thinking, reading, writing and speaking. It governs our day-to-day mind[1], the part of our intelligence that we use to figure out problems and process information. So it is said to rule the various systems that pass information around: language, school, journalism, the telecommunications industry. In a national chart, it indicates the culture's intellectual life: its media; educational, research and transportation systems; range and quality of discourse; linguistic peculiarities and so on.

An opposition adds a strident tension to any chart: it is as if two energies are playing tug-of-war. We have looked at Pluto as the engine of hidden power in the USA, and the key signature of its territorial prerogative. Its opposition with Mercury is the closest planetary relationship the US Pluto makes, and their interplay tells us more than any other in this chart about the manifestation of power in American society.

Pluto and the Media

This is the aspect of the US chart that signifies the power of American media—newspapers, video and especially television; a power that has been raising alarm among citizen groups comprised of parents,

---

[1] Jupiter, by contrast, governs the kind of thinking that involves not just cognition but paradigm shifts. By analogy, Mercury governs grade school, whereas Jupiter rules over higher education; Mercury governs travel within a relatively local area, while Jupiter governs travel to a foreign place.

anti-monopolists and other cultural watchdogs. Their alarm might be summed up in the bumper-sticker distress call *Kill your television.*

To understand with metaphysical detachment the fraught topic of power in America, we must first strip it of its connotations. Interpreting a chart is like painting a still life: if we want to truly observe the object, we start by forgetting what we think we know about it. What would astrology, straight out of the textbook, make of a Mercury-Pluto opposition when found in a group chart? It would probably say that *the group's information system may be undermined by an underground power source.*

The system in question is a mass media whose immense reach extends well beyond America, into popular culture throughout the modern world—from Shanghai street vendors hawking knock-offs of J-Lo perfume to Nigerian gangsters using street language inspired by Eminem CDs. And what is the underground power source? How does it work, and what are its implications?

To answer this we need to factor in what we have learned about the relationship between the country's resources (second house), and the powers-that-be that seek to control them (Pluto)—powers increasingly unrestrained by reason or law. In the current era, information itself, and by extension the media that conveys it, has become one of these resources.

As we begin to look at this all-too-familiar situation from an astrological perspective, it becomes easier to understand the muted and compromised state of American public discourse. Mercury governs the ideas the media ushers into currency, and the opposition with Pluto suggests that these ideas are subject to sophisticated manipulation (e.g. the "echo chamber" effect of the mainstream news) that keeps a few carefully selected stories in the forefront, while "controversial"[2] and/or unexpurgated information is pushed underground (onto the web; into the increasingly endangered alternative print media; dismissed as "conspiracy theories.")

Reading between the lines has become increasingly necessary if one hopes to extract a modicum of verisimilitude from the mainstream media. As its products become increasingly outlandish, the media's lack of integrity becomes increasingly obvious.

---

[2] Notice that the adjective *controversial* does not so much describe the noun it's supposed to modify as serve to distance the user from the topic, via a posture of faux-neutrality.

The Paper and the Government

Since Pluto crossed the USA chart's Ascendant in 2000-01 (to be discussed in detail in Chapter Eleven), there has been a significant rise in public concern about complicity between the press and the government—a pairing that cannot help but result in information (Mercury) pollution (Pluto). An example of this phenomenon so trenchant as to be downright operatic was the Judith Miller affaire of 2005, an indictment of American journalism disguised as a *don't-kill-the-messenger* (Mercury) parable.

Miller, a celebrated *New York Times* reporter who was in-like-Flynn with the Bush administration, was arrested for failing to disclose her sources. Her contacts had supplied Miller with a steady stream of skewed data supporting the case for war with Iraq, which the "paper of record" had duly printed—thereby legitimizing a military disaster that had been widely decried by the public and almost universally denounced by the wider world before it began. With its weapons of mass destruction, its spies, its warmongers and manipulation, the whole media débacle was a toxic swamp of Plutonian intrigue, with hapless Mercury (clarity, facts) sinking beneath the slime[3]. The incident was one of several recent indicators of an implosion going on within the *New York Times*, America's most highly esteemed journalistic institution: a death (Pluto) of credibility (Mercury) that has been coming to light since this epochal transit began.

---

[3] Journalist Miller—free speech heroine (Mercury) or parrot of the hawks (Pluto), depending on your point of view—announced her "early retirement" from the *New York Times* in November 2005. Miller's flawed reporting—since exposed as not merely erroneous, but the intelligence equivalent of cooked books—was at first shielded (Pluto) from critique (Mercury) by none other than *New York Times* publisher Arthur Sulzberger Jr. himself. "I can do whatever I want," Miller was reported to have told a colleague, glowing with reflected power in her role as the Bush camp's spokeswoman. "They call me Miss Run Amok." Sulzberger later published a shamefaced apologia about the *Times'* dissemination of discredited *"intel"* (a term increasingly popular with functionaries who seek to prevent a lie being traced back to its source), though he lauded Miller as a freedom-of-the-press martyr when she went to jail to protect the mysterious individual she would only refer to as a "White House "staffer" whose trail led investigators to Dick Cheney's office door.

To romanticize Judith Miller's stonewalling as First Amendment heroism is an ironic spin to put upon the episode, whose true meaning can be inferred, as astrologers know, from its timing. When the grand jury first asked Miller and her colleagues to testify, it was October 2004: the American electorate was poised to elect a president feared and despised by the people of the world. The year's postponement marked the difference between a few weeks before the presidential election and well after Bush was safely tucked into office. It is hard to avoid the conclusion that Miller and her inside-the-Beltway friends knowingly delayed sharing their direct knowledge of a top-level crime that could have changed the outcome of the election.

If natal Mercury-opposite-Pluto can be said to have a worst-case scenario, it is Pluto chronically threatening to drag Mercury away from its purpose (neutral observation and reporting), in order to shill for Pluto's purpose (unbridled behind-the-scenes power).

The essential teaching of the pairing is that information (Mercury) can have life-or-death impact (Pluto). The *New York Times* illustrated this truth with unwitting precision when it violated its mandate to provide the public with clean information in the Judith Miller tale; and it is not an isolated instance. The "paper of record" has long identified itself with Washington's tireless mischannelings of the national Pluto.

Intellectual Property Cartel

Part of America's current crisis of self-revelation concerns media hegemony, bias and corruption, all of which have been duly outed in a flurry of bestsellers (e.g. *Weapons of Mass Deception*) and films (e.g. *Outfoxed*) exposing the news industry as an intellectual property cartel. But we have seen that myths grow up around Pluto, keeping it strangely isolated in the chart. These serve to protect the planet, perversely, from scrutiny and integration. Collective stories surround America's Pluto just as personal stories surround an individual's Pluto. Obsolete notions and fantasies about free speech (Mercury) in a plutocratic economy (Pluto in the second house) abound in the national ethos.

One of these myths is that the availability of five hundred television channels means freer choice and higher quality programming—a notion that falls away when we consider the ramifications of the fact that the same four corporations own everything from TV satellites to billboards. As industry watchers know, these mega-companies do not really compete with each other. Like a mafia family (also ruled by Pluto), they form a cartel that operates through a carefully controlled arrangement: Fox movies have to be sold to HBO, Warner cable has to take Fox because they're the one with sports teams, and so on; all of which keeps the power locked in, and independent producers shut out[4].

---

[4] At least as sobering are the implications of one giant company owning all the phone lines. To paraphrase telecommunications lawyer, Chris Witteman: If anti-trust efforts to stop AT&T continue to fail, it will own most of the wires to an American's home phone and computer, *and* from his cell phone company's towers to the cell phone company's switch, *and* those from his internet café to the network's central office, as well as the wires carrying his emails and VoIP telephone traffic—not to mention the wires over which he might want to, say, Google information that may or may not be flattering to his government and its favored companies. Like AT&T.

Clues in Plain Sight

As we have seen, Pluto's clues tend to be hidden in plain sight. Accordingly, evidence of what the US media has become is often openly flaunted, while Americans' grade-school-textbook notions about free speech remain bizarrely unchanged. Take the example of political reactionary and media mogul, Rupert Murdoch. He is now a household name; but though the public knows who he is, they do not seem to know *what* he is. His monopolistic holdings are more likely to be mentioned in popular magazines in the gushing tones of a personal-success story than they are to be condemned.

It is hardly classified information that the media has become a corporate commodity with an entrenched lobby in Washington, right up there with Big Oil and Big Pharma. Cheerfully reported in the news as if it were the most natural thing in the world is the fact that media goliath Clear Channel poured millions of dollars into G. W. Bush's reëlection campaign. Accepted as common knowledge is the fact that Colin Powell's son was allowed to run the supposedly apolitical Federal Communications Commission—that august body set up to protect the airwaves, which were once seen as belonging to the common weal every bit as much as the oxygen we breathe.

And in case the children of the 60s had not yet noticed the writing on the wall, it was announced a few years ago that even *Bill Graham Presents* is now owned by the conglomerate responsible for the kind of radio and television broadcasting that would make ol' Bill spin in his grave.

Connecting the Dots

Wherever it is placed, Pluto points to a highly charged situation that nobody wants to name. The aspect in question suggests fear of recognizing the truth (Pluto) even when discussing known facts (Mercury).

It is in keeping with Pluto's operation that even where dots exist, they are not connected. Connecting them would be too disturbing. One of those features of modern life that seems to be shrouded in mass denial is the notion that the free press Americans learned about in fifth grade—one of the most frequently touted sacred cows of US democracy—is in fact a mega-business in bed with the government.

Over the course of G.W. Bush's first term, Big Media tried to gut the last few FCC restrictions that have safeguarded the media from

---

And now this monster monopoly wants to charge Web sites for the right to allow users through those wires. See www.media-alliance.org

total consolidation. This has provoked no widespread outrage, largely because the rulings have been virtually blacked-out by mainstream news outlets—all of whom naturally support the effort to kill the safeguards. At issue here is the threatened loss of an iconic American concept: that the airwaves are public property that cannot be bought and sold. But because the loss is already well underway, there is almost no coverage of what is going on.

In January 2005, the proposed rule-gutting was struck down in court; and the Bush camp, no longer even bothering to hide its interest in the issue, temporarily stopped pursuing it[5]—a reprieve that was due to a small but vocal group of free-speech advocates who rallied a grassroots protest. It is telling that they used the world wide web to raise the alarm. All eyes are now on the internet as a last bastion of free exchange of ideas. At the moment (late 2006) there are two Congressional bills which seek to suspend network neutrality. This is a development to chill the blood of those who have come to depend on the internet as a refuge from government media control.

In any case, the internet is not where most of America gets its news. The information-dispensers-of-choice in the USA are still overwhelmingly corporate TV and radio. And since they exclude themselves from self-disclosure, any details of how the government manages the industry remain the inside scoop of those folks who are web-savvy enough to know where to find unexpurgated news on their computers, or of those folks who read books and watch documentaries— a tiny minority of Americans. With Pluto obscuring the issue in typical don't-ask-don't-tell fashion, most of the country remains oblivious.

No Escape from Escapism

When they do appear, the mainstream media's much-hyped attempts to observe itself are so unserious as to come across as intentional red herrings. For example, the novelty of "embedded" war reporters—a self-parodying idea if there ever was one—to cover the attack on Iraq in the Spring of 2003 suggested a deliberate attempt to steer viewers' attention away from the urgent and vital questions they had been in the process of asking about the invasion.

More ghoulish entertainment than information dispensing, the embedded reporters gimmick was paraded before the television audience and then lost its buzz as quickly as Peter Jennings' new hairstyle.

---

[5] In September 2006, the FCC was once again lobbying for the new rules. See http://www.civic.moveon.org/save_the_internet?track_referer=706%

Group Charts

I have proposed that the worldview described by a group chart is held, on a consensual level, by those individuals who identify as members. If our wish is to transcend the folly of the collective in which we live, we must follow the same logic that accrues to transcending the limitations in the individual chart. This means first of all seeking out a dispassionate observer who can help us pinpoint our blind spots.

Looking at the world through a foreigner's eyes every once in a while would be quite an eye-opener for Americans who believe that the corporate news describes—in the words of Uncle Walter Cronkite—*the way it is*. By contrast, Americans who read international newspapers and web sites are informing themselves outside of the Pluto-Mercury pattern. They are less likely to be in the thrall of their country's group-think.

We would not expect viability from a rotting organism; and we will not get the truth *about* the mainstream media *from* the mainstream media. Putting one's credence in National Public Radio, for instance, without looking at where they get their funding, fails to take Plutonian logic into account; as does launching a liberal radio station under the auspices of Clear Channel.

Tale Told by an Idiot

If a system of information is corrupted to the core, we would expect it to share characteristics with other life systems in decay. In Nature, when an organism is about to die, it may go through a flailing disintegration, a penultimate frenzy of faux-vitality. Think of a chicken with its head cut off, madly running around the barnyard. Then think of the evening news.

In the fractured format of today's popular news programs, with their jumble of popping visuals and speed-crawling sound bites, we see a similar pre-mortem hysteria. The plan seems to be to pile on over-stimulating production techniques to keep viewers from thinking about what they are seeing and hearing.

In content as well as form, the corporate media's fragmented worldview comes across as a tale told by an idiot, signifying nothing. Affecting the look-and-feel of sports programs, the nightly news reduces all information, no matter how tragic or globally significant, to the same level of glittering meaninglessness. Watching each week's breathless mini-drama crowd out the one reported the week before, one cannot help but conclude that the intention is to enable the public's amnesia and encourage its ignorance.

When "investigative reporters" were covering the assault on Fallujah of December 2004, for example, they tried to rivet viewers' attention on mock-scientific pie-graphs supposedly showing how much of the terrorized city had fallen, day by day, to US forces. At no point did they question why 500-lb. bombs would still be dropping on a place that had, in their reports from the previous week, been declared "pacified."

Skewed Presentation

This lack of cohesion extends to the print media, where story placement and frequency of mention betray the same corruption: e.g. a media-watch study found The *San Francisco Chronicle* to be twelve times more likely to report the killing of an Israeli child than a Palestinian child. It has become commonplace to find a story of considerable significance—e.g. a communiqué from the Iraqi branch of Al Qaeda claiming to be negotiating with kidnappers to spare Red Cross worker Margaret Hassan's life—buried in the back pages of the paper, while inflammatory stories alluding to the same group's brutality are placed on the front page.

Although critical thinkers might view both reports with equal skepticism, at issue here is the fact that conclusions of any value are arrived at in spite of the way news is presented, not because of it.

Faux Scandals

Inconsistencies such as these bespeak a systemic lack of *integrity*, in all senses of the word. The center cannot hold in an entity that is decomposing.

One wonders how the university journalism departments of today negotiate the disparity between the old-school tenets of ethics, neutrality, intelligent debate, etc. and the new realities of rightwing radio diatribes and "infotainment."

In a curious subplot, the demise of journalistic integrity in America has been the subject of a recent spate of mini-scandals (Pluto) involving plagiarizing reporters (Mercury), served up with the perverse glamour of celebrity crimes. It is almost as if Americans hope that by watching a B-movie about disgraced *New York Times* reporter Jason Blair's isolated malfeasance, they can staunch the deeper wound: that of a media whose viability is going down the tubes.

Government Abuse of the Press

As the natal opposition suggests, disinformation (Mercury) has been dished out by the press to meet the needs of every government in power (Pluto) since the colonies first forged themselves into a union. What has made the current period noteworthy is that a national conversation has begun on the subject, punctuated by episodes of venality so over-the-top as to be almost comical.

Since the current Plutonian period began, at the millennium, Washington has been caught paying big money to "columnists" like Armstrong Williams to advertise administration policies under the guise of reporting them; it has planted a phony reporter, Jeff Gannon, in the White House press corps to lob friendly questions at the president; and it has issued hair-trigger indictments against any journalists with the temerity to "leak" information unflattering to itself—all the while using the press for leaks of its own. Thus has the Bush presidency, like Nixon's before it, embellished one of the classic subplots of the Mercury-Pluto theme: that of the White House making an enemy of the "liberal press."

Moreover, journalists are being murdered. Pluto's opposition to Mercury in the US chart has manifested as literal death, in unprecedented numbers, for reporters in Iraq, the Philippines, Haiti and elsewhere who are not "embedded" within the safe confines of the US media machine. This hideous development extends the logic of control (Pluto) over information dispersal (Mercury) to its ultimate reaches.

Truth: the First Casualty of War

It is the war in Iraq—whose astrological impetus was Pluto's ingress into the US first house in 2000—that American historians will one day name as having set the epochal precedent for government control of the news. Despite the *New York Times* 2004 *mea culpa*—in which the esteemed publication conceded that it might have been just a tiny bit hasty in accepting Bush's call to war—America's news media clearly continue to get their scripts from the White House.

Just as political agencies are being privatized, watchdog agencies have become thoroughly politicized, precluding any capacity for self-correction. The *New York Times*, despite its reputation among liberals as a bastion of even-handedness, can be counted on to report with lightning speed any Hezbollah rockets landing in Israel while neglecting to mention that they were launched in response to hundreds of Israeli shells coming the other way.

In the American mainstream media, facts (Mercury), buried but still available, have been superseded by a far more formidable force: that of political power (Pluto).

Curiosity

Individuals whose charts contain the Mercury-Pluto opposition may be possessed of an extraordinary focus of mind that can latch onto a chosen subject like a drill. But although this capacity can bestow an intense mental rigor, seldom does one see that free-ranging openness that gives Mercury its reputation for loving ideas for their own sake.

In the US chart, Pluto has overpowered Mercury, crippling its capacity for curiosity. The anti-intellectualism for which the US has long been notorious has deepened into a dumbing-down trajectory that is studiously aided and abetted by the business-government alliance that rules from Washington (Pluto in the second house). Without curiosity, one lacks sufficient mental vitality to question—let alone respond to— what one is being told. What remains is numb credulity.

Plutonian Linguistics

Throughout modern history, propaganda has been demonstrably effective in subverting the natural human tendency to be repulsed by war. Propaganda is manipulation (Pluto) of the mass mind through words and ideas (Mercury). Nowhere is it more thoroughly evidenced than in the language used by the corporate news.

In the weeks before the bombs hit Baghdad in March 2003, military monikers such as "*Operation Iraqi Freedom*" began appearing in newspaper stories without quotation marks or qualifiers, signaling that the government's version of the invasion was the only version one was going to get. Throughout the war, the American media has kept up with the White House's shifting wordplay every step of the way.

An example of Plutonian linguistics that has received an atypical amount of critical parsing is the tailored phrase "enemy combatant," invented to get around protections that international law would extend to these unfortunate men and boys, were they called something else.

Under the Radar

Other official coinages are more covert. Pluto is in its element when under the radar; and it is a well-documented irony that propaganda is more persuasive the more unremarkable it is.

After the Iraq war had been going on for about a year, for example, Washington strategists temporarily decreed that non-military Iraqis would stop being called "civilians"—presumably because the term came across as too sympathetic—and newspapers dropped the word without missing a beat. Allusions to "insurgents" started to appear instead.

During this period, White House surrealism also dictated the language the press used to refer to the various puppet regimes Paul Bremer & company were trying to set up in Iraq. Few questions were raised when the media started throwing around terms like "president" and "prime minister" to describe the dubious Mr. Allawi, a hand-picked veteran of the CIA and British espionage, and his disgraced predecessor, Ahmed Chalabi, immediately after the Pentagon began trying to bestow these risible titles upon them. The US media, alone among the news agencies of the world, started to linguistically legitimize Iraq's ever-changing gaggle of collaborators—collectively referring to them as "the interim government of Iraq"—well before the ghastly charades at the ballot boxes that began in January 2005. Calling this committee of stooges a "government" was clearly meant to sidestep the question of whether such a thing could exist in a country being occupied by a world-class military with no intention of leaving.

In some instances the media's manipulation of language is apparently intended to be subliminal; and this is Pluto at its most Plutonian. A recent photo in the *San Francisco Chronicle* of a prisoner at Guantanamo referred to him as being "caught" on such-and-such a date. Given that this young man had been neither tried, indicted, charged nor even accused of a crime, it would seem that the accurate word might be "detained," or some variant thereof. But someone, somewhere, decided upon the verb "caught"—a word associated with escaped convicts and rodents.

Terms of Debate

The damage done by the media's skewed presentation of the war goes beyond misinformation. It has steered the debate itself fatally off course.

At first, the debate was about whether the occupation was necessary, legal or moral. A surprising number of editorials during the antebellum months of 2003 came out denouncing the invasion as a mass-murdering snow job by oil profiteers. But during the presidential campaign of the following year, it was not about *whether* but *how* troops should be deployed in Iraq. Soon the war debate—if that is what it could be called—began centering around tactical details such as armor, provisions and numbers of soldiers. As 2005 began, the intrepid American press began busying itself with the Grand Guignol of the Iraqi "elections."

One can only imagine the profound jadedness that must have descended upon the spirits of these network employees stationed in Iraq, dispatching bromides about *the will of the Iraqi people,* while outside their secured hotel rooms a full-blown military occupation exploded in free-fall.

Corporations

Massive power plays are always a potential when Pluto is opposed by another planet. In the case of the USA, the dynamic between the powers-that-be and freedom of expression is a particularly obvious expression of this. Less overt but gaining more and more national attention is the phenomenon of corporate power, which is also indicated by this polarity. To understand why, we need to refer back to the astrological houses.

Mercury in the US chart resides in the eighth house, which deals not with business *per se*—that's the second—but with the profits of business[6]. It is the house of joint resources and financial mergers, which, along with sex and death, belong to the eighth house through its association with Pluto. (When individual companies merge, their singular identities die and a whole new thing is created; just as individuals die metaphorically in the sexual act, when vital energies are pooled in a momentary orgasm and/or in the procreation of a new human being.) So among other things, the eighth house governs all institutions that involve shareholders. What effect does the Pluto opposition have on this part of American life?

It has fortified and intensified the capacity of corporations to do just about whatever they want. Pluto has raised to an art form the *hostile takeover*, an eighth-house/ second-house exercise in consolidation and monopolization which is no longer limited to the domestic sphere (Pluto trine Neptune in the ninth house[7] of foreign markets). On a historically unprecedented scale, American mega-businesses have been buying, extorting or appropriating resources from indigenous owners in Africa, Central America and the South Pacific—everywhere there are US companies; which is to say, everywhere on Earth.

But this is the symptom, not the cause. The generative shift behind what we might call the Plutonization of corporate America, though it is all but ignored by the public, is the key to our understanding of what's going on. As reported in the fascinating documentaries *Corporation* and *The Century of the Self* (first aired on BBC television), under the nose of an oblivious populace American corporations have been granted certain definitive legal rights that have resulted in a new species of super-business.

---

[6] This is a *derived signification*, by which an analogous relationship is supposed between pairs of houses: thus, the first and the second houses (the self and its fruits) parallel the seventh and the eighth (a relationship and its fruits). Astrology sees partnerships as having second-house resources just as individuals have them.

[7] We will look at the US Neptune in Chapter Nine.

We have seen that Pluto, which rules mutations as well as mergers, governs the sort of changes that have a creepily unnatural feeling to them—the sort one reads about in science fiction. This is what has happened to US corporations: like Dr. Frankenstein with his hybrid monster, the federal government has tinkered with some of the most basic legal distinctions between human entities and financial entities, equipping monster industries with the license to pursue profits into heretofore virgin terrain. As radical as it once was to confer inviolable freedoms to citizens, this re-imagining of business is no less radical (from *radix*; Pluto governs roots). Soulless financial abstractions are now winning court cases and achieving territorial powers that in some instances outstrip those of persons.

It is a development to send shivers down the spines of humanists everywhere. And yet it makes Plutonian sense.

Secrecy

We have seen that Pluto governs secrecy, an issue that has recently been pushed into the public's consciousness from two separate angles: the government's secrets from the American people, and the people's secrets from its government.

Since the "war on terror" was metaphorically declared, Washington has made a veritable fetish of secrecy. The Oval Office has claimed the right to stonewall requests for information from every quarter—from citizen groups to special prosecutors drawn from its own ranks; even going so far, in a particularly nonsensical moment, as to reclassify documents it had previously declassified.

At the same time, the National Security Agency has out-Orwelled Orwell. No shred of customer information or personal data is apparently too tiny to escape the bank and library record-checking[8]; no progressive group too random to be infiltrated by FBI agents (sneakily costumed to blend in, one imagines, among the tree huggers and peaceniks). The revelation in early 2006 of illegal wiretapping by the NSA, which was discovered to have struck secret deals with the big phone companies to access citizen data, managed to semi-incense

---

[8] In the How-Soon-They-Forget Department: In 2002, a Pentagon data-mining program called "Total Information Awareness" that sought to check everything from credit cards to vet reports was made public, universally reviled and summarily dumped. Except that it wasn't dumped; it just changed its name. It turns out the program had simply slinked into the shadows like its sponsor, John Poindexter, moving from an open secret to a secret secret until journalists broke the news a couple of years later and made it an open secret again.

Congress for a few months before being mutely accepted as business-as-usual.

These abrogations of citizen freedom, along with the despicable national embarrassment of the war in Iraq, will be seen by history to have eroded the last remaining bastions of support for the Bush administration.

Ignorance vs. Stupidity

But the government of G.W. Bush is unique only in its blatancy. As we will see in Chapter Twelve, the transit of Pluto over the nation's Ascendant—which corresponded with the Bush presidency—has revealed with grotesque clarity certain themes that have been there in the American story since its beginning. As inadvertent agents of this revelation, Bush et al have done nothing more than bring America's corruptions to the surface. Of interest at the moment is what they have helped reveal about Pluto opposite Mercury and the American mind.

As a multi-leveled archetype, Mercury governs more than just information acquisition. It has to do with the proficiency with which we use our minds: our intelligence, which a teacher of mine once defined as *the ability to pay attention.* Unconscious Pluto can impair the Mercurial ability to pay attention; to take in reality.

Ignorance—to not know enough—is unfortunate. But *stupidity*—to buy into polluted information out of intellectual laziness—is downright dangerous.

Lies

Perhaps the most damning result of a corrupt government is that lying loses its ability to offend and disgrace. In America's current Plutonian crisis, the stigma (to say nothing of the criminality) attached to presidential lying seems to have disappeared.

Propaganda is capable of making people believe both everything and nothing at the same time, as Hannah Arendt has observed[9]. Fear-inflaming scenarios are fabricated by Washington, instantly repeated by all the news networks at once, and the next day refuted (remember anthrax?); but rather than protesting against the lies, the public retreats into cynicism. The last nail in Mercury's coffin will be when the public stops objecting to being deceived because they hold everything they hear to be a lie anyway.

---

[9] See Arendt's classic *The Origins of Totalitarianism.*

Cynicism vs. Common Sense

Of the myriad social degradations of contemporary American life, cynicism is the most insidious. Not too long ago, cynicism was seen as a character flaw: among politicians, it was a grievous slur. But as popular culture has forsaken any muse but commerce, the media has lost credibility as a zone of ideas; and fewer and fewer systems of public accounting remain to represent and support ordinary citizens. People begin to feel powerless, and then they get cynical. Cynicism is no longer merely an affectation of critics and teenagers. In America it has become normative.

But though it may be hip, as the poet Amiri Baraka reminds us, cynicism is not revolutionary. Those who believe in working for consciousness must maintain a distance from the toxic cacophony that is the mainstream media. To do so we must apply two basic traits of a healthy Mercury: curiosity (the word derives from *cura*: to care) and common sense[10].

Curiosity and common sense are ours from birth: astrology considers them to be part of our animal nature. The essential gift of Mercury is our everyday intelligence, our instinct to question: that voice in our head that would say, "Okay, now the Bush administration spends 65 million in the Ukraine; turns out the CIA has been there for some time. They say it was to ensure an honest election over there. Does this sound plausible? Is that why the CIA usually goes places? Let's think this through. Does our government seem to worry about rigorous accuracy here in American elections? Let's look at the track record. Have Bush's calls for democracy in other countries resulted in self-determination in those countries? Like, in *even one* of them? If I were to put money on it, what would I bet was most likely to be true here?"

To be a conscious citizen in the millennial era, one must detach from this deadening mass experience. If Americans were to turn off their televisions *en masse*, it would really, really help.

---

[10] See astrologer Raye Robertson's timely essay on the famous pamphlet written by an American radical in 1776: *Pluto, Chiron and a Return to Thomas Paine's Common Sense*. http://www.byjovepublications.com

EIGHT

OF THE PEOPLE, BY THE PEOPLE AND FOR THE PEOPLE

AMERICA'S URANUS

The next planet we will look at in the US chart is Uranus, governor of *revolution*. Like Neptune and Pluto, Uranus is an outer planet—unpredictable and life-altering. Astrologers see these three bodies as representing epoch-making cosmic forces. When the native is aligned with them, they use her will as their agent. Their function is to stretch human understanding as far as it can be stretched.

Uranus' purpose is to incite within us an urge to break through and break out: to explode the rules that define our context. When Uranus is strong in an individual chart, natally or by transit, we may find ourselves feeling unusually impulsive, daring or exceptional. An event may come along that seems to necessitate our defiance, or a spontaneous inner willingness may bubble up within us to open ourselves to risk. Nicknamed The Great Awakener, Uranus bestows a new alertness to areas where we have been falling asleep—regardless of whether or not we want to wake up. The planet plays tricks, like a prankster at a party who catches us spacing out, sneaks up behind us and pops a balloon in our face. Uranian surprises are not malevolent, but neither are they merely whimsical. They give us a swift kick in the status quo.

A Reputation for Originality

In the US chart, Uranus occupies the sixth house in Gemini, not far from Mars across the Descendant. The relationship these planets have to Saturn in the tenth house ties Uranus into the chart by means of a smooth, harmonious angle, showing how fated it was that America's originality would feed into its strong reputation.

Uranus governs entrepreneurship and ingenuity, national features that have put the country on the world map in sixth-house arenas (medicine, work methodologies). The sixth house is that of *techniques* and Uranus is the planet of *advanced technology*: the placement speaks to America's ability to invent new ways of getting things done. In the realms of manufacturing, science, telecommunications, the military—

you name it—this group soul cannot stop originating new machines and revolutionary ways of using them, even when the old ones work just fine (consider the hyper-technologization of American healthcare).

Of particular interest here is Uranus' rulership over the concept of independence. The strong trine that unites this planet to Saturn at the top of the chart hints at the importance of the idea of freedom (Uranus) to the choice of governmental structure (Saturn).

Uranian notions—such as the idea that every individual is unique—are always breathtakingly new when they break through the threshold of mass consciousness: they are seen as wild and crazy, and they often stay confined to the realm of ideas. But the trine to Saturn tells us that America's Uranian impulses were not meant to remain merely conceptual. The idea of individual freedom was destined to be institutionalized, written into the very framework of the country.

Uranus and Democracy

In an elegant expression of the *Law of Correspondences* (see Page 201), Uranus was officially recognized as a planet in 1781, not long after America had had its revolution and soon before the French had theirs. The planet is associated with all independence movements, wherein one (usually newer) group rebels against another (usually older) group. On a philosophical level, Uranian ideas are those that champion the rights of the individual over those of the state. Thus Uranus is traditionally linked with democracy, while Neptune, the planet of unified, undifferentiated masses, is linked with communism.

Uranus is the first of the three planets that orbit beyond Saturn. The ordering of the bodies in the solar system is a primary clue to their significance: Saturn is about form and tradition, so Uranus is the first planet to *go beyond* form and tradition. The dark side of Saturn is enslavement to tradition, and Uranus signifies the will to break through that bondage and repudiate antecedents. Historically, when the time had come for humanity to get wind of this radical new concept, along came a bright new idea in government: one that championed the right of individuals to overthrow tyrants and think for themselves. Defiance and dissent are at the Uranian core of true democracies[1]. This is the promise contained within that beautiful trine in the US chart. Has the USA kept that promise?

Certainly the word *democracy* is a current favorite in the mainstream American media, who take their cue from White House

---

[1] In this context we are excluding the ancient Greek and Roman models, which were more like proto-democracies.

language-spinners. But beneath the veneer of verbiage, American political realities are becoming more and more estranged from Uranian impulses. So removed—in spirit and practice—has American democracy become from its key tenets that its most heated proponents seem to be deriving their inspiration more from vague and distant references in their grade school textbooks than from direct experience of the society in which they live.

Uranus: a Mental Planet

Democracy, like all Uranian constructs, depends upon a high-level use of the mind. Uranian thinking is independent, crisp and explicit. Unlike Neptune, which is associated with the water element, Uranus is associated with the air element at its most stubbornly abstract. Uranus represents intellect without the baggage of subjectivity. This is why it governs science, whose classical goal is knowledge stripped of prejudice and illusion.

In the opinion of the eighteenth century radicals who drafted the US Constitution, emotion was not an ally of clear thinking. Democracy was to be protected at all costs from the caprices of charismatic leaders and the vagaries of mass mood. When constructing their elegant theoretical arguments, Jefferson, Adams et al were not after pulse-quickening rhetoric; they felt it detracted from sound reason. They avoided appealing to deities. They were against regalia. They were not into brass bands[2].

What would these sober gentlemen make of the hyperbolic bombast that saturates every reference to *democracy* in America these days?

Democracy as Rationale for Empire

From its beginnings as a Uranian challenge intended to empower the individual, *democracy* is now a buzzword used to disempower the individual. Pimped by America's current leaders, democracy—as a word, as a concept—is being pressed into service as a foreign policy ruse. The war in Iraq, in its fourth year at this writing, gives us the preeminent example of the word's new meaning. Soon after their initial arguments for invading Iraq were universally discredited, the cartel now in Washington seized upon the "democracy" argument. First the mushroom cloud scenario was used to appeal to a hideous collective fear; next the "democracy" scenario started being used to appeal to a

---

[2] The prophetic vision of the Declaration of Independence beggars description. The reader is encouraged to take another look at it, at http://www.law.indiana.edu/uslawdocs/declaration.html.

collective ideal with which Americans identify heart and soul.

This political curveball exudes a cynicism so morbid that it surpasses all the others. When modern American politicians invoke the iconography of Uranian freedom, they are exploiting the most fluid angle in the US chart: the highest and finest aspect of America's self-image. When presidential scriptwriters invoke the American Revolution, they are taking advantage of America's desperate yearning to believe in itself.

In these days of national identity crisis, the government's appeals find fertile ground. The White House's extolling of "democracy" as a rationale for imperialistic assault has been taken up by the mainstream American media, as well as by savvy pundits who ought to know better. We have recently seen even such thoughtful journalists as *The New Yorker*'s David Remnick solemnly analyze "this experiment in democracy" being attributed to Baghdad's impotent, revolving-door puppet governments. One isn't sure whether these commentators are reciting a memorized essay question from a childhood social studies class or whether they imagine that these ideas bear some relation to actual circumstances.

It is a timeworn verity of American propaganda that when a president uses the word *democracy* in a speech, the public more or less takes leave of its senses: eyes moisten en masse, Pavlov's-dog-style, and amidst all the snuffling and flag-saluting, woe betide anyone who dares to insist upon what the term really means. America's disconnection from its Uranian origins has widened to the point where *democracy* is now being touted as a rationale for a future series of ongoing invasions of sovereign states Washington would very much like to control. As we saw in Chapter Five, the neo-con doctrine ominously entitled "The New American Century" tells us that Washington intends to install, one by one in various handpicked countries (they've gone so far as to publish a list of them), a series of militarily imposed "democracies" around the world. This is certainly a new take on the word. In this context it is meant to signify *the kind of government America thinks it has*. But it actually means *the kind of government our leaders want these countries to have*; which is to say, not democracy at all.

This campaign of take-it-or-leave-it "democracy" is an idea that could only fly in a country where most of the citizenry has no sense of world history, ancient or modern. Perhaps the only thing more absurd than the claim that a government "of the people, by the people and for the people" *could* be established right now in Iraq—a state that was starved to attrition for thirteen years of "sanctions", destroyed with guns, bombs and depleted uranium poisoning, then allowed to devolve into a civil war that is claiming the lives of 100 civilians a day—is the notion that an American-style government *should* be imposed in Iraq: an ancient civilization whose ancestors came up with the Code of Hammarabi thousands of years before America's Founding Fathers were born.

Self-Determination vs. Washington's Determination

Even if this conceit were to be accepted at face value, the question immediately arises: what if these unfortunate democracy-starved people, once possessed of self-determination, opted for scenarios Washington didn't like? Such as the Iraqis voting to boot the USA out of their country and returning control of their natural resources to themselves? The probable reason why questions about self-determination remain largely unasked is that everyone subliminally understands, already, that giving Iraq back to the Iraqis is nowhere in the plan. As one insider has darkly joked: US policymakers would sooner give up Washington DC than give up the Persian Gulf.

Amidst all the lip service to *democracy* currently burning up the nation's airwaves, the US-funded Israeli assaults on Hezbollah in Lebanon and Hamas in Gaza constitute a stunning testament to the hypocrisy behind the cant. Israel's open declaration to crush Arab resistance in the Middle East was provoked by an election that was not merely nominally democratic—it was actually democratic—but whose results proved unappealing to the "great democracies" of the world.

In January 2006, the people of Palestine overwhelmingly voted into power a group they see as their champions: Hamas; to the great dismay of the US and Israel, who'd been counting on their own candidate—not the people's—to prevail. Once the votes were counted, and after American interests tried and failed to find fraud, the international community was cajoled and blackmailed into cutting off aid to the already destitute Palestinians. This embargo, combined with Israel's stepped-up round-the-clock shelling, has created at this writing a humanitarian catastrophe in Gaza that meets every criterion of genocide.

Though Israel named the "kidnapping"[3] of its soldiers as the provocation for its assaults upon Palestine and Lebanon during the summer of 2006, in the big picture it was the expression of democracy in

---

[3] The verb speaks volumes. The three Israeli soldiers in question were, of course, prisoners of war, captured in the kind of border incidents that are as common as salt in the region; but their selectively humanized stories generated reams of press in the USA. Meanwhile, there are almost ten thousand Palestinian political prisoners currently held in Israeli jails—most of them civilians; others of them, in violation of international law, elected officials; some of them kidnapped from their beds—all of them thrown into holding tanks notorious for torture. These detainees get virtually no coverage in the American mainstream media.

88

Palestine that was the true provocation. The Arab people spoke, and received collective punishment for their pains[4].

Israel's assault on Lebanon in July/August 2006 leveled the region's infrastructure and racked up so many war crimes that Amnesty International was forced to investigate. US-built bomber planes wiped out roads, bridges, power plants, water refineries and the tourist and fishing industries upon which the country depended, via a monster oil spill that is the worst ecological disaster in Lebanon's history. The onslaught was condemned in every corner of the world—except in the only government with the power to make it stop: the USA. The siege was so hideously extravagant that it received denunciations even from American allies like Jordan and Egypt. Yet at this writing most Americans seem neither to perceive the asymmetry of the warfare[5] nor to realize that their own hard-earned taxes—to the tune of ten million dollars *per day*—paid for Israel's air strikes upon these Lebanese villages, bombing apartment complexes, targeting ambulances and hospitals, gunning down fleeing refugees, killing whole families as they slept.

One can only wonder whether most Americans think of villagers like these when their president tells them that Arabs "hate America." An even more compelling question is whether they imagine there could be any way these villagers could possibly *not* "hate America" under the current circumstances.

Occupation in the Name of Democracy

In Chapter Seven we discussed the problem of ignorance as an inborn karmic challenge for the USA. In the current context the situation has become acute, for White House propaganda and an endemic lack of curiosity have kept the US public grossly in the dark about the Middle East—the one spot on the globe where the world now hangs in the

---

[4] Collective punishment, a notorious tactic of the Nazis featured in many a WWII movie, has become official policy with the Israeli army in Palestine and Lebanon. As astrologer Rob Hand remarked after Israel's massacre of innocents at the Jenin refugee camp in 2002, this seems to be a case of what Jung would have called *enantiodromia*: the Israeli state becoming what it was born to oppose.

[5] Israel asked the Pentagon for a special type of cluster bomb with shard bomblets to release upon Lebanon, where civilian casualties reached the 91% range—more than a third of them children—all the while claiming that even the slaughter at Qana was merely an unfortunate accident. By contrast, armed with munitions whose targeting capability was far less precise, Hezbollah killed very few civilians: out of 156 Israelis killed, 118 were soldiers. In the face of these damning numbers, Washington's spin about Israel simply "defending itself" became more and more absurd; but was nonetheless resoundingly supported with resolutions championed by both parties of the US Congress.

balance.

The American public has been led to believe that the carnage in Lebanon and Palestine was and is a battle between two more or less equal sides; which fails to take into consideration Israel's overwhelming superiority of force, maintained by state-of-the-art American weaponry. The perception also prevails that religion is the only engine driving the conflict, the same perception that the American mass media has been using exclusively to present the war in Iraq. Only at the fringes of public debate is anything said about the stark realities of Third World indigenous populations (Palestinians and Lebanese) fighting colonization by First World governments (the USA and its junior partner Israel, which has been fashioned into a First World state by Washington).

Neither is this ignorance merely geopolitical. There is very little understanding in America of social realities in the Middle East, either— though the class disparities in places like Washington's little friend Kuwait are pretty hard to miss. It is ironic indeed that Americans, as identified as they are with the idea of democracy, have not noticed that there is a polarization of almost feudalistic proportions within the so-called "moderate" Arab countries—a gaping abyss of wealth and power between the masses of people and their rulers—of the sort that American schoolbooks categorize as inferior and anachronistic, to say nothing of unjust. Certainly Washington has noticed this polarization, as have the sheiks and kings in Egypt, Jordan and Saudi Arabia—all of whom are becoming increasingly fearful of their own angry, restive populations. On the Arab "street", the divide between the franchised and the disenfranchised in these countries is notorious; and is understood to be a major source of the area's violent potential. Without this information, the American public remains at a loss.

So here again is that other troubling divide: the one between the American public's perspective on the region and the perspective of the greater world. This second divide is widening exponentially even as the tensions there explode. Though the US public hears Israel's opponents described invariably and incessantly as "terrorists," the people of Palestine view Hamas as national heroes and their only hope to get their land back. In Lebanon, too, increasing numbers of the population have viewed Hezbollah as freedom fighters since the group formed in 1982— in resistance to Israel's last occupation. Ordinary people saw, with their own eyes, members of Hezbollah moving into their villages and setting up hospitals and schools[6]; and they ended up voting them into ten per

---

[6] As it turned out, the 2006 summer assault on Lebanon was an abject failure for the US and Israel—not only in terms of lost moral high ground, but in terms of strategic and military objectives—with the whole world as witness. In the wake of Israel's self-avowed

cent of the seats in the Lebanese parliament.

As for Iraq, if the American public is allowing itself any soul-searching at all about the devastation their leaders have wreaked, it seems to be confined to the simplistic surface of the *missionaries-for-democracy* trope. It may be that the public is so desperate to identify with the noble ideals in their childhood history books that it fails to see what is so transparent as to be staring it in the face: that the reason America is in Iraq has little to do with government and less still with democracy. It has to do with wresting economic and political control of an oil-rich region as a critical part of a campaign of global dominion very clearly outlined in the official National Security Council Strategy— a document which, far from being classified information available only to insider wonks and conspiracy theorists, has been formally signed by President Bush and duly posted on the internet (http://www.whitehouse.gov/nsc/nss.html).

Those who see Iraq as being prepared for Uranian democracy would do well to apply that good old American rule of thumb: *Follow the money.* Is Washington investing in the civil society of this wrecked and ravaged land, as would a wise paternal mentor guiding a new entity towards self-governance? All we need to do is look to America's second-house representatives for the answer. Even before the most recent escalation of implacable violence, the Pentagon's contractors were not lifting a finger to build schools or hospitals or sewer systems in Iraq. They were putting their millions into military installations. Sixteen permanent bases have gone up so far. This is not what you construct in a potentially autonomous state. This is what you construct in a staging area.

The Will of the People

While citizens of every other country in the world can see the American government's intentions as plain as day, in the USA the latest official story continues to fool far too many. For this, as we have seen in Chapter Seven, we can thank a mainstream media that legitimizes each new red herring as fast as Washington can drag it across the path. For much of 2005 American pundits wasted their time debating such faux-issues as, for example, where Iraq's "foreign fighters" were coming

---

attempt to exterminate all resistance in the region, Hezbollah's popularity has skyrocketed across the Arab world. At this writing, as the group begins to rebuild Lebanon's demolished infrastructure they are gaining grateful supporters even among the most heretofore Western-leaning segments of the Lebanese population.

from[7]—a concept that made no sense from the Arab perspective, which is that Iraq is one of the historical centers of the Arab world.

At this writing (September 2006), with all memory of the torturous international haggling that led up to *Shock-and-Awe* apparently forgotten, and the subsequent pretense about exciting new elections drowned out by catastrophic civic breakdown, the press and the politicians are now framing the chaos in Iraq as a distressing domestic problem—as if the American presence had no meaning except to prevent things there from getting worse.

The truth is, of course, that desperate violence always and everywhere accompanies military occupation. Were the American public to take even the briefest break from the mainstream news and its parroting of White House nonsense, common sense might suggest to them that the fierce resistance in the Middle East—much of it in Iraq self-destructive, at this point—gives voice to the current will of the people through the only means Washington and its client states have left them.

Collective Nervous Breakdown

The American psyche is in sad shape, as Pluto (planet of breakdown) now passing through the USA's first house (of identity) makes clear. America's national consciousness has diverged into two disparate streams:

1. The idealized story about why the USA is in Iraq, funding Israel's occupations, and champing at the bit to attack Iran, Syria, Venezuela, Korea, Cuba et al—which dominates discussion on the surface; and
2. The appalling truth of what's actually going on, which courses beneath the surface.

Those in the first camp, who purport to believe the government's version of things, are living in a soul-sapping suspension of belief. The cynics and dissenters in the second camp, meanwhile, suffer the hardship of disempowerment. And America as a whole stumbles along in a state of massive dissociation.

Meanwhile, Halliburton, Bechtel et al continue to raid the killing fields of Iraq with impunity. An embattled and outnumbered US military stacks up casualties by the thousands while the civilian death toll mounts into the hundreds of thousands. And when every few months the

---

[7] Few American commentators take into account that the current division of much of the Middle East dates from the artificial boundary-fixing of the treaty of Versailles in 1919, when whole countries' geographical identities were changed to facilitate the management by France and England of their colonies.

Pentagon requests more blood money, Congress throws more billions into the death pit, reassuring their constituents that they are taking a stand for *democracy*.

Democracy vs. "Democracy"

As we have seen, Iraq is not the only example of Washington tossing around the term *democracy* in a way that suggests they have never looked it up in the dictionary. None of the governments on Washington's Good Countries List has anything akin to democracy going on. The sanctioned brutality against women and dissenters in Pakistan and Saudi Arabia is legendary; they are among the world's worst offenders in terms of corruption and torture. These are countries where the judiciary deals with petty criminals by chopping off their hands, and where young girls are stoned for adultery. Wretched, abandoned Afghanistan, with its Abu Ghraib-style detention camps and its heroin crop that has quadrupled since the American invasion, is the most recent graduate of Bush et al's beneficent democratization program.

Even if one stretched the term *democracy* to its most implausible inclusiveness, it would be hard to find states less democratic than these recipients of Washington's friendship and billions in aid. The story Washington is churning out about "the march of democracy" is not merely a distortion of truth. Just as Orwell predicted, it is the opposite of truth.

Other Democracies Washington Doesn't Like

Over the past fifty years, the handful of places in the world that have actually managed, despite lethal superpower interference, to elect populist, autonomous governments—such as Guatemala, Nicaragua, Chile, Haiti and now, Palestine—have had their revolutions toppled, one by one, by counter-revolutionaries funded by Washington. The American public once heard the truth about these coups years later (Allende); now one can follow along in real time (Aristide, Chavez). What has changed is the blatancy of American policies designed to undermine governments that refuse to kowtow to Washington.

American leaders no longer pretend to be disinterested observers of other countries' governance. Nor have they learned anything from their failed interventions abroad, except that they can pretty well count on being safe from the American public's censure if the press is told to spin the intervention as democracy-supporting and/or humanitarian. From the merciless bombing of Yugoslavia under Clinton to the disastrous military meddling in Somalia before him, Washington's touted "humanitarian" adventures abroad should be, by now, a tip-off of the most ominous kind. There is always a reason for the US government's highly selective interest in trouble spots around the globe, as our exploration of the US Pluto has shown[8]. And it seems that no degree of White House meddling, no matter how obvious or skewed, offends the unskeptical American public so long as the media portrays it as the ever-vigilant championship of democracy.

In a recent example, Washington's prize attack dog, political consultant Dick Morris, went so far as to claim credit for helping Vicente Fox win Mexico's presidency in 2000. Six years later, he is widely believed to be the designer of the smear campaign—unprecedented in Mexican politics—that unleashed a last-minute torrent of vicious ads against the populist candidate, Lopez Obrador, which helped insure the election of his opponent: Washington ally Felipe Calderon.

Putting the Uranus Back in Democracy

The more we consider the true meaning of the system of government to which the word *democracy* refers, the more disturbing it becomes to hear its name taken in vain. In order to honor the Uranian roots of democracy, we must celebrate and encourage the human desire for freedom from oppression, and support all those bold movements worldwide that attempt to champion the individual voice.

As always, we must start where we are. If one lives in America, one must look at what America is doing. To say one has a government *of, by, and for the people* means taking responsibility for how one's employees in office are running it. If one accepts the metaphysical view, one must accept that each of us incarnated into a given location for reasons that have as precise a meaning as the day and time we were born. It is a karmic relationship with very literal ramifications: the American taxpayer pays the salaries of these criminally insane public servants. They and their lethal machinations quite literally belong to the voters.

As conscious beings trying to become more conscious, we have choice on multiple levels. Just as we choose (or not) to confront the shadow places within ourselves, we choose (or not) to confront the shadow places in the groups to which we belong. Confronting these realities would mean shaking off denial about the monstrosities that continue hourly in Iraq, especially in those areas where resistance to the occupation is most dedicated. And especially at night. American forces

---

[8] As of late 2006 Washington was back in Somalia elbow-deep, funding new warlords and boasting about sending shiploads of food. The punch line of this story, of course, is that Sudan has oil—60% of which now goes to China, Washington's rival. At its current level of consciousness, America's Pluto is simply not capable of leaving such a situation alone.

staged most of their bombing raids in places like Fallujah at night—the better to psychologically destabilize the target populace. This despicable practice is the very definition of *terrorism*. These are crimes against humanity, and they must be named before they can be rectified.

As we look more closely at the meaning of Uranus and its placement in the US chart, let us consider anew the shimmering ideal so close to the heart of the modern world. Let us take a moment to imagine the cultural shift that would occur if we all stood up for a democracy seen not through the brittle distortion of cynicism nor through hazy memories from grade school catechism, but through the bold, clear lens of Uranus.

NINE

THE DARK SIDE OF GLAMOUR
AMERICA'S NEPTUNE

Next we come to a part of the American personality as elusive as it is intriguing: its collective fantasies. These are represented by the planet Neptune, ruler of inspiration and longing.

Readers of astrology textbooks may know Neptune as the governor of bliss, inspiration and psychic sensitivity—mundane associations with no small appeal to metaphysical seekers. Even Neptune's less favorable associations—martyrdom, overwhelm and substance abuse—have an undeniable allure. Neptune is probably the most glamourized planet in popular astrology; which is fitting when one considers the planet's long association with glamour—in the prosaic sense (cosmetics and fashion) and in the esoteric sense: the illusionary nature of the material world, known to the Hindus as *maya*. Indeed, astrology students already possessed of a Neptunian sensibility may find, when interpreting the planet in their own chart, that its complex range of meanings is obscured by the same utopianism of which Neptune is itself a symbol. Reading the delineations may make a reader feel like she is but a sprite made of stardust who stumbled into the wrong dimension.

But let us not underestimate Neptune: the fact that it is amorphous does not mean it doesn't pack a punch. Neptune has a very dark side. It is true that Neptune governs ambrosia, the beverage of the gods; but it also governs street-corner hooch and the slow, systemic poisoning that goes along with it. Neptune gives us dreams and visions, but also nightmares and delusions. When manifested without awareness, Neptune's collective function, in particular, deserves a very careful look.

Planet of Yearning

Neptune refers to the human longing to pour one's identity into universal consciousness, a sublime experience that beggars description in any other terms but the spiritual. Mystical, artistic and psychic explorations are among the few pursuits subtle enough to properly express its agonies and ecstasies. This is the planet of mists and waters, governor of poets inspired by the muse and sailors bewitched by the siren. It refers to yearnings that do not belong to the material world and cannot be satisfied by material pleasures. Trying to respond to Neptune with anything other than a soulful perspective is like trying to put vapor into a cardboard box. Neptune's purpose is to get us to know the truth of the infinite; attempts to take this energy into the finite world tend to run aground.

So what happens to Neptune in a place like America, where the dominant belief system proclaims physicality to be the be-all and end-all of reality, and where every desire is fair game for commodification? What happens in America is the material plane gets glamourized.

Marvels and Wonders

In the US chart there is a *square aspect* (a ninety-degree angle, signifying agitation and stress) between Neptune and the planet Mars (activity, desire, aggression). Neptune occupies the ninth house, which is associated with foreignness: exotic places, expansive ideas and travelers. The ninth house in a national chart governs immigration—at this writing, a subject roiling with animosity (Mars)—while Neptune, of course, governs the sea. This pairing sheds light on where the public discussion about immigration gets its dramatic imagery. Linguists have made note of the fact that the media is awash in watery metaphors when referring to the issue: immigrants are seen by some as a *rising tide* that will *pour* into the USA and *swamp* its social services unless walls are built—in the collective imagination, they are more like levees—along the Mexican border.

On another level the meaning of the ninth house encompasses a wide range of idealistic impulses, which in this case are broadened even further by the occupant planet: Neptune governs utopianism. Neptune is associated with the concept of the infinite, and the ninth is the house of belief systems. So we get a picture here of a national wellspring of confusingly deep yearnings—religious, ideological, philosophical—sought through a vast array of channels. Factor in the busy, mutable Mars (in Gemini, the sign of multiplicity and variety) and you get a kaleidoscopic torrent of collective dream fragments: a ceaseless quest for transcendent bliss at odds (square aspect) with the scattered efforts to attain it.

Neptune governs marvels and wonders, notions of heaven, Valhalla, never-never land. As a testament to its can-do entrepreneurship, America has fashioned several wonderlands out of bare sand: the faux-magic kingdoms of Hollywood, Las Vegas and Disneyland. These have been populated with an ever-shifting plethora of twinkling human and cartoon "stars." The Neptune-Mars square bespeaks a frenetic appetite for the outsized and the other-worldly, which helps us understand the prodigious amounts of energy Americans pump into fantasy.

This is the placement that explains the country's lust for nonstop recreation and material dreamlands. They come from Neptunian drives that have been displaced from their origin in the soul.

Divine Discontent

Ultimately, Neptune feels the mortal coil to be an onerous weight. This translates into an urge to escape duty and restriction, whether we see our burden in existential terms or simply as the boss forcing us to show up for work. What may appear to be irresponsibility is actually a fear of being trapped by the confines of the earthbound self, which is why independent action and clear decision-making are repellent to the Neptunian mindset; it would much rather seek out some deep, wide pool to dive into and disappear. The drug-taker who seeks solace in a mood change is motivated by the same impulses as the devotee in an ashram: each wants freedom from the prison of individual consciousness. On a collective level, unaware Neptune manifests as conformity, group hysteria and blind faith in undeserving leaders. Awash in group feeling—swaying to the beat in a dark dance club or gripped by the game in a crowded stadium or cheering with our compatriots after a rousing speech—we free ourselves, at least temporarily, from the burden of upholding a lonely, separate ego.

Part of the difficulty in using Neptune consciously is that the spiritual purpose at its core is rarely positively modeled in the Western world. A full understanding of any chart must factor in the macrocosmic context behind any chart placement; and the epochal backdrop here features the disensoulment that humanity entered into with the modern age[1]. American society in particular fails to honor the divine discontent that is universal to human experience—that craving to lose ourselves in something larger than ourselves. In our day and age, such stirrings, if they are named at all, are likely to be pathologized by the secular priests—the medical and psychiatric scientists—as the lapses of a weak ego or an unstable mind[2].

---

[1] See Richard Tarnas, *The Passion of the Western Mind*; and *Cosmos and Psyche: Intimations of a New World*.

[2] Pathologized, and then cashed in on. "A recent study has found that every psychiatric expert involved in writing the standard diagnostic criteria for disorders such as depression and schizophrenia has had financial ties to the drug companies that sell medications for those illnesses..." *San Francisco Chronicle*, 5/06.

It is no wonder that Americans are beset by addictions of every stripe[3], which represent the effort to seek the numinous without disturbing our allegiance to the literal. It is no wonder that we fall prey so readily to trends of fashion and ideology, which seduce us to pool our sensibilities together with large numbers of our fellows, and thereby divest ourselves of individual choice.

Deeper View

This is where astrology comes in. Using its timeless symbolism to plumb the meaning of current scenarios, we have at our disposal the archetypal framework necessary to look at human dilemmas that would be incomprehensible otherwise. The alert observer will have noticed that our world is no longer served by the conventional ways of seeing things. A deeper view is urgently required.

When the Pentagon attacked Baghdad on March 20, 2003, Saturn was conjunct the USA's natal Mars and squaring natal Neptune to the exact degree, with Pluto still within orb of the national Ascendant[4]. Unconscious Mars and Saturn together can manifest as the crudest kind of masculine assertion, narcissistic and defensive; and we have seen that Pluto governs destruction and death. But of interest at the moment is the role played in this configuration by Neptune, governor of the mass emotionalism that accompanies war.

Mass Emotionalism

Mass emotionalism is like individual emotionalism, only exponentially stronger. This vast sea of undigested feeling is analogous to the psychic contents that slosh beneath the threshold of consciousness in an individual, and cause, as each of us knows, so much trouble when

---

[3] One of the next big public health issues will doubtless be juvenile drug addiction, a prediction one doesn't have to be an astrologer to make. Absent a change in the current policy (i.e. of waiting for official studies to corroborate the obvious, instead of nipping it in the bud), the trend will ripen until it becomes epidemic. As illegal drug use has become a normative rite of passage for adolescents from even the most conventional families, younger and younger Americans are being prescribed pharmaceuticals to the point where *legal* juvenile drug use is becoming normative, too. Whereas aggression and mood swings were once seen as part of the vicissitudes of growing up, they are now being given acronyms (e.g. IED) and ceremoniously listed in the Diagnostic and Statistical Manual of Mental Disorders. The use of anti-psychotic drugs to treat children for problems like these increased more than fivefold from 1993 to 2002.

[4] In the June/ July 03 and Dec03/ Jan04 issues of *The Mountain Astrologer Magazine* of 2003 are several articles analyzing the transits that accompanied America's lurch into overt, full-scale militarism. See especially TMA #108: Editorial, Tarriktar; and TMA #109: *Bush, Iraq and Saturn Forum.*

ignored. More than at any other time in American history, we must take the collective unconscious seriously.

Nation-states no less than individuals have troubling feelings that must be raised to awareness and worked through, lest they fester and cause psychic harm to the host. Much has been written about the wounds that linger in the American psyche from its interlude with slavery and from the disaster that was the Viet Nam War; these energies are still festering, hidden in the recesses of the mass mind, unhealed and awaiting resolution. And with every month that passes, by virtue of Washington's violence in the Middle East and elsewhere, more wounds are inflicted upon the American soul. These are abominations too. They are national decisions with immense karmic reach, in which all American citizens participate—knowingly or unknowingly, for cosmic law makes no such distinction.

Sentimentality and Depression

America has not yet found a way to use its Neptune to purge collective feelings like shame, grief and guilt. The USA has no tribal keeners to ritualize sorrow; no funerary priestesses to dignify and release national pain. This nation has not come up with a galvanizing art form such as the trancelike mass dancing that South African demonstrators used to transform their suffering into the creative will to break apartheid. With no means to process these energies, what happens to them?

They manifest as public sentimentality, which—unlike true emotion—has no movement in it, and no ability to heal us. There is a big market in America for newspaper photos of homecoming soldiers embracing toddlers; for stuffed animals and *I-♥-Grandpa* mugs. But sentimentality is not real emotion; it is a thin substitute, arising from ignorance of the role tragedy plays in the deepening of the soul[5].

And then there is the gray scourge of depression—not a disease, from astrology's point of view, but a symptom of stagnant Neptune—that has reached epidemic proportions in the United States. New drugs are invented every year to suppress this mass inundation of feeling, but it is like trying to dam up the ocean instead of learning how the tides work. Psychotherapy and groups like AA may help on an individual level, but Americans lack a mechanism to do so as a nation.

For a people so self-avowedly pro-active, it is noteworthy that the rituals America has come up with in regards to tragedy and trauma

---

[5] But a new mourning ritual has recently arisen in American cities that does seem genuinely Neptunian, given its noncommercial and spontaneous origins: the funereal t-shirts, worn en masse by loved ones, that feature a photograph of the dead—typically young men killed by gunfire in their own neighborhoods.

are for the most part obdurately passive—rendering its citizens feeling helpless and ineffectual in the face of the great griefs of the world. Accustomed to seeing everything—even human misery—as a commodity to be consumed, Americans take in the suffering all around them in the form of "news," making of it a superficial and intellectual exercise instead of an empathetic experience. Instead of confronting it, as a group, and ennobling it through meaningful catharsis, they then put the terrible content out of their minds as best they can (so long as it involves strangers far away), as conventional notions of psychological health encourage them to do. Millions of viewers of the evening broadcasts see nothing perverse about sitting on the couch drinking a beer while unthinkable inhumanities are nonchalantly presented on the screen in front of them. The normal thing to do, it is presumed, is to watch one's fellows struggle with disaster and war, then brush the teeth and go to bed.

Indeed, it is a wonder there is not more depression than there is. Expected to witness horrors night after night but given no means of flushing the feelings out of his heart, the television viewer has no recourse but to numb out; or perhaps, on an impulse, to drive to the local murder victim's house and leave a teddy bear on the sidewalk.

Hijacked Grief

Mass feeling is a formidable force, one which shifts unpredictably like the weather at sea. A prodigious expression of Neptune occurred when, shortly after 9-11, an unprecedented sense of togetherness opened hearts in the United States and around the world in a soulful period of mass grieving. But ever so quickly America's unscrupulous leaders moved to harness the power of these tears, jerking them effectively for five years and counting, in order to justify completely unrelated[6] foreign and domestic agendas. For Neptune also governs the stagecraft of national politics: the confetti and balloons and giant flags flapping against a blue sky. Neptune's swelling chords and cinematic imagery can provoke a flood of group fantasy, impelling otherwise rational citizens to support the insanity of war. Neither reason (Mercury) nor pragmatism (Saturn) has anywhere near the impact on a crowd.

At issue is the current American government's campaign to inflict great harm upon many innocent people in the Middle East and around the world with whom the ordinary American citizen has

---

[6] Or maybe it was not completely unrelated, as a disturbing amount of evidence is beginning to suggest. See, for example, http://www.911truth.org.

absolutely no quarrel. It is an old story. In order to cajole consensus opinion, warmongers in every age have appealed to ideals of racial purity, religious entitlement and national superiority[7]. As extravagant as they are utterly vague, such notions constitute a vulgarization of Neptune's quest for spiritual meaning. Without the illusions of distorted Neptune, people would vote for life over death every time.

Homeland Insecurity

It is time to take a sober look at the phenomenon of nationalism, an issue that has recently moved from the background to the raucous foreground of the American persona. To the dismay of critical thinkers at home and abroad, an outbreak of "patriotic" fervor overtook the country immediately after 9-11 and became entrenched with the subsequent transit of Saturn in Cancer (2003-2005)[8].

Cancer is associated with safety, home and native land; and Saturn, in its unconscious state, manifests as fear. With Neptune setting the stage by means of an agitated, drama-prone collective unconscious, the dark side of the Saturn transit grabbed hold; and sheer panic and dread became institutionalized as foreign policy. The official term for the unseen enemy provoking all this frenzied defensiveness is *terrorist*, but the astrological signature tells the tale: America was and is in the primal grip of stranger-phobia.

In its highest expression, Cancer inspires a genuine identification with the land—as when we connect emotionally with our country's purple mountain majesties and amber waves of grain. But this self-protective water sign, especially when paired with Saturn, is also the sign of fortifications, defenses and walls. Given that the American populace was already groomed by their leaders to fear first and think later, the dark side of Saturn in Cancer was in full bloom as it crossed the US Sun and Jupiter/Venus in late 2003-04. Among the transit's most visible

---

[7] Several hundred thousand Iraqis are estimated to have died as of this writing since March of 2003—a number one must glean from international relief groups, because the Pentagon makes a point of not counting the non-American dead. Accommodatingly, the mainstream media, when it mentions the Iraqi dead at all, divides the perished into categories: "insurgents", "terrorists" and "civilians", implying that some of these terminations of human life were well worth it and others were unfortunate. Exponentially more unfortunate, from this point of view, were the three thousand deaths on 9-11, which these observers seem to feel occupy a whole separate ontological category because they were American.

[8] Roughly every thirty years, when it passes through Cancer, Saturn transits over the USA's Sun and Jupiter; which highlights the harrowing issues of security—and loss of security—that are a big part of the American birth chart. This is a theme we will return to later.

results were platoons of newly-minted federal wardens wearing the badge of "homeland security." Another was the burgeoning of "gated communities,"[9] a bizarre residential trend that looks like nothing so much as a voluntary incarceration of the wealthy. *In*voluntary incarceration has also flourished. These years saw economists heralding the birth of a new mega-industry: prisons, which started springing up like mushrooms after a rain[10].

Mass Yearnings

It is a grand irony indeed when a culture that forces its female executives to wear sharp-seamed suits suddenly goes all mawkish when the band starts playing God Bless America. Uncle Sam may denigrate emotional wisdom in every part of society from politics to business, but when that trumpet starts to play he tears up like a girl. Perhaps this is Neptune's revenge on the patriarchy: *If you do not acknowledge Feminine Knowing, I will make the biggest and toughest among you weep at baseball games.*

Among the talking heads in Congress and the media, when the subject turns to the military, a veritable whitewater of nationalistic feeling comes crashing and flooding over the most thorough and substantive counter-arguments. Swept away without a trace are, first, common sense, and second, any consideration for the other peoples of the world. And for good or ill, one gets the idea that, in the case of at least some of these legislators, their patriotic sentiments are quite genuine—perhaps the most genuine emotions these gentlemen ever allow themselves to feel.

What would it look like to consider questions of extreme national import without patriotism? Is it even possible to look dispassionately at an ideal that we have been socialized to equate with honor, loyalty and all-around decency?

It does become possible when one separates out the values one wants to keep—honor, loyalty and decency—from the idea of belonging to a specific country. Not all Americans wish, of course, to disabuse themselves of the belief that being a true-blue American makes them better than everyone else. But for those interested in distinguishing their

---

[9] It is estimated that between five and ten million American households are now surrounded by some form of locked fence or wall, with residents gaining entry to their homes by means of a plastic card.

[10] By the summer of 2005, prisons and jails were adding more than one thousand inmates each week, putting 1 in every 136 US residents behind bars. – *S .F. Chronicle, May 2006*

own opinions from the fog of conditioned response, the first requirement is a desire to understand the way Neptune works.

We have suggested that Neptune's miasmic force, which seems at first blush so gentle and benign, has the capacity to mess with the minds of the most rigorous thinkers. Under its influence even clear-minded citizens can become steeped like a teabag in a warm collective emotionalism more compelling than any fiction she could have come up with alone.

Neptune in the ninth house of the US chart combines an aching yearning with an all-encompassing incertitude, causing ideas to melt one into the other in a chaotic grasping for higher truth. The resulting vision in the American mind is a jingoistic mishmash of ideals that increase each other's emotional charge while diminishing each other's meaning. What makes American nationalism so uniquely persuasive is its confusion of:

1. love of country (nationalism) with
2. the economic system (capitalism);
    which is itself conflated, as we have noted, with
3. the form of government America believes it has (democracy).

Democracy in Perspective

Many of its citizens derive genuine inspiration from what historians have called The American Experiment: the founding 230 years ago of an astoundingly sophisticated, multi-tiered union from thirteen hardscrabble colonies. And on paper, the concept of democracy—for its ingenuity is based on its conceptual purity, as we have seen—is a worthy and elegant creation if there ever was one.

But Neptune is a transpersonal planet[11], and when it pumps its energy into a feeling—and the native fails to understand the feeling's spiritual source—the feeling goes a little nuts. Neptune's idealism needs to be balanced by the other energies in the chart, and when it is, a natural order prevails: Neptune is checked by Mercury's critical thinking, Saturn's practicality, and Jupiter's ethical discernment. But without these checks and balances Neptune will overtake the rest of the chart like a tsunami overtakes villages along the shore.

As every American schoolchild knows, the Founding Fathers wrote a similar system of checks and balances into the Constitution, as part of their infinitely affectionate yet reasoned approach to the

---

[11] As we saw in Chapter Eight, the three outer planets are not bound by the dictates of the personality. Uranus, Neptune and Pluto are called *transpersonal* because they represent powerful universal energies that cannot be understood in ordinary intellectual or psychological terms.

phenomenon of human beings working together for self-governance. The Congress was mandated to guard over the excesses of the executive branch, and the Supreme Court was designed to guard over the excesses of the other two. Again and again, the document spells out the hope that the populace would watch democracy at work, keep it healthy and have the wit to notice when it is being taken away.

But from the crowded field of today's culture wars, we find the loudest champions of democracy distinguishing themselves by their utter obliviousness as to whether their own government is acting democratically. The sublime ideals with which the American republic started its life (Neptune in the ninth house) have been pressed into service as a front for the old us-against-them dualism (Mars in Gemini) with the original values getting lost in the shuffle.

So it is that Neptune—governor of euphoria and idealism— becomes fuel for the grotesque hypocrisies of America's foreign policy as well as for its increasing abandonment of civil liberties. The planet's dark side is mass emotional chaos. With no grounding in historicity or moral relativism, nationalism has degraded the idea of democracy until it becomes as flat and meaningless as a Hallmark card.

Ersatz Nationalism

Taking off the blinders of negative Neptune would allow us to confront the fact that nationalism has become, quite simply, anachronistic. The uppermost captains of industry and government already know this. In today's world of multinational corporations, where entire islands are bought and sold to the highest bidder, and whole countries are used by others as banking vehicles, for an increasing number of wealthy citizens nationalism is no longer a motivating reality[12]. The corporate billionaire may doff his hat and even shed a tear when the flag is unfurled at a civic event, but his accountants know— even if the public does not—that his allegiances belong to no one country.

At the very top where wealth and geopolitical power merge, national identifications and their attendant loyalties have acquired a new meaning—one which seems to depend, interestingly, upon the average citizen maintaining the old meaning. Recall that even the awkward fact that fifteen of the nineteen vilified 9-11 hijackers were Saudis did nothing to disturb the chummy transnational alliances between Bush's oil men and Saudi Arabia's oil men. Though the nationalities of the

---

[12] In August 2006, it was reported that wealthy Americans who stash their savings in offshore tax shelters cost the US treasury a total of seventy billion dollars a year in lost revenue.

suicide-pilots were widely publicized—and at a moment when Americans were howling for blood and ready to lynch—the powers-that-be, who had compelling petro-political reasons to shield the Saudis from blame, spared no effort to steer public opinion in other directions. The result was that, even five years later, the very country that supplied the majority of the hijackers escaped scot-free as a focus of popular vengeance. It is hard to imagine a more blatant tip-off that America's leaders claim exemption from the simplistic, *with-us-or-against-us* nationalism they encourage and exploit in the masses.

That this incongruity was not immediately denounced as such by the American public is a testament to nationalism's irrational power. Neptune is an emotional planet, not a mental one. Upon the collective mind it can function as a mass narcotic.

Beyond Nationalism

With origins in tribal survival, nationalism as a human organizing device started out as a reasonable enough way to service a sociological need. But the world is smaller now. Nation-states are no longer the *sine qua non* of group identity. The bottom line in global survival is this: our identification with our country must no longer trump our identification with the human race.

Over the past couple of centuries, the vision of our shared residency on a fragile planet has begun to replace the old chauvinisms. It is a vision that has given rise to human rights organizations, to the peace and justice movement, and to environmental groups worldwide, all of which prioritize global cooperation over the caprices of governments. It is to universalism that we must now pledge our primary allegiance.

A potent symbol entered our collective visual vocabulary in the 1960s when the first NASA photographs of Earth were sent back from the Moon. No longer a gaggle of distinct countries and tribes, we were jolted into seeing ourselves as a single unified world, iconicized by a delicate little blue ball that was alive, precious, and home to us all. That famous picture[13] may become a powerful consciousness-raiser over the next few years. It is the modern world's link to the ancient dictum that all people everywhere are inextricably connected.

---

[13] When the German Greens Party first achieved electoral legitimacy in the 1970s, instead of filing into chambers with the customary partisan flag they marched in with a great big balloon depicting planet Earth, hoisted jubilantly above their heads. In the same spirit, the American peace group Not in Our Name has chosen the NASA photograph of Earth as its emblem.

A Purer Form of Neptune

Every spiritual system the world over promotes some version of this idea, and it is far closer to the essential truth of Neptune than any of the various other crowd-rallying sentiments in currency. It is to be hoped that the visceral poignancy of Earth's current condition, beset by ecological crises that are by definition global, will arouse nations from their nationalistic stupor and inspire them to start cooperating, as squabbling children must when their mother is in danger.

The prospect of replacing nationalism with universalism has about it a sense of evolutionary inevitability; and among the world's visionaries it is already clear that no other version of Neptune will work anymore. Meanwhile, behind the grotesqueries of American popular culture—its enthrallment with the illusory, its preoccupation with the maudlin—is a hunger for higher meaning. To bring Neptune back into balance, this hunger must be recognized, and used as a starting point.

TEN

THE TEMPLE IN FLAMES

PLUTO IN SAGITTARIUS

At this point we have considered the essential nature of the group soul that is the USA by looking at the significant themes in the American chart. Now let us consider its ongoing drama.

One of the ways astrologers study this unfolding process is by following *transits*, which describe the interactive dance between the patterns in the sky at birth—frozen in time and space, in the form of a natal chart—and the patterns in the sky at any given moment.

Learning to Tell Time

To study a natal chart is to examine an entity's potential, which does not change *per se*. But planetary cycles do keep on moving and changing, and astrologers use those changes to track developmental passages in the entity's evolution.

Planetary cycles constitute a complex clock, signifying certain lessons that are due to be learned, en masse, at certain moments in history. We look at this clock to see what time it is for the world. In this way transits confer meaning upon events. After we've seen "what time it is" in the abstract language of astrology, we are able to view with new eyes the events that arise to symbolize the lessons of that time.

Some planetary cycles are very long and gradual, like those of the three outer planets. Pluto, for instance, takes more than two centuries to go through all the signs; so to look at where Pluto is transiting in a chart gives us a very big picture of what's going on for the native. Because it moves so slowly, such a transit stays focused on one particular area of the chart for a relatively long while. There is a cosmic logic to this: profound lessons take longer to take in.

Spotlight on the Natal Chart

A transit operates like a spotlight cast on the natal chart: the moving planet lights up a certain spot of the entity's unmoving potential. (We might say that each planet has a different-colored lens: Saturn's spotlight is red, Jupiter's is green, Uranus's is a shimmering silver,

Venus' is a lovely blue.) But no matter what the color, or character, of the transiting planet, they all function to light up something in the natal chart; and that is where our interpretation should be focused. All transits have the same basic purpose: to get the native to understand the spotlighted part of the natal chart at a deeper level than they ever did before.

In other words, transits, properly read, say more about the natal planet than about the transiting planet. They ideally raise to consciousness something about the natal placement, which, at that particular moment, needs to be understood more deeply. They identify when the soul has an appointment to learn something specific about the way the self (and by extension, the universe) works.

Whatever it Takes

This learning may be taught through internal or external events; the gods don't care which. Though prevailing cultural opinion has it that literal events are more significant than consciousness shifts, astrology does not make this distinction—which is why transits, like dreams, need to be decoded. In our study of key transits to the USA chart, rather than seeing them as having *caused* this or that to happen in or to the country, we will read them as signals of this group soul's intention to explode into new levels of a particular awareness—keeping in mind that any number of things could have led to the same state of awareness. If it hadn't been that one thing that happened, it'd have been something else with the same charge.

Whatever the cosmos has to do to lead the soul to a particular awareness, it will do.

Pluto through Sagittarius

The first transit we will look at is the one that sets the tone for the others during these times. This is the passage of Pluto through Sagittarius (1994–2009), which establishes the background of the current world situation.

Sagittarius governs religion and other formalized beliefs; Pluto is the planet of death and rebirth. As discussed in Chapter Three, the function of this transit is to break down and reformulate ideologies that have grown obsolete. Like every other transit of Pluto, this one comes around every 250 years on average; and each time it does, there are holy wars of one kind or another.

During its thirteen years in Sagittarius, Pluto zeroes in on those institutions that purport to hold the truths of a civilization. It subjects these to a ruthless elimination process, one that fuels efforts by believers to rid their faith of impurities. These may be inspired crusades or woeful miscomprehensions of Plutonian law, but their common thread is an urge to strip down some belief system to its essentials; which often feeds into an obsessive commitment to a singular point of view.

In the secular arena, there is a wholesale destruction (Pluto) of commonplace verities (Sagittarius), leaving the populace in a philosophical vacuum. In the arena of the sacred, the past several years have seen the great sky-god religions of recorded history—Judaism, Christianity and Islam—held up to scrutiny. For the most part, they and their cultural offshoots have been reacting with the toxic excess typical of entities in decay.

Putrefaction requires purging. What is being purged here are belief systems that many have considered immutable. The trauma of Pluto in Sagittarius is that it turns inside-out and upside-down worldviews that have given meaning to the lives of millions upon millions of people.

Old-Time Religion: Past its Expiration Date

While for many Westerners the intellectual credibility of the church was lost long ago, for many more its moral credibility started biting the dust with this transit of Pluto through the sign of religion. These believers may not have looked to church teachings for philosophical consistency, necessarily, but they'd at least expected ethical leadership. This has changed.

Theological sacred cows have been dropping dead everywhere you look. The fiery Islamicists who burst into global awareness around the millennium, betraying the peaceful premises of their ancient faith in the process, are only the most obvious example of the crisis. Also grown rank and shrill is that American "old-time-religion," which is in fact not nearly old enough to have carved out a place among the universal verities, nor new enough to help with the unprecedented dilemmas of a millennial society in acute distress.

Fundamentalist preachers who violate their own fire-and-brimstone injunctions with adultery, alcohol and embezzlement have certainly been around for a long time; but the extravagantly public posture of the current crop of culprits has made their offenses into an American tabloid staple[1]. The pedophilia cover-up scandals that have racked the Catholic Church have revealed the "infallible" papacy to be quite fallible indeed. The Episcopal Church is being riven by the issues

---

[1] Into this category we might also place secular radio personalities who crow about the superiority of Christian principles while sending their maid to buy them cigar boxes full of pill-mill meds from drug dealers in parking lots.

of ordaining gays and women. A book questioning the core tenets of Vatican orthodoxy—Dan Brown's *Da Vinci Code*—has been a runaway success, and *The Judas Gospels* have just hit the bookstores. Our grandparents would have found this situation incredible: out-and-out heresies are now subject to pop culture commentary. Nor can Granny ask her friendly neighborhood priest how to cope with these developments—he's on the lam in Mexico.

As we have seen, a do-or-die extremism characterizes whatever sign Pluto occupies. In the sign of spiritual search, Pluto has been intensifying and polarizing belief systems worldwide in order to rid the mass mind of its outworn perspectives. As the transit has destined, we are all warriors for the truth these days, whatever we fancy the truth to be. Every public figure with an agenda is bearing the cross and proselytizing the word. Anti-globalization protesters, Zionists and Right-to-Lifers all wield the fiery sword.

Religious wars constitute a primitive example of this process at work, as does the election of a simple-minded leader who reduces complex moral issues to Sunday-School clichés while wreaking havoc upon civilizations he knows nothing about. The American presidential elections of 2000 and 2004 resulted in a regime whose most telling feature is xenophobia with religious overtones. Though for many Americans the scenario has felt monstrously wrong, it is a symbolically appropriate outcome given the transit involved.

Seeing the Big Picture

Let us step back and use planetary archetypes to see the recent period from the big picture. From a macrocosmic point of view, the pattern of mass ideological breakdown that is inevitable under Pluto in Sagittarius is happening right on schedule. It makes astrological sense that a cult-like oligarchic cartel has secured control of the most powerful country in the world. Indeed, the apocalyptic imagery employed by G. W. Bush's ludicrously shallow spiritual advisers provides clues about a greater plan that far outstrips their understanding.

Pluto uses life-or-death intimidation tactics to force humanity into breakthroughs of awareness, and with this transit the Dark God is drawing a line in the sand. As America's big-talking president has himself said: "*You're either with us or against us.*" It was one of those truth-out-of-the-mouths-of-babes statements he tends to make, which double as inadvertent encapsulations of what astrological transits are up to. How true it is that each of us must launch ourselves into a private soul-search, asking ourselves where we stand in this new millennial terrain.

As I write these words in 2006, we are in the last dregs of Pluto through Sagittarius, with two more years to get our collective values straight. For the past 5,000 years or so, in the Western world the business of establishing essential group values has belonged exclusively to religion; and for most of this period these values were pretty much cut and dried. In the Holy Roman Empire there was only one Church in town, which meant only one definition of right and wrong. There was no confusion about what was moral and what wasn't; it was all written down. There were functionaries whose job it was to interpret God's truth, and you believed what they said, or you were toast. One True Faith: the no-nonsense solution to the Sagittarius problem of establishing an ethical consensus.

Things have gotten rather more complicated since then, and not just because we have several One-True-Faiths competing for the title. Over the past decade we have seen wrenching destruction (Pluto) across the globe, involving clashing versions of higher truth (Sagittarius). The image that comes to mind for the whole transit is a church set aflame and burning to the ground. When passing through this sign, the Dark God initiates a merciless clearing of the stage of old talismans and figureheads to make way for new ones as yet uncreated. At this point in the 21st century, the spires crashing and burning around us are doddering old ideologies that have lost their ethical logic and cannot withstand modernity—otherwise even Pluto would be unable to get rid of them.

Today's gay-marriage resisters and abstinence-only promoters are in the same club as the bearded old theologians calling for the honor killings of young girls: they are fighting an unstoppable decay process. By Plutonian Law, anything that has outlived its usefulness must undergo the throes of death, which, unless welcomed with grace, can bring out the ugliest in any creature.

Righteousness: the Dark Side of Belief

When Pluto makes a direct or retrograde station[2], an event often arises that exemplifies the overall significance of the planet in the sign through which it is passing. In September 2004 with a direct station of Pluto hanging in the sky, the most sacred temple in Shi'ite Islam was

---

[2] Direct and retrograde stations occur when, from Earth's point of view, a planet seems to stop and change direction along its orbit, intensifying whatever transit it is making to the natal chart at the time. Stationing planets are astronomical anomalies, and thus very strong. (Astrologers reason that if something in Nature breaks a pattern, it has a point to make. In this case the regular pattern is movement, and the departure from the pattern is lack of movement.) The stationing planet seems to be caught, freeze-frame, at a certain degree of the zodiac; and for a few days around the exact station, exerts a steady, concentrated influence.

destroyed by high-tech American weaponry. Enraged Iraqis pledged to take up the arms of any fighters martyred defending the shrine while US Marines warned journalists that if they stayed to witness the massacre, they would be killed.

It is hard to imagine a more quintessential expression of religious terrorism than the bombing of this ancient site, nor a more deviant misuse of this particular planet in this particular sign. Yet the White House, in the face of countless desecrations like this one that have occurred since the 2003 invasion and before, continues to talk about "winning Iraqi hearts and minds." In order to understand this outlandish incongruity we need to look a little more closely at the latest spin the White House is putting on its incursions, current and proposed, into the Middle East. The conceit is that America is in the process of introducing the backward Arab world to what are presumed to be the self-evidently superior virtues of Western civilization.

If the soul of Sagittarius is religious faith, its shadow side is hypocrisy. When this transit is factored in we see revealed another layer to the military mindset currently driving Uncle Sam: the staggering arrogance of American religious fundamentalism. Pluto in Sagittarius (which is very strong right now in the first house of the US chart, as we will see in the next chapter) has turned even the most morally indefensible viewpoint into a great sanctimonious crusade.

To bolster its case against a foe, instead of appealing to global standards like those of the Geneva Convention, the White House has been tossing around the word "evildoer" as a means of justifying all manner of violent engagements. Patently uninterested in international law, Washington has been accusing non-allies of being in breach of divine law. The current American president explicitly claims he is acting on orders from his god; his favorite preacher, Billy Graham's son, has declared Islam to be an "evil" religion. One of his generals went on television declaring, in an unmistakably *nyah-nyah-nyah* tone, that Allah was less "real" than the Christian god.

The raw idiocy of these pronouncements makes them an easy call for observers interested in the archetypal forces beneath them. Unenlightened Pluto reduces complicated theological ideas to crude elementals, the better to see dangerous attitudes in an unvarnished state.

Religious Projection

Herein lies the grand irony of the current Sagittarius transit. The US is at the moment in the thrall of religious zealots who are destroying a country they claim is in the thrall of religious zealots. It is a contradiction that becomes darker the more closely one looks at it.

Contrary to the portrait painted by the American powers-that-be, pre-invasion Iraq was a predominantly secular society, not a religious one. Meanwhile the USA—the world's great secular democracy, setter of the global standard for humanism and reason, whose elected officials are presumed to reflect a cool-headed plurality of views—has been behaving like a bunch of compulsive fanatics, setting out to proselytize a group of unwilling converts into the Christian American Way.

Recall that Neptune resides in the ninth house of the US chart. This puts the planet of other-worldly schemes in the peripatetic house of religion: what we have here is the signature of the missionary. Recall too that America's Mars squares its Neptune, predisposing the nation to cloak its aggression (Mars) in presumptuous evangelisms (Neptune). This underlying theme became more and more explicit as Pluto in Sagittarius started provoking this natal square by transit (2004-07).

The US media has at this writing reduced all cultural perspective on Iraq to the inter-tribal conflict trope, but a glancing familiarity with the recent history of the region offers a different view. In sharp contrast with its neighbors, modern Iraq, with its celebrated educational and scientific establishment (Iraqi hospitals were renowned throughout the region before the ruinous sanctions) had been a fervently nationalist society after freeing itself from the British. As strategists in Washington knew quite well, Iraq's many sects were presided over by a secular dictator who disdained the mullahs. Saddam Hussein was a sworn enemy of Osama bin Laden, though this salient fact is completely absent from the official story[3]. Saddam's distrust of the jihadists was well-known in the Arab world, and was presumed to stem from his fear that they posed a threat to his rule. There was no Al Qaeda in Iraq before the war.

But within a few short years, Al Qaeda has indeed set up shop there, and whatever religious factionalism that did exist in the country has been exacerbated by Washington, quite by design[4]. In a divide-and-

---

[3] The leader of the September eleventh hijackers himself despised Saddam, another highly relevant fact—but one which would have totally messed with the White House's conspiracy theory had it been common knowledge among the American public. According to the 9-11 Commission, Mohamed Atta considered Iraq's dictator "an American stooge set up to give Washington an excuse to intervene in the Middle East." But of course this detail did not receive air play; and at this writing, four years after the catastrophe in Iraq began, a full half of the American people still believe Washington's story of an Iraq-9-11 link. When one considers America's ignorance of what its own government is up to in critical matters such as this, one begins to see the US populace is the trusting wife in an embarrassingly public betrayal: always the last to know the truth.

[4] It was the Pentagon, not the Iraqis, that coined the phrase "the Sunni Triangle," an artificial geographical designation with artificially religious implications—it was and is a

conquer policy that has worked tragically well, whatever sectarian differences there were to begin with in Iraq have turned into gaping rifts. When it came time to stage national elections, Washington carefully manipulated Iraq's Muslim factions—stamping out all voices of resistance to occupation, shutting out the forces of moderation, undermining secular reformers, stacking the roster of candidates with whichever sects would be most likely to do the occupiers' bidding, and using the increased factionalism to shore up power. Though the significance of this chicanery has been largely lost on the American public, none of it has been lost on Iraqi nationalists.

The bigger picture of what is happening in Iraq, however, is that despite clashes of tribal identity, religion is still not the central issue there. The occupation is. The groundswell of loyalty to a leader like Al-Sadr, for instance, is more a case of the people looking to a religious figure for nationalistic reasons than looking to a national figure for religious reasons. Al-Sadr is seen as a champion of the urban poor by many from a variety of faiths.

But the US military has all but banned any independent journalists at this point and thus maintains almost complete control of the news from Iraq[5], and the mainstream press has dropped any discussion of the war that does not revolve around the intertribal-violence story.

Get Out of My Country

It does not take a foreign policy analyst to understand that in an occupied country, national sentiment is strengthened and hatred towards the occupiers increases, the more destruction they wreak. Americans have no trouble understanding this concept when they watch the movie classic *Casablanca*, for instance, or read Hemingway's *For Whom the Bell Tolls*. But somehow the American public's identification with resistance movements fails to extend to people who are of a different race and/or who are resisting aggression by the USA itself. The Vietnamese, for instance, have yet to see their patriotic valor romanticized in American film and literature.

In the US at this writing, the sectarian-violence scenario has monopolized the war debate to the point where the fundamental

---

multi-ethnic region—though the way the American media throws the term around, one would think the region had gone by that name since before the Ottoman Empire.

[5] Not only is independent reporting shut out; an expensive propaganda campaign has unabashedly replaced it. According to the *San Francisco Chronicle* (9/06), the US military has put out a bid for a two-year $20 million public-relations contract that calls for extensive monitoring of US and Middle Eastern media in an effort to promote "more positive coverage" of news from Iraq.

immorality of the occupation has been rendered moot for much of the public. Reports from the international media, by contrast, maintain that the Arab-on-Arab bloodshed is primarily still between resisters and collaborators: first targeted are the cops, the oil refinery workers, the Western-friendly journalists and the foreign contract employees—that is, those whom the resisters see as working for The Man.

Their home-made bombs no match for Uncle Sam's Blackhawk helicopters and white phosphorous, it is upon their more vulnerable fellow Iraqis that the resistance fighters are increasingly turning their wrath[6]. They are targeting those they see as having sold out, such as the desperate recruits who join forces with the US in order to cop a week's wages and then sell their gun and boots to buy bread for their families, desert the force and make their way back to their villages in hiding.

Guerillas Tend to Win in the End

The probable outcome of this Sagittarian war can be guessed by looking at historical precedent: a nation that has been colonized before and then gotten free will stop at nothing to keep their country from being colonized again. To the chagrin of partisans on both sides of the debate,

---

[6] It is noteworthy, moreover, that observers close to the terrible violence (see http://dahrjamailiraq.com/) do not take at face value the Pentagon's reports about who the perpetrators are of all these car bombs and mosque burnings. It is no secret that the occupation has espionage units on the ground in Iraq (some of the CIA's loathsome sabotage techniques, e.g. the "Salvadorean solution," have even found their way into the American vernacular), yet there is little curiosity among the US public about what these agents actually *do*. Perhaps when Americans hear about the existence of these spies, saboteurs and "special forces," they visualize these gentlemen sitting quietly behind desks in the Green Zone coming up with plans to stop the violence. If so, this would be stretching naïveté to the point of denial.

A very dark Keystone-Kops-like story made the papers briefly in 2005 about a British unit crashing their tank headlong into an Iraqi jail. The soldiers were apparently trying to rescue a couple of their own undercover operatives who had been caught by Iraqi police red-handed: in plain clothes, carrying unexplained explosives. The story was quashed before the public had time to ask: *Wait a minute—what exactly were these lads from "our side" doing carrying bombs? What were they planning to do with them?* It was a smoking gun if there ever was one, but the episode failed to raise suspicions in the general public that the occupation forces want anything other than civic order in Iraq.

Meanwhile, many neocon-watchers are of the opinion that civil war has all along been Washington's second choice of how to weaken and thereby more easily manipulate Iraq, should the first choice—making the country into a clear-cut puppet state—fail to go according to plan. This would explain the otherwise incomprehensible coincidence between the attempts by Iraq's prime minister to sit down and negotiate between factions and surprise moves by Washington that provoke more violence (e.g. the Pentagon's arrest of a popular nationalist leader on 6/24/06—the very night before talks were to take place between the leaders of antagonistic sects).

this grim and shameful chapter in American history is likely to go on for a long time.

War advocates fatally underestimate the Iraqi people, who are, as a group, far more politically and historically informed than most Americans. Iraqis are well aware of the significance of the black liquid that lies beneath their sand; they have figured out why foreign powers will not leave them alone. And they will probably prevail for the same reason that the North Vietnamese did: guerilla movements tend to hang on until the bitter end, while their occupiers lose heart, money and time. The Pentagon has obscene amounts of money and military hardware on its side, but the Iraqi people have on their side the fact that they are fighting for their homeland. By contrast, the exhausted young American soldiers kicking down the doors and manning the checkpoints know, on some level, that they are only fighting for Halliburton.

The Religious Menace Closer to Home

As we have seen in previous chapters, Washington has made use throughout its history of American xenophobia to pursue its business-driven interests. The claim that Islam is why Iraqis "hate America" is just the latest Pluto-in-Sagittarius spin.

As the transit winds to a close, the American public would do well to turn their attention inward, and consider the fact that their government has itself become an elite club of demented ideologues who have been directing their fantasies of Armageddon onto a faraway land with completely different theological traditions. With Pluto positioned in such a way as to uncover issues of collective psychological mirroring (to be discussed upcoming), America's own Sagittarian crisis is being projected outwards onto a widening swath of people who are depicted as alien fanatics. The Iraqis' racial and cultural exoticism makes it all too easy for Americans to see them as such, while making it difficult to see that their own US government is in the hands of what is, for all intents and purposes, a religious cult.

Separation of Church and State

As Americans from everywhere along the political spectrum are vividly aware, there is ideological breakdown at home as well as in Iraq. In our chapter on Uranus we looked at the violence currently being inflicted upon the US Constitution—whose principles underlie the nation's democracy as surely as holy writ underlies a theocracy—by the current "faith-based" president's hand-picked lawmakers and jurists. In recent years we have seen Congress turning its attention to the inclusion of "under God" in the Pledge of Allegiance, the mounting of the

Christian ten commandments in government buildings, and the advisability of deep-pocket churches to run state prisons.

If there is such a thing as a secular sacrilege, this is it. Only under a Pluto-in-Sagittarius-transit-gone-wrong could morally infantile politicians presume to dismantle a sacred cow as fundamental to American thought as the separation of church and state.

Other Structures Toppling

Pluto exerts a quiet, steady pressure upon the subject of its attentions. Whatever sign it is passing through, it burrows into the foundations of the institutions governed by that sign, taking advantage of any weakness that is already there. Sooner or later, without fanfare, the structure topples like a termite-infested house.

In addition to religion and the ideological foundations of government, Sagittarius governs long-distance travel and education. In the years since the transit began there have been mass bankruptcies in the airline industry, which conventional wisdom originally chalked up to 9-11; and though astrologers would concede the existence of a link, we do not see it as a causal one. What is clear is that what used to be a delightful adventure for many has become more like a nightmare, as air travel has been officially appointed ground zero of the elusive "war on terror." The typical visit to an American airport has mutated into a time-wasting charade of bureaucratic and dehumanizing "security" rites, with passengers herded like sheep through corrals of conveyor belts and ordered, without a hint of irony, to take their shoes off in front of strangers (god forbid someone try to staunch the indignity by making a joke about it: there are signs posted that warn that Security is No Laughing Matter). Pluto's dark hand has reached even into the sky, as strapped-in passengers may now be forced to watch videos advertising military jobs on their little television screens[7]. *The New Yorker Magazine* could have been quoting an astrologer when it said of the airlines that "The entire industry…[i]s ripe not so much for a makeover as for mass euthanasia, followed by the birth of something new"[8].

Equally evident are the corruption and degeneration of America's public school system, triggering mass alarm on the part of anybody who remembers the solemn eulogizing of "a good education" that was at one time the unquestioned goal for every American child. Outrageous financial mismanagement seems to be standard operating

---

[7] Trying to staunch the largest personnel deficit in 26 years, American Airlines has struck a deal with the Pentagon to allow the in-flight videos to be shown on commercial flights.

[8] Anthony Lane, 4/24/06

procedure on every level of the system, with embezzling secretaries turning up in struggling school districts and ivory-tower greed being unmasked among velvet-cloaked chancellors. Since the planet of decay has entered the sign of education, one hears the phrase "our school system is broken" virtually every time the subject comes up. As students trying to learn in plaster-chipped facilities with broken-down bathrooms know only too well, America's urban schools are quite literally rotting.

Religion Deconstructed

As happens with every sign that Pluto passes through, we find ourselves back at the beginning with Sagittarius, looking at it with new eyes. We have seen that Pluto engages in a kind of deconstruction of whatever sign it enters, reducing specific forms to essential impulses—universal human impulses that had been obscured by institutional inauthenticity or simply taken for granted. For twelve to fifteen years we get to see the nuts and bolts of the sign being taken apart.

What are the nuts and bolts of Sagittarius? The fact that it is a *fire* sign in *mutable* mode tells us that the sign imparts a restless, aspirational hunger for meaning; one that drives us to know *spirit* in the elemental sense of the term. Although it is true that of all the twelve signs Sagittarius is the one most closely connected to institutionalized beliefs, when defined astrologically the word *spiritual* is not limited to literal religious affiliation. The broader meaning of this passionate fire sign is *hunger for wisdom* wherever it can be found.

Pluto has almost finished purging Sagittarius, getting us ready to start out afresh with the issue of spiritual search. This will entail formulating new approaches to our old spiritual practices or making up new ones from scratch: either way we are being inspired to create rites that more effectively serve Sagittarian purposes than the old ones did. The ultimate effect of the transit will be that humanity as a whole adopts a relatively more personal, individualized and direct approach to its chosen articles of faith.

Taking Back the Holidays

One indication of the shift into a new Sagittarian era is the nascent consciousness that has arisen about how the so-called civilized world has sacrificed its sacredness to the marketplace, and how our holidays have been rendered both mundane and maudlin as a result. A growing number of Westerners mourn the loss in their culture of the rites ancient peoples practiced as a matter of course. Pluto has uncovered the meaninglessness and sterility of what pass for spiritual practices, forcing us to admit that the modern world has forgotten how to celebrate the divine without the involvement of a priest or a rabbi or an imam or a retail outlet.

A key feature of these lost rites is the honoring of the gods on their appointed days. In astrological terms this means that people have lost touch with the patterns in the sky that map out sacred juncture points over the course of the year. Nowadays, for many Americans these seasonal portals are remembered only because of the calendar on the wall, or because the bank is closed, or because commercials for holiday specials start to appear on TV. They are not remembered because of what they mean.

Feeding our Hunger for Ritual

But as we have noted, Pluto's point is to expose the decrepitude of a sign's extant expressions, and give us a crack at using the sign more fully. We are being reminded here that human beings have always had and will always have a hunger for ritual, a hunger that grows ravenous in a disensouled world. The Plutonian challenge is to regain control of these once-holy days, so that they can do again what they were designed to do: serve as markers of numinous turning points. Among those Westerners left cold by the bleached-out spectacles that pop culture tries to sell them in the name of the changing seasons, a movement was bound to arise to rewrite the spiritual scripts.

As descendants of the Judeo/Christian/Islamic tradition and myriad others besides, Americans have inherited a symbolic vocabulary of rich classical rituals. Ancient solstice lore is creeping back into the public's consciousness, inspiring curiosity about the archaic origins of such secularized clichés as the yule log and the mistletoe. Novelists and filmmakers are de-sentimentalizing the holidays of their youth, making them their own. Madonna has discovered the Kabbalah. Satirist Bill Talen is spreading the gospel with his Church of Stop Shopping. More and more meaning-seekers, high-and low-profile, are re-consecrating the sacred portals. The culture wars are raging, which leaves a lot of room for unique expression.

From the Ashes of Smoldering Temples

Pluto in Sagittarius—the sign of ethical judgment—has been a journey of fire. In foreign affairs, extreme ideological positions have been staked out on many fronts, with virulently destructive results. The transit has exposed the flagrant ways societies fail to live up to their stated ideals. Long-denied practices such as torture by the American military and grossly unequal standards of justice based on racial, economic or religious affiliation have exploded from their hiding places, begging questions worldwide about what constitutes right and wrong.

On the American domestic front, moral battle lines are more sharply drawn than at any other time since the divisive 1960s, with just about every citizen—even those who see themselves as apolitical and non-ideological—hotly polarized around any issue that can be construed as an ethical one, from birth control and homeless policy to vegetarian school lunches and the spaying of stray cats.

The transit has shown us the dark face of Sagittarius glaring out at us from every corner of the globe. But it has had a perverse benefit: that of exposing to a new awareness the human capacity for arrogance, xenophobia and intolerance. More observers than ever before have offered up thoughtful insights—to more listeners and readers and internet surfers than ever before—about how the craving to believe in something can get channeled, at our peril, into enforcing belief instead of embodying belief. It is not a new revelation, but the transit has given it a fierce new collective scope.

Sagittarius is the sign of foreignness. Pluto in this sign forces a confrontation between the self and that which is unfamiliar to the self: this is where Sagittarius gets its connection with mind-expansion. Thus the transit has profoundly impacted long-distance travel, education and spiritual learning, inviting us to reconsider what these classic horizon-broadening experiences are all about.

Sagittarius is the sign of rectitude and morality. New biotechnologies such as cloning have prompted ethical discussions that would have been moot, if not unimaginable, a short time ago. Medical advancements such as fertility enhancement have combined with a kaleidoscope of new family patterns and gender-identity possibilities to render obsolete once-unquestioned ideas about sexual morality. Many people's conventional notions about what is sacred and immutable have been deeply disturbed.

Has Pluto in Sagittarius wiped out religion?

Perhaps religion as we have known it. The zeal that has burned so fiercely during this transit has not really been about religion; it has been about the human shut-down mechanism that obscures religious vision. The propensity to clamp down and stop growth comes from the planet Saturn, which, when not used wisely, distorts and contracts whatever it touches. As we will see in the following chapter, Saturn and Pluto together created the current religious climate. Saturn (resistance to change) + Pluto in Sagittarius (theology) = fundamentalism, which is not about vision but fear. The transit's job has been to flush it out of hiding in order to usher it into retirement. Fundamentalism will always exist in fits and starts in the human condition; but now that it has been named and stoked into high cleansing fires, its time as a world-determining force is ebbing. Pluto is moving into Capricorn and has other fish to fry.

But before we leave Pluto in Sagittarius, we must bring its core meaning home: home to the personal self. The transit has forced humankind to subject to a long and thoughtful examination the interior process of truth-seeking, whether or not we thought we wanted to. For the sincere seeker, this examination has been a blessing. It has inspired a redefinition of what integrity means to each of us personally. We have been cajoled into dedicating ourselves to whatever path we have chosen, nurturing more conscientiously whatever ideals we hold dear and putting our beliefs into action.

ELEVEN

LIGHTNING STRIKES THE TOWERS
THE PLUTO-SATURN OPPOSITION

Now that we have a sense of the themes ushered onto the world stage by Pluto in Sagittarius, we will turn to a transit that cranked them up to fever pitch.

With the thirteen-year passage of Pluto through the sign of religion forming the backdrop, transiting Saturn entered the scene. Straight across the sky from Pluto, Saturn hit the Descendant of the USA chart. This took place as Pluto was on the chart's Ascendant for the first time in the country's history. It was this opposition between Saturn and Pluto[1], the most widely-discussed astrological configuration in recent times, that defined the millennium for the USA and by extension the world.

The Flaming Arrow

Faith-based terrorism of one form or another is a typical expression of Pluto in Sagittarius, as we have seen; and prior to Pluto's 1994 ingress many astrologers had speculated about the likelihood of religious strife during this cycle[2]. But the events of September 11, 2001 painted the definitive picture for all of us. On that day the fiery arrow that is the symbol of this sign took the form of speeding airplanes,

---

[1] This transit extended between Fall 2000 through Spring 2003. A discussion of the full chart for the WTC bombings {Sept. 11, 2001 8:48 am EST, New York, N.Y.} is beyond the range of this book, but interested readers are encouraged to read Richard Tarnas' excellent monograph at http://www.gaiamind.org/WTCNotes.html.

[2] The most seminal example of this historical pattern—alluded to in an amazing gaffe G. W. Bush made on September 16, 2001 when he used the word *crusade* in a speech castigating the jihadists—was the Saturn-Pluto opposition of 1099 {Libra-Aries}, when the Christians desecrated Muslim holy sites in their siege of Jerusalem. See Jacob Schwatz's essay at http://www.asteroids.com/WTC.htm.

crashing into New York's proud commercial towers and changing the numbers nine-eleven from a date into a mythos[3].

The Twin Towers

Those familiar with the tarot doubtless recognized the televised image immediately: the Tower is the card of cataclysmic change, wrenching a people out of complacency. The Walker deck's version of this card depicts the pope (the church) falling off one side of the tower, and Caesar (the state) falling off the other, as a bolt of lightning shatters the structure in the middle. The World Trade Center towers, symbols of mercantilism, corresponded to the planet Saturn, planet of the corporate marketplace. The fact that there were two towers (and two planes, and two attack sites) corresponded to the sign Saturn was in: Gemini, sign of the twins. The transit was illustrated in pure archetypes, and as such became emblazoned into the collective mind as a nightmarish group vision of extraordinary power.

Rot Within the Structure

From what bow did this arrow shoot forth? Not from a source Americans recognized. Not from one of their familiar old-fashioned enemies, like Russia, nor from any nation on a map. Recall that Pluto, planet of the underground and invisible, governs terrorism as well as the criminal underworld, the CIA and their associated conspiracies, provocateurs and secret plots.

Pluto's purpose in Sagittarius has been to undermine those societal values that need an overhaul, and the opposition brought this purpose to a head. The World Trade Center attacks expressed the principle that when the time has come for immense change, a culture's civilized self-image (Saturn) will be traumatized (Pluto), and its unacknowledged underbelly revealed. Where there is rot (Pluto) in any structure (Saturn), it will be uncovered.

Energies that have been covered up for a long time become distorted and ugly; but if one wishes to understand, one keeps looking. An investigator examining a rotting structure would be foolish to demonize the forces behind the rot and quit the scene in disgust. If he wants to know what created the rot he will keep looking. If the desire is to understand the process, one suspends judgment and keeps looking until one sees the whole pattern.

---

[3] The first bombing of the World Trade Center, in 1993, took place under a square (90° angle) between Saturn and Pluto. In astrological cycles a subsequent opposition often acts as the other shoe dropping.

The rot revealed by the Saturn-Pluto opposition was the dark side of global ideology and power politics, and our job as investigators is to look at the whole pattern.

Ignorance and Incredulity

The sign Saturn was in at the time, Gemini, tells us the transit had something to say about the access to and use of information[4]. Saturn in Gemini is always a statement about deficient or faulty data. On one level it was suggesting a need to postpone action until sufficient knowledge had been acquired. On another level it was a critique of a certain chronic irresponsibility that afflicts the American sensibility as regards the use of information—a national character flaw that in part provoked the attacks and would determine the period to follow.

Saturn (responsibility) was proclaiming that actions based on ignorance (Gemini) of America's role in the world are not responsible actions; they are reactions, and they cause terrible harm. Incredulity, a product of insufficient information, as well as propaganda, a system of disinformation, are among the themes signified. Both of these expressions of dark Gemini were everywhere in evidence immediately after the disaster.

Among average Americans there was very little understanding, then or now, of the rage harbored by the Muslim suicide-pilots who right away became the object of national vilification; nor that of the Muslim world in general of which these men seemed to be the emissaries. Instead there was shock, appended with repeated declarations of incredulity. The whole nation was seized with one staggering mass expression of "*Huh?*"

Immediately an ad hoc educational campaign was launched by the media, wherein Americans began to see anti-American activists on television in areas of the world that they would not have been able to find on a map until that September day. There is no doubt that most Americans were unaware of the ghastly mass suffering in Iraq under the thirteen-year-long campaign euphemistically referred to as "sanctions," which the U.N. had been bullied by the White House into authorizing and which had claimed the lives of an estimated half a million Arab children. But the Muslim world was not unaware of it.

---

[4] This theme was emphatically underscored by the presence of Mercury, the ruler of Gemini, on the Ascendant* at the moment the towers were hit.

*Mercury hits the Ascendant for only four minutes every 24 hours. This fleeting cycle added the final touch to the timing of the WTC attacks—the detail of specificity to complete the astrological moment—like a second hand on a grandfather clock whose minute and hour hand are already in place, pointing to the hour, when the second hand sweeps up to meet them. And at that moment you hear the chimes.

The provincial American president, who had not even traveled abroad until his new job demanded it, was a fitting national symbol of this collective ignorance. When Saturn in Gemini crossed the USA Descendant in 2001, it was making an announcement about the country's irresponsible approach towards being informed. It was declaring that in a post-9-11 world such an approach would be untenable.

We looked at the differences between the higher and lower vibrations of Saturn in our discussion of its natal placement; the same contrast pertains by transit. When Pluto connects with Saturn in the sky, it seeks to bring Saturn into a higher vibration by first making an exaggerated point about the flaws in its current expression. As we have seen, low-level Saturn expresses as polarizing exclusionism, of which jingoism and bigotry are all-too-familiar examples.

High-level Saturn, by contrast, would involve a profound and spiritually mature level of world leadership. It was into a deeper level of Saturn's function that the opposition was meant to push the American people. At this level, human suffering—whoever the victims and wherever their suffering takes place—is recognized as one of the Dark Mysteries, and must be witnessed with a humble and universal perspective.

Less a Cause than an Effect

At first blush, the events of 9-11 seem to be the cause of which the current world situation is the effect. But the astrological view is to see things rather the other way around. Events are understood not in terms of agency, but in terms of symbolism and timing. From this point of view, 9-11 was less a cause than an effect.

Around the millennium just before the Saturn-Pluto transit hit, the buzz in Washington was all partisan gossip about sexual misbehavior and campaign finance. But when Pluto and Saturn moved into position, decades' worth of clandestine foreign policy patterns with vast global consequences very quickly began to surface. Though the authenticity of Osama bin Laden's various communiqués is not entirely certain, one of them raises three issues that seem to get right to the heart of the matter as regards America's doings in the Middle East:

- foreign troops in lands sacred to Islam,
- the bombing of Iraqi civilians, and
- arming Israel against the Palestinians.

Context Around Nine-Eleven

At this writing, there is a welter of confusion about the circumstances surrounding the World Trade Center attacks. The White

House immediately snapped into lockdown mode when questions were raised—to the point where now, five years later, the members of the victims' families are taking their own government to court to sue for answers. The effort to process the disaster has been complicated by reports of incomprehensible incompetence on the part of the relevant agencies; and these, together with impossible logistical inconsistencies in the official explanations[5] and implacable stonewalling from Washington, have created an aura around the event that is hauntingly reminiscent of the JFK assassination—a similarly epochal wound in the national psyche that has never healed. As with that dark episode, one wonders whether political scientists, investigative journalists or citizen speculators will ever be able to piece together the many-tiered forces behind the 9-11 phenomenon on the level of evidentiary fact.

But on the level of social and political themes, there is a lot to piece together; so much that it is difficult *not* to see the forbidding sense it all makes. The pithy patterns that shed the most light on the meaning of the disaster were readily apparent in America's foreign dealings at the time of the attacks and leading up to them. They were quite available in the mainstream American media[6]. But as the Gemini transit made clear, the American public—whose national chart features Saturn squaring its Sun/Jupiter in Cancer—is not known for an appreciation of geography, history or geopolitics.

Clues at Ground Level

The cry for blood was hot and high after New York was attacked, and when Bush's ministers named a country to go after, the public was all too ready to support the mission. But Americans wouldn't have had to look very hard for reasons not to invade Afghanistan.

Among the great benchmarks of the modern era was the crumbling breakup of the Soviet Union not long after its botched

---

[5] Information on the various controversies is lucidly presented at http://www.911truth.org/article.php?story=20041221155307646

[6] Americans who read past the front pages of their newspapers would have known, for instance, about the bombing missions their government was conducting in Iraq in the years before the invasion, during the period of "sanctions"; about the billions in military aid being shipped to Israel to use against the Palestinians; about the desperate straits of the common people in the lands controlled by Bush's allies the sheiks; and about America's extensive military installations throughout the Middle East. It was common knowledge—in terms of broad themes if not in terms of details—that Washington's leadership was oil-industry-backed, that its diplomacy was oil-industry-driven, that the world's biggest oil fields resided in Arab lands, and that these three facts had something to do with one another.

invasion of that country, wretchedly poor but strategically located. The Soviets' attempt to crush Afghanistan's warlords had been an abject failure; and one would think that would have given Washington policymakers pause before their own incursion there–*would* have, that is, unless the desire for a natural gas pipeline were stronger than the desire to avoid a messy war[7].

But perhaps the most fascinating in the snarl of background threads that led up to the WTC attacks was also the most counter-intuitive—which may be why, even now, it seems to have not sunk into the American mass mind. In the rash of post-attack publicity surrounding this mysterious new villain, Osama bin Laden, an old-boys'-club of connections started to come to light—not just economic but dynastic—between bin Laden and America's very own ruling family. Before the news was discreetly retired from the front page, Americans were able to pick up a paper and read about Osama's relations to the Saudi royal family, George Bush Sr.'s relations to the Saudi royal family, and—with absurd inevitability—George Bush Sr.'s relations, via the Carlysle Group, to bin Laden himself: a six-degrees-of-separation situation of the type that is less the exception than the rule among the world's petro-billionaires.

For years before this came out, moreover, it was well known that George Senior was head of the CIA when finishing touches were put on the system of partnerships which now controls the world's oil wealth. Less widely discussed were the functions and geopolitical ramifications of this shadowy network, of which W. and his Washington cohorts—not to mention Saudi allies and every other wealthy Arab family from bin Laden to Saddam Hussein himself—were the heirs.

This handful of facts and connections would not, all by itself, have settled the irresolution that nags at the nation's mind and heart about 9-11. But it would have helped frame the right questions, and asking questions was what Saturn in Gemini was warning Americans to do in order to come up with an appropriate response to events at ground level.

Questions at Sky Level

The astrologer's ambition, however, is to seek out the truth behind the facts. This entails looking at events from sky level. Here global lessons are inferred from timing, on both a micro and a macro

---

[7] American interests were set on securing control of the region because they needed to cross Taliban country in order to avoid political trouble elsewhere along the route of their pipeline (see Page 46). Once their negotiations with the Taliban had fallen through, the US and Britain sent troops to Afghanistan—in early 2001, well before the WTC attacks.

scale. By pinpointing the cycles that were occurring during the period, we see large epochal teachings struggling to come to group consciousness.

The immense historical threshold that the USA crossed in 2001 was marked by a literal astrological line: the horizon axis of the American chart—one pole of which, the Descendant, represents dealings with *The Other*. When Saturn hits the Descendant in any natal chart, the native gets a teaching about relationships. In a country's chart, the teaching is about the nation's relationship to other countries.

The Descendant is the gateway to the seventh house, which poses the question: *Who am I in relationship to you?* Each of us has been tested in one-to-one relationships, trying to play nice; trying to balance. Nation-states work through knots and tangles, too, with other nation-states. Nobody said relating was easy. And with Saturn transiting here, you have to work at it even harder. You have to earn whatever cooperation you get. When it crossed this cusp in the chart of the USA, Saturn began a cycle whose function has been to showcase American foreign policy and its attendant responsibilities.

Saturn is the planet of definition and clarity. In this placement it was highlighting the USA's long-term isolationism, for the purpose of urging the country to transcend its collective narcissism. Transits such as these always augur some kind of chickens returning to the roost. With the planet of karma on the cusp of foreign dealings, the American people were given an unmistakable heads-up that international chickens would be headed their way.

Hear No Evil

So who are these chickens? How might the American people have interpreted this clue from the heavens?

At this point we find ourselves once again up against the dilemma discussed in our chapter on Mercury. How can Americans watch out for the chickens if they don't know where they are coming from or why? Millions of ordinary Americans—the one segment of the world population who stand the best chance of correcting the alarming trajectory the world is on—are overwhelmingly estranged from the rest of the globe by a glaring paucity of information, while being suffocated with a deadening pall of disinformation.

The problem is not just a failure to pay attention. Saturn in Gemini, wherever it resides, is the signature of state censorship. Saturn governs all institutionalized restriction, and in Gemini it indicates authoritative control over language and data. Saturn (delay, shutdown) was just moving into Gemini (media access) when Bush Junior rescinded the provision that gives access to a president's records twelve years after he leaves office. In perhaps his most symbolically pungent first act as president, he proposed that disclosure be indefinitely postponed. Thus were the American people presented with shades of things to come.

Early on, some of the manifestations of this campaign of curtailment, such as the proposal to take the French out of French fries, came across as farcical. At this writing, the Bush administration's carefully orchestrated censorship of dissent, punishment of whistle-blowers, First Amendment shredding and intrusion into citizen privacy have gone so over-the-top that the French fry move makes one feel downright nostalgic.

Soon after the hijacker attacks and the subsequent invasion of Afghanistan, Saturn in Gemini made its shadow side known. Big Media began to define its identity in postmillennial America, clamping down on free expression on many fronts. The music giant Clear Channel established a do-not-play list of presumably un-American songs (John Lennon's *Imagine* made the list) and its corporate cousin Viacom refused to rent billboard space to a peace group. The gradual deregulation of and government control over the mainstream media, discussed in Chapter Seven, got fully underway. By the Spring of 2003, while the Iraqi invasion raged, the front pages of American newspapers were featuring G.I.s tenderly ministering to wounded children rather than showing pictures of the horrible results of the American cluster bombs that had turned those children into orphans.

These restrictions reflect more than mere intellectual inhibition, governed by Saturn. They fall into the category of mind control, governed by Pluto.

Censorship and Criminalization

All presidential censorship in America since September of 2001—from the ban on the networks' airing of Bin Laden's tapes to the refusal to submit subpoenaed federal documents—has been justified by the claim that divulging the information would aid and abet the machinations of a faceless yet larger-than-life horde of lethal international outlaws. This imagery derives not from Saturn, but from Pluto, the Dark God of the Underworld.

At the millennial opposition these two archetypes introduced themes that have been playing themselves out ever since, in the compulsive secrecy Washington has exhibited about its own machinations, as well as in its obsessive data-collecting on the people it claims to be shielding from outside harm. At the height of the transit, the White House came up with the ludicrously misnamed "Patriot Act," which vastly expanded the criteria for the censorship (Saturn) and criminalization (Pluto) of individuals and groups seen by Washington as antagonistic to its purposes. Soon these criteria were stretched even further to apply not just to suspected "terrorists" but to presumed "terrorist sympathizers:" a net big enough to snare troublemakers such as immigrants with and without documentation, non-Republican professors, peaceniks, outspoken movie stars, animal rights activists and who knows who else (no one seems to know—least of all the labyrinthine federal agencies in charge of collecting these staggering reams of data[8]).

Astrologers suspect the involvement of Pluto whenever they see attempts to radically control and negate something. This is the only planet that can reach down into the guts of a concept and mess around with its essential structure. The "Patriot Act" is the consummate example of this principle at work, in that it is designed to undercut the most basic rights of citizenship: it allows the very definition (Saturn) of national identity (Ascendant) to be rendered moot by the government's ability to simply revoke it (Pluto).

A couple of months after the WTC attacks, the Saturn-Pluto transit reached exactitude: each planet occupied the same degree of its sign, one of several peaks of the three-year transit. There was a perceptible shift in the spirit of inquiry about what had happened: the numbness had worn off and an urgent collective curiosity seemed to replace it. It was at this point that a handful of uncowed US critics—and of a great number of international ones—began sniffing around the roots of America's investment in the Middle East. There was newly energized discussion of that nasty Iran-Contra business, and how several of its key deal-cutters had gradually crept back into powerful roles in Washington. The long-moribund affair with the Shah of Iran started to turn up in the newspapers. Intrigued Americans started looking up the Crusades in Wikipedia.

Shock and Awe

Saturn highlights unfinished business; Pluto pinpoints corruption and cover-up. Both of these themes played out with burgeoning blatancy as the two planets continued their back and forth dance over the months

---

[8] Americans are now hearing, with a weary sense of predictability, about a series of breaches that reveals that their government seems neither to know what data it has nor how to keep track of it. The military has admitted to several such snafus, but perhaps the most darkly comic example of the trend was the news in the summer of 2006 that a federal agency charged with "fighting identity theft" had lost two government laptops containing the sensitive personal data of millions of people.

that followed, making retrograde and direct turns as they performed their several-year-long duet. Each turn marked a shift in America's consciousness of the Americans-versus-non-Americans theme.

At this writing, all but the *my-country-right-or-wrong* contingent have come to know what millions of protesters worldwide knew on February 16, 2003[9], a month before the Pentagon invaded Iraq: that the war would be an unmitigated disaster. But in the Spring of 2003, Saturn, parked solidly on the US Descendant, was like a stone wall separating America's consciousness from the rest of the world's. When the staged video clip of Saddam's statue crashing to the ground amidst a small crowd of Iraqis[10] was played over and over on the network news, it offered American viewers an image of the invasion that was almost unrecognizable from the way international observers were seeing it.

Before long, however, the American people themselves began to see that their leaders' prediction of Iraqis showering their "liberators" with flowers of welcome had been a tad overoptimistic. White House spin had ill-prepared the public for the scenario of traumatized civilians fighting their new colonizers tooth and nail. The Plutonian subplot behind the invasion became unmistakable during the terrible chaos that followed the siege of Baghdad, when American soldiers did not lift a finger to protect Iraq's antiquities, guard its hospitals, restore its water or protect its women and children. They were too busy securing the all-important oil fields.

See No Evil
The task of the astrological investigator is to attend to the imagery flashing before our eyes in historical moments such as these and decode the symbols in the sky to see what they mean.

We can infer from the Saturn-in-Gemini part of the transit that the cosmos was introducing the theme of not-knowing (Saturn=not; Gemini=knowing) as it related to the rest of the world (the Descendant). This was a warning to Americans that they could no longer afford the luxury of ignorance. Saturn's job is to keep tabs on our karma—energy we put forth that will sooner or later come back to us. The placement of Saturn in Gemini during its fateful opposition with Pluto tells us that

---

[9] On that day the Saturn-Pluto opposition was three degrees from exactitude; Jupiter was exactly opposed to Pluto; Mars was opposed to Saturn, and the Full Moon brought everything to a head. Unprecedented numbers of people amassed in public demonstrations in every major city on Earth.

[10] Did you ever wonder where those random bystanders got all their little American flags?

misinformation, lies and ignorance—whether innocuous or fatal—have amassed karma for the country and will continue to do so until addressed.

The warmongers' snow job on an unskeptical American public demonstrated this point with woeful precision. That Iraq's resistance to invasion could have surprised anybody is a testament to the difference between what is common knowledge in America and what is common knowledge in the rest of the literate world. Every one of Iraq's schoolchildren has grown up knowing about the British occupation of their country, its hard-won revolution in 1958, the twelve years of deadly sanctions and the current imperial intentions of the United States. Americans, by contrast, could hardly be bothered to remember back to 1983, when, during Iraq's war with Iran, Donald Rumsfeld himself had been dispatched by then-president Reagan to pledge undying American allegiance to none other than Saddam Hussein.

The forces of karma do not bend to government spin, but most Americans did. From the onset of the weapons inspections, it was whispered that the committee behind this war had been planning to invade Iraq all along, a campaign that would be facilitated by pre-disarming Iraq's military. This premise has been since corroborated by the Dover Street memos, of course, which revealed Washington's bluff and posturing reaction to the U.N. investigation to have been a long, drawn-out charade. But at the time, most Americans allowed themselves to be distracted like credulous children by news reports that stayed riveted on the weapons-of-mass-destruction trope as if the whole episode were some sort of treasure hunt or board game: the Search for the Smoking Gun.

But soon all that was smoking was the rubble of a ruined Iraq.

Plutocratic Intentions

Transiting planets provoke their natal counterparts. During the several years that Pluto hovered over the US Ascendant, the chart's natal Pluto was roused like a waking beast. As discussed in previous chapters, Pluto resides natally in the second house of the USA, the signature of plutocracy. The links between huge but secretive corporations and the politicians they finance—and by extension, the laws that those politicians enact—are by now old news to all but the extraordinarily naive.

As the siege of Baghdad raged in the Spring of 2003, one was not surprised to see running stock quotes posted beneath the battle reportage on the network news, as the media made no bones about the war-as-marketplace rationale—at least for certain favored companies—

that was driving the bloodshed and destruction. Battle cheerleaders like CNN, which made its mark during the first Gulf War, became beneficiaries of the boom no less than war suppliers like Lockheed and postwar builders like Bechtel. Indeed, America's vice president—a truly Plutonian figure with a reptilian demeanor and a penchant for backroom-dealings—had himself gone to Iraq in the early 1980s to negotiate a pipeline that was then-President Reagan's pet project—a bit of data one would think remarkably apposite but about which the American mainstream media has been silent as the grave.

Mr. Cheney has been less lucky avoiding publicity about his extensive ties to the notorious Halliburton, Kellogg, Root, and other companies whose contracts—awarded without any bidding—have been earning billions from not-rebuilding Iraq.

Cracking the Code of the Descendant

Now that we have looked at the two archetypes that starred in the show, Pluto and Saturn, let us look in more detail at the points in the US chart where they landed: the horizon line, or Ascendant/ Descendant axis[11]. The fact that their opposition straddled that all-important line was as crucial a feature of the transit as the signs these planets were in. It focused the cosmic klieg light on a part of the chart structure that is as basic as a skeleton is to a body—and as often taken for granted.

Whatever planet hits this axis by transit, in any chart, is going to give the native a teaching about the existential conundrum of the Self vs. the Other. For the USA to have received one planet on each pole was a sign that the collective intelligence was getting a teaching about what psychologists might call *mirroring*. The fact that Saturn was involved meant that failure to integrate the teaching would have clear consequences; the fact that Pluto was involved raised the stakes to a global-risk level. This means not only that America must learn mature relating skills but that if it does not, the whole world pays the price.

---

[11] The Ascendant and Descendant are two of the four *angles* that establish the structure of every natal chart. Although for abbreviation's sake astrologers often speak of these two points separately—as if they each had a discrete meaning that could be understood alone (the Ascendant: "self-awareness"; the Descendant: "awareness of others")—they are in fact poles of the same axis and operate as one integral unit. By definition 180 degrees apart, they represent twin faces of the native and as such balance and reflect each other. For example, if one has Sagittarius at the Ascendant (as the USA does), one's fiery, emotional, idealistic disposition is meant to be balanced by the dry, abstract, data-driven energies that come from others (or from the act of relating itself, which ideally brings these energies out in the native).

The USA and the Rest of the World

Modern astrology has learned a lot from psychology as regards the Descendant and by extension the seventh house[12]. Let us continue our examination of the Saturn-Pluto transit by applying some of the most valuable of these principles to the context at hand—that of a national entity and its *alter egos* ("other selves")—and see if they fit.

We have defined the seventh house as that of the generic Other, friend and foe. For the entity that is the United States, that means *the rest of the world*. The double transit of Pluto and Saturn put tremendous pressure on this arena, forcing America to look at its relationship patterns with non-Americans—not just current but long-evolving[13]; not just overt (Saturn) but covert (Pluto).

The Ascendant-Descendant opposition of Saturn and Pluto coincided with the return of critical attention to disturbing questions not raised since the sixties about the CIA and FBI's involvement in counter-revolutionary sabotage around the world. Most emblematically, the assassination of the democratically-elected President Allende in Chile—probably the best-known of a series of hundreds of such incursions since 1945 initiated by the United States—started to be considered from a new point of view: one that asks, *Why was the storming by Kissinger's men of the presidential Palace in Santiago acceptable, whereas the idea of a suicide bomber hitting the White House would be heinous to the point of devilry?*

The answer, of course, is: That was *them;* this is *us.*

Herein lies the central issue of the seventh house, and the code we must crack in order to plumb the deeper meaning behind the relationships any of us draw into our lives. The first law of the seventh house is that one must see beyond the *us vs. them* paradigm if one wants to avoid the transiting planet's coming right back at us—and in its least benign form—come the karmic deadline.

---

[12] The Descendant is one of the chart's four *angles*; it establishes the meaning of the seventh house (see Page 207, Appendix I for definitions of these terms). The closer planets are to the Descendant, the more emphatic the seventh-house lesson. Saturn was an astounding one degree away from the USA Descendant when the planes hit the towers, and Pluto was one degree away from exact opposition.

[13] This is inferred from the duration of the cycles. Though Saturn and Pluto oppose each other roughly every thirty-five year (the last time was in 1965, when American combat in Viet Nam began in earnest), the placement of Pluto on the Ascendant was unprecedented in the lifetime of the national entity (to be discussed in the next chapter).

The Laws of Projection

In order to make sense of the ever-more-astounding hypocrisies streaming forth from Washington, let us consider how a psychologist might interpret the blaming patterns of married couples. The law of projection is seen to be at work when the complaining spouse condemns in his partner the very features he needs to see in himself, but cannot. Each of us knows this ploy. Even if we can't see ourselves clearly enough to catch ourselves at it, we certainly recognize it when our friends do it. When we listen to a friend ranting about someone who's pressing her buttons, we may notice in the accuser's diatribes an uncannily accurate description of the accuser herself[14].

Projection and the Father

As family therapists know, projection gets particularly heated when the parties in question are personally related. Bush the Younger's righteous denunciations of dictatorship were a centerpiece of his call to war, but of course his own father was among those policymakers who supported the bloodiest dictators of a generation. It could be argued that Bush allies Mobutu and Suharto made Saddam Hussein look like Mr. Rogers.

George Senior was also supposedly the object of a murderous plot hatched by Saddam, and thus the star of a vengeance fantasy W. was thought to harbor; though one must decode the language of projection to see the simple tit for tat. In George Junior's 2003 State of the Union address, he implied—with horrible smugness—that his men had murdered scores of purported terrorist masterminds (they are "no longer a problem," he said, with a wink and a nudge). Yet had Saddam's forces succeeded in killing his father, we can be sure that nothing less than the noble term *assassination* would have been pressed into service and that Washington would have reacted to the murder as if to the martyrdom of Jesus Christ. As to the military retaliation, given the hundreds of thousands of Iraqi casualties from sanctions and invasion combined, one shudders to imagine the tsunami of vengeance that would have been meted out had the elder Bush been hit.

---

[14] The metaphysical understanding of projection differs from the psychological in one major respect: projection is not necessarily a fantasy. Natural Law stipulates that we can and do attract individuals who play out the very themes that we are denying in ourselves. Saddam may well have been a brute and a mass murderer; projection does not address accuracy or exoneration. It merely explains the choice of sins with which the accused is condemned and the exaggerated and myopic fervor of his accusers.

Projection of Crimes against Humanity

Many commentators on the military psyche have speculated about the mindset that allows soldiers to see it as a sworn duty to kill, in this case, Iraqi "insurgents" (Pentagon-speak for virtually any military-age Iraqi male) and then turn around and vociferously condemn any violence that comes back at them. Whatever the psychological mechanism that allows this incongruity, it is being stretched to the very limit in Iraq.

As has been widely noted since the invasion, the very generals who drummed up war fever with stories of purported Iraqi chemical weapons are themselves responsible for unleashing upon their victims munitions of almost unimaginable toxicity, such as white phosphorous—a napalm-like substance that burns through the skin to the bone—and depleted uranium, seen by some as a radiological scourge with the power to destroy Iraq's genetic future. Even more widely noted is the fact that the very president who regaled Americans with tales of Saddam's torture chambers has himself been conducting an all-out campaign to use unspeakable "interrogation procedures" upon the several hundred unnamed, unlawyered apprehendees within the soundproof cells of Guantanamo, and at the American gulags that are being discovered to exist in Europe. Moreover, the current inhabitant of the Oval Office is only the latest to refuse to extradite the estimated 1,000 torturers whom Amnesty International says are now living safely in the USA, most of them graduates of the infamous School of the Americas in Ft. Benning, Georgia—renamed but not forgotten by those who seek justice for war criminality.

From the Pentagon brass who boasted about the shocking-and-awesome effect their latest mega-bombs would have upon the terrified residents of Iraq, and who waited—with stomach-turning cynicism—until immediately after the American elections in November 2005 to launch a massacre in the town of Fallujah that demolished thirty-six thousand homes and murdered four to six thousand civilians—from these men we hear righteous accusations of "terrorism" when a ragged Iraqi blows himself up defending his home.

And after it seems that nothing could top their accumulated hypocrisies, in June of 2006 we hear—from this government that has erected around itself the most expensive and opaque public relations machine in American history[15]—a pronouncement dismissing the

---

[15] In early 2006 it was reported that the Bush administration had spent 1.6 billion dollars on public relations and advertising over thirty months' time.

suicides of three men at Guantanamo who hanged themselves in their cells, after four years without trial, as nothing but "a cynical PR stunt."

Pot Calling the Kettle Black

The strangely archaic phrase that became a media cliché— "weapons of mass destruction"—serves our study of the Descendant by exemplifying projection in its baldest guise. When mentioned in debate it was markedly unaccompanied by any reference to the fact that the USA is by far the number one producer, seller and deployer of such weapons in the world.

This oddly contradictory stance is not new, as an expression of America's distress over the presumption of foreign countries (that is, those *not* on Washington's Good Guys List) to arm themselves. Among disarmament activists much has been made of the irony that the USA, the only country responsible for killing hundreds of thousands of innocents with an atomic bomb, should thereafter claim to be the arbiter of which nations can possess nukes and which cannot. In the context of the current bellicose posturing against Iran, this irony is newly relevant. Except that it is not, strictly speaking, ironic at all. It is quite predictable. This is exactly how projection works.

Face in the Mirror

The axiom behind the Ascendant and the Descendant proposes that both are houses of identity. First-house action (*I did this*) shows us who we are in a direct way; seventh-house action (*you did that*) shows us who we are in an indirect way. When we're too unconscious to create friendship, we create enmity. Though we may prefer the former to the latter, from a cosmic point of view the two have the same valence. In fact, either one has the same valence as the self. To paraphrase Robert Hand: "People we relate to are as indicative of our level of consciousness as we are ourselves."

This is an understanding that would take the bite out of the whole *he-said/she-said* game were we to apply it to our personal relationships. It is an understanding that could deflate moral righteousness and defuse international violence were we to apply it to group relationships. Every instance of *us vs. them* thinking can be opened up to a higher level by identifying the mirroring mechanism at its core.

Were Americans to heed the lesson of the Descendant transit, it would free them from the blinkered perspectives they get from their mainstream news and make the phenomenon of mirroring embarrassingly easy to see. Consider that after the fall of Baghdad, US newspapers repeatedly used the term *looting* in their headlines to refer to chaotic mobs in the bombed-out stores and museums of Iraq. Meanwhile, in the business section, the triumphs of American corporations contracted to move in and seize that country's oil fields could have been—but were not, of course—described with the same verb.

It may be over-optimistic to imagine that such a shift in perspective could be espoused widely enough to render moot warfare in the world. But we are in an endgame as far as old global paradigms are concerned. Ambitious leaps of consciousness are no longer a luxury but a necessity. The secret of the Descendant—"We have met the enemy and he is us" (Walt Kelly)—must be told.

Friends and Foes

The Descendant refers both to our interchanges and to the *alter egos* with which we have them: partners, rivals, friends and peers. Pluto's opposition to this angle in the chart of the USA exposed several generations' worth of hidden patterns motivating the nation's feuds and alliances.

We have referred earlier to Pluto's association with domination and genocide, thugs and warlords. Soon after Saturn and Pluto opened the Pandora's Box of American foreign policy by opposing each other over the horizon axis, America's military bankrolling of Israel moved from being an open secret to high-profile news. The indictment for war crimes of the Pentagon's old friend General Pinochet hit the headlines. And a coup in Venezuela was linked to the CIA without our having to wait a decade to hear about it. Each of the American government's rapports with foreign governments since the transit began has been met with a new level of suspicion from those observers unconvinced by official explanations, and the stonewalling from Washington has taken on a new fierceness as the worms have come crawling out of the can.

Pluto is also the planet of betrayal. The crisis in Iraq has thrown a spotlight upon the White House's history of embracing and then demonizing puppet-strongmen all over the world. Turning the idea of loyalty on its head, the USA has traditionally exhibited no real allegiance except to those American business interests for whose benefit a given country needs to be stabilized. With stunning consistency, Washington has trained, armed and then repudiated despot after despot—men like Pol Pot, Trujillo and Somoza. Even in the censored American press one can find mention of how the Pentagon supplied guns to the same mujahidin in Afghanistan that its soldiers would later gun down; and about how it supported and then betrayed dissident Iraqis during the first Gulf War.

Just what kind of karma is America accumulating through relationship patterns like these? We might ask ourselves what fate we would expect a good storyteller to divvy out to a fictional lover who woos, jilts and then murders his ex.

World-Scale Wrongdoing

What are the consequences of a superpower's world-scale wrongdoing? The United Nations was set up to be the venue to try such cases, but the United States, as the only country with the might to refuse to play fair, has excluded itself from war criminality jurisdiction.

The current administration of G. W. Bush, culpable as it is, is only the most obvious in a long, sorry history of disdain. From issues ranging from global warming to the prevention of nuclear holocaust, decades of painstakingly eked-out international efforts have been summarily dismissed and undermined by Washington. If the world body's other members had any faith left in the USA's integrity after this shameful legacy, we can be fairly sure that the contemptuous game-playing Bush et al demonstrated over the arms inspections has killed off any last vestige of that faith.

What is the karmic blowback for sabotaging the only international peacekeeping body in the world?

If a schoolchild is caught cheating on a test, we expect there to be a punishment. If a doctor is convicted of malpractice, his license gets taken away. The laws of karma do not exempt the high and mighty; sooner or later, whether the perfidy is individual or collective, blind universal law will prevail. And ultimately, the gods do not care who or what is the agent of a particular injury, who received the harm, nor in what form responsibility will ultimately have to be taken. To them, it is nothing personal. But as mortal beings, we must try to fathom our stance towards these issues.

Personal Responsibility for Collective Wrongs

The phrase "an accident of birth" reflects the prevailing assumption that our birth data are among the few things in this life that are incontestably arbitrary. But from a metaphysical viewpoint, of course, it is no accident at all. We are each denizens of a certain place and members of a certain generation for a reason. Our collective identity is one of the many layers of who we are.

If one believes that we each somehow choose our soul's lessons, it follows that we must express ourselves not in some theoretical elsewhere but where we are, alert to what is happening now. In times like these, each of us must actively cultivate his or her own unique heart connection to the greater world of which we are a part. Otherwise, we descend into a state of victimhood, denying yet absorbing the toxicity in the atmosphere all around us, condemning or ignoring its perceived source, and making our lives very small.

A New Kind of Grown-up

When Saturn (adulthood) and Pluto (makeovers) appeared across the USA chart's most important axis, it signaled quite an opportunity for the USA: that of a whole new vision of adulthood. The transit augured the mass transcendence of whatever perfunctory ideas Americans were raised with about what it meant to be a grown-up—and in its place, the substitution of a vision of adulthood deeper, more solitary and more sincere. Pluto's presence in the opposition tells us that America's new vision of adulthood would have to include the awareness of the deep collective shadow. The nation was being dared to face the darkness within itself without looking away: this is the ultimate task of all entities that take up the challenge of Pluto. And then, to be grown-up enough to do something about it: this is the real meaning of Saturnine responsibility. We will return to these two ideas, and how they might inform the lives of each one of us, in the chapters ahead.

What might it look like to take in the lesson of this opposition on the highest collective level? One can imagine a war criminal humbly asking pardon for his crimes, or a country solemnly paying reparations for its sins against humanity. One can imagine each member of a group daring to confess to his complicities and shames—thereby unleashing a tumult of creative energy that would be the inevitable result of stepping out of denial.

At Ground and Sky Levels

In this chapter we have identified the Saturn-Pluto opposition that straddled the horizon axis of the USA chart as being the key astrological signature of the phenomenon now referred to in mythopoeic shorthand as *9-11*, and of its aftermath, the invasion of Iraq in 2003. We have considered these catastrophes at ground level, in terms of the international relationships that led up to them—geopolitical clues hidden in plain sight. We have explored the Saturn/Pluto issues of ignorance and mind control that militated against clear sight on the part of the American public.

We have also considered the crises at sky level, cataloguing the lessons about power and responsibility that the USA was and is being challenged to learn. We have looked at the cosmic significance of the Self-Other dyad—how it can be distorted, through unconscious projection, in collective entities just as it can be in relationships between individuals. And we have speculated upon the potential of these teachings to be taken in by the collective intelligence of the United States, and how if they were—even in small measure—what a difference that would make in the world.

There are many levels of meaning in collective traumas like 9-11 and the war in Iraq. There are as many disparate ways to respond to horrors and griefs such as these as there are individuals who experience them—which is a very large number and, one fears, an increasing one. There were millions of Americans whose immediate reaction to both tragedies was to wave a flag; and in the United States the impulse to wave a flag is still predominant whenever these terrible episodes are mentioned.

So let us go ahead and wave flags, if inspired to do so—it is at least a response, and we must respond. Those of us who would wave flags, let us wave the flag of New York, the flag of Iraq, of Afghanistan, of Chechnya, the Balkans, the flags of Chiapas and East Timor, the flags for all of the African states whose people have been suffering so relentlessly that we can barely imagine how they endure. Those of us who would light candles, let us light one for all the precious dead, and for every man, woman and child alive. Let us send up a prayer to whomever we pray to that we meet the years ahead with a dedication to clean the blood off our hands and put not one more drop upon them.

TWELVE

COSMIC ECHOES

RECENT AND UPCOMING TRANSITS

Ongoing after 9-11, a string of significant transits came around, one after another, to evoke and disseminate the Pluto-Saturn opposition's relentless teachings. These created a series of "cosmic echoes", offering variations on the twin themes of responsibility (Saturn) and power (Pluto).

Saturn Time for America

From late 2003 through 2004 Saturn was hovering around the middle degrees of Cancer. This part of the Saturn cycle always inspires suspense among American astrologers because it pits the planet of karma against the Sun in the US natal chart[1]. Astrologers who use this chart to track America's vicissitudes keep a close watch on *any* planet that is transiting through Cancer, knowing that whatever it brings out will express the country's core issues. Saturn transits, especially, tend to spur relatively obvious and epigrammatic episodes when it passes over America's Sun cluster—episodes that resonate across the cultural landscape.

Karmic Birthdays

Every three decades when the transit comes around (Saturn has a cycle of roughly 29 years), astrologers watch it like a hawk. This time they got a double-whammy: Saturn conjoined the Sun of the sitting president and the Sun of the country at the same time. Because his birthday is so close to the USA's own birthday, George W. Bush's natal Sun falls within the same zodiacal range and is hit by the same transits[2].

---

[1] Remember that when Saturn crosses this placement it also meets up with America's natal Jupiter/Venus because they reside near the U.S. Sun—as well as with natal Saturn which squares them both. Since all three pieces of this natal configuration make up an integral whole, any transit that hits one piece of it impacts the others too.

[2] George W. Bush was born on July 6, 1946, 7:26 am EDT; New Haven, CT (41N18, 72W55); from the hospital records.

Bush's Sun resides in the elusive twelfth house of his natal chart, suggesting that his self-image bears little resemblance to his public persona. Protected by the benign sheen of a Jupiter/Moon conjunction in Libra, during the years just prior to the transit he had been coasting on the puerile charm by which he was commonly known. But soon after the Iraq war began, Saturn, the planet of accountability, started heading in his direction.

Beneath the easy manner he projected on television, one saw a dazed and frightened little boy trying to bluff his way through a situation he was in way over his head. Though it was widely recognized in America and abroad that George-Bush-the-individual was not the force controlling his administration, he was its figurehead, apologist, spokesperson and buck-stops-here—and the spotlight was on him. His effigy was being burned in massive street demonstrations that were erupting all over the globe that spring and summer in protest of the pre-emptive bombing of Iraq. In the wide world there was no more hated man.

These were not optimal circumstances in which to welcome a Saturn transit.

Fahrenheit 911

There was a lot of conjecture among astrologers about what form Bush's comeuppance would take. As it turned out, I think we must bestow the Saturn Visitation award to Michael Moore's "Fahrenheit 9/11."

The movie burst upon the world scene right on time, opening to packed movie houses in the United States despite efforts by Disney to dump it and by Republican "citizens' groups" to keep theatres from showing it. It blew the minds of many viewers who usually get their news by way of Rupert Murdoch and gave progressives a point of focus and a shot in the arm. It was released within days of the exact conjunction.

The anger and partisanship that immediately sprang up around the movie were symptomatic of a telling feature of Saturn transits: they tend to be aggressively resisted when the native harbors unacknowledged pain. Students of human nature no less than students of Saturn know that when we have not admitted our wounds we do not like to be reminded of them, and if someone comes around poking and prodding we usually react with blame. In this case it was the whole country getting poked and prodded by a big irreverent filmmaker in a baseball cap, holding up a mirror and demanding that the nation look at itself. But the collective mind was nowhere near ready in June of 2004 to face the wound of 9-11;

nor is it ready at this writing. So it was that during the summer of 2004, Michael Moore's movie incited an outpouring of vitriol for daring to expose some linkages in the political arena that were very uncomfortable for many Americans to consider.

As always, however, if we want to understand how transits work, we need to approach the subject metaphysically and strip the archetype down to its value-neutral essence. Saturn is an impersonal force, no more capricious than gravity—which it rules—whose job it is to bring things down to Earth. Saturn transits bring low that which has soared high, but not out of grudges or vengeance. Gravity does not sling mud; it only ushers downward mud that has already been slung up in the air. Much to the chagrin of his critics, Michael Moore did not invent the material he depicted[3]. He merely traced old material back to its origins, in part by showing previously unpublicized footage that allowed his targets to self-reveal.

With exquisite minimalism (Saturn), the movie's most famous sequence spoke volumes. The president was being videotaped in an elementary schoolroom where he was on a good-will visit. A federal agent is shown approaching him, and we see the man whispering in the president's ear—presumably telling him that the WTC towers had just been hit. The camera is then held on Bush for several long minutes, during which time a look comes over his face that is utterly incongruous given the content of the presumed message. Calm, affectless and vacant, his reaction is incomprehensible from the point of view of a man to whom news of the calamity is being broken for the first time.

There it was, right in front of America's eyes—but the evidence was left un-decoded. Far and away the most talked-about scene in the film, that chilling visual of the president's face hit a deep nerve in the viewing audience. It was certainly a clueless expression, as many critics and spectators pointed out, but it was by no means the *kind* of cluelessness that might be expected under the circumstances. This made doubly curious the lack of satisfying attempts by pundits, pro or con, to explain the universal discomfort Bush's non-reaction provoked. Unanswered questions are uncomfortable, but un*asked* questions are far worse: they stay lodged in the pit of the stomach.

One wonders, in retrospect, how people would have reacted if Moore had *fabricated* the image of their president at that climactic moment: sitting in a kiddie chair reading a story about a pet goat, with

---

[3] The primary objections raised by Moore's detractors, such as unconsecutive data, singled out stylistic inconsistencies of the sort that are standard in documentaries— criticisms which, in and of themselves, do not account for the virulence of the attacks the film provoked.

that look on his face. Surely offended critics would have roundly accused the filmmaker of straining the bounds of credulity. But Moore didn't have to make it up. Real life gave him that image, and audiences were invited to make of it what they would.

As Saturn takes about two years to make its way across the US Sun cluster, the meaning of its passage is revealed gradually, like chapters in a well-told story. Thus astrology allows us to see the over-riding patterns of significance behind world events which otherwise would seem as random and senseless as—well, as the repeated claim from a president that "No one could have imagined planes into buildings" after his administration had received multiple and detailed advance warnings of exactly that.

Accepting Responsibility

Whether our perspective is astrological, political, philosophical—or whether we just want to duck under the covers and not look at it at all—everyone who identifies as an American felt a sense of fatal decision in the air during the summer of 2004. What was it about?

The transit tells us it was about accountability. Even more specifically than the Pluto-Saturn opposition that preceded it, the transit of Saturn on the US Sun introduced the theme of accepting responsibility on a national level. The point of the period was to disclose how well or poorly America understands its global impact, to teach it to acknowledge what it puts out into the world, and to get it to respond to the consequences of its misdeeds.

In any chart, the rule of thumb with Saturn is that whatever is juvenile and reactive in the entity will be revealed as such (in Cancer the typical reactive devices are denial, withdrawal and defensiveness). We may feel that Saturn itself is creating the insecurity, but this is not how planets work, as we have seen. Saturn merely exposes the inadequacy of our attempts to resist consciousness change. When we try to protect ourselves with our old familiar mechanisms, we create suffering.

Saturn's larger purpose is to forge an adult character. This involves the development of definition and discernment: the necessity to concretize whatever the native has been muddling through in vague, undefined form. Where we have relied upon some parent figure, we will be challenged to shift the responsibility to ourselves. When Saturn passes through Cancer, the sign of security, one is called upon to make *oneself* safe—not through fearful over-reaction but through reasonable, conscious planning. Wherever one has given power away to an authority figure (as in "Oh well, I'm sure Dad/ my boss/ Michael Chertoff knows what he's doing"), one will find that playing the helpless child is an obsolete gambit.

Understanding Karma

Karma is an elegantly simple concept: *Whatever is put forth will come back to its source.* What makes this concept seem more complicated than it is, however, is humanity's tendency to confuse karma with the notion of *blame*, which is an invention of the human mind (to be discussed in more detail in Chapter Fourteen). Neither self-blame nor projected blame has anything to do with cosmic principles; but we still have to deal with the fact that, all over the globe, the human impulse to judge and blame is running rampant as whole societies and factions of societies struggle in this postmillennial period to come to grips with the breakdown of familiar structures and—far more troublingly—with the fears this breakdown provokes.

Those who desire to maintain clarity amidst the morass may find it in astrological symbolism, but we must acknowledge that there are two discrete levels going on here—the subjective and the cosmic—and try to separate them out. Our task is to take human reactivity into account but not mix it up with the principles encoded in the sky.

This means examining Saturnine law on its own terms. If you throw a ball up in the air, it will slow to an arc and head downwards. If you study hard for a test, you're more likely to pass than someone who doesn't study. If you bury land mines into terrain, sooner or later they have to be unearthed or exploded. When you drive people off their land, bomb their cities and kill their innocents, you are going to get a backlash.

Intersecting Transit Cycles

Saturn's passage through Cancer from 2003-05 set the tone for the whole world to learn a series of lessons about homeland, safety and self-protection. Because the US chart features four planets in this sign, the transit's impact on America was particularly acute, as Saturn passed over each of the planets in its Sun cluster one by one. The country's sense of vulnerability was exceptionally high. Against this backdrop the USA had the choice of either responding or blindly reacting to collective anger from within and presumed threat from without.

These volatile energies were represented by Mars—which was coming up to meet Saturn in Cancer—and from Pluto, which was still slowly making its way through the US first house. As noted, the quicker planets move across the slower-moving planets in intersecting orbits, adding specificity to the whole transit picture. A complex dance of archetypes ensues: the longer-term themes (e.g. Saturn's teaching of responsibility/reactivity and Pluto's breakdown of ideological verities) are crisscrossed with shorter-term themes (e.g. aggressive spurts from Mars and highlights from the Full Moon).

Mars' strongest showing during the Saturn-in-Cancer period was in the late spring of 2004. First it conjoined its natal position in the USA chart—this was America's Mars Return—and a couple of weeks later it opposed both transiting Pluto and transiting Sun. This compound transit was behind that season's threatening posture towards Venezuela and the pre-regime-shift (6/30/04) violence in Iraq. Mars is always strengthened by its return to its natal position, and whenever it is empowered by the dark compulsions of Pluto at the same time, we are likely to see scenarios of over-the-top militancy. Both April and May's eclipses[4] of 2004 coincided with newspaper headlines expressing the sadistic depths to which unconscious Mars can go, as exemplified by hostage beheadings and carpet bombings of densely populated cities. It was during this Mars/Pluto period that the first reports of torture started to trickle out of Iraq[5].

The outright madness of a group's collective shadow is forced into consciousness with transits like these: destruction and violence in an *Us vs. Them* context is the least enlightened form a seventh-house Mars[6] can take. But when we remember that Saturn in Cancer was there in the background, triggering chronic insecurities that reside deep within the American psyche, the crazy violence of Mars and Pluto become perversely understandable.

Transit configurations reveal layers upon layers of meaning— some layers seeming to contradict others, just as they do in a human personality—that cannot be summed up with simplistic explanations. But in an effort to find the astrological logic of the dangerous mass mood

---

[4] Astrologically speaking, eclipses are intensified lunations whose cycles have been closely watched throughout the millennia. For the sake of this discussion we can consider them extra-strong New Moons and Full Moons, whose effect is like that of a klieg light cast upon whatever else is going on in the configuration. Their involvement punctuates the scenario with a fateful potency.

[5] When Mars next returned to Gemini in the spring of 2006, the pattern was repeated (a return to its natal position, then an opposition to transiting Pluto) and so was the surge in violence. During the week that Mars opposed Pluto in the sky (April first through seventh), the number of casualties in Iraq spiked after a lull of two years (the length of a Mars cycle). By this time Washington had turned its bellicose rhetoric (Mars) upon Iran, and the Pentagon came out with the astonishing announcement that it had not ruled out tactical nuclear weapons (Pluto) as a means to chasten the newly upgraded foe.

[6] This is the position Mars occupies in the US chart, and thus the position transiting Mars occupies whenever the country has a Mars Return.

that prevailed in the spring 2004, we can say that Saturn was stoking America's Cancerian fear of appearing weak and thus open to violation by outsiders (seventh house). This served to complicate the martial strutting that was going on with an emotional poignancy all the more perilous for being largely unconscious.

The configuration was telling us that America's fear is the root problem, not its aggression.

W's Transits

There was much transit activity in George W. Bush's chart during that spring of 2004, with Saturn setting him up to be tested and other planets passing through to contribute their specific themes.

The exact conjunction of Saturn and Bush's Sun occurred three days after the configuration described above, in the twelfth house of his chart where demons are hidden and deeply rooted. Called by some the *house of karma,* the dreamlike twelfth house suggests unresolved problems and restive ghosts dating from a past that pre-dates the native's birth.

In an astounding repetition of the Martial theme, Bush's birthday transits featured the red planet exactly conjunct his Ascendant—mere minutes of arc away. He was a walking embodiment of the all-encompassing mood of militancy that—for its own mysterious soul-driven reasons—the nation has been using him to personify. It was at this exact timing that he came out with the apposite declaration, *"I am a war president."*

To Which Law Do We Turn?

For five years and counting, the USA has been confronting head-on the reality that extreme power (Pluto) entails extreme responsibility (Saturn). Revelations have been pouring forth about industry-wide corporate corruption at the same time that the turpitude at the core of national politics is becoming more and more visible with every week that passes. Americans are opening up to the truth about the inhumanities to which America and its allies subject presumed foes in conflicts both actual (Afghanistan, Iraq, Palestine) and rhetorical (the "war on terror"). All of this has stimulated a universal call to identify culpability, with critics demanding that the worst of the perpetrators submit to the rule of law. But what law are we talking about?

Is military law the corrective for America's deficient sense of responsibility? Although a military court does not lay claim to the same standard of justice that we expect from a civilian court, in the current chaotic climate many observers seem to be searching for solace in military rigidity. In its own unabashedly undemocratic way, military justice appeals to the Saturnine need for structure. It was military law that sentenced to one year in prison the hapless soldier who had the bad luck to be photographed committing the more visible of the Abu Ghraib atrocities; and it was military law, around the same time, that meted out the exact same sentence—one year in prison—to Camilo Mejia, the conscientious objector who refused to return to Iraq because of the inhumanities perpetrated by the US army there. The stunning irony of this equation does not seem to have registered as such with the American people, most of whom have disavowed their responsibility to assess anything the Pentagon does.

But even the dubious legitimacy of military law has been cast asunder in Iraq, given that many of the occupation forces seem not to answer to the army at all, but to civilian companies the Pentagon has been using as subcontractors. What law applies in this case? Perhaps there are regulations that guide policy in the shadowy businesses whose employees have been imported into this post-draft war to help with the dirty work. Is this where Saturn's buck stops in Iraq? Should we look to Titan Corporation and CACI and see if they keep an eye on their "soldiers of fortune" by means of an honor code?

Or should we turn to civilian judicial law to assign American accountability? The Supreme Court, which took upon itself the task of choosing the chief executive in 2000, has been stacked by this same gentleman with jurists who can be counted on to do his bidding. Once the check-and-balance of last resort, this venerable bench clearly takes its cue now from the White House no less than the legislature does. Neither is the once-sacrosanct Constitution, as has been widely noted, a hedge against the politics of the day. While impugning the Bill of Rights as a hindrance to "homeland security," the American president is currently backing a campaign to create out of whole cloth a Constitutional amendment to ban same-sex marriages because they offend a key segment of his constituency.

Public Opinion

In what court, then, will America resolve its accountability issues? Perhaps the buck stops in the court of public opinion. In theory, this is what is supposed to happen in a democracy (recall that when Spain's last prime minister lied to his people, they simply fired him). But American elections are quite literally sponsored by corporations these days; everyone knows that only those with access to these channels of power have a crack at the presidency. A glance at the campaign contributions for even the most rinky-dink elected office—virtually identical for candidates from both parties in the current duopolistic system—tells the tale. Americans know that as things are now, only in a movie or on television could a truly populist candidate become president.

More fundamentally, if issues of collective responsibility are to be decided in the court of public opinion, the public must *have* an opinion. This leads us to a question we have asked before: how informed can a populace be that gets its information from Fox News? How judicious can a court of public opinion be in a society where scientists are denied grants and removed from positions of power when their findings contradict governmental policies? What level of intellectual inquiry flourishes in a country where publishing houses are enjoined by the government to blacklist over-candid insiders?

America's simple-minded president is an embarrassment, to be sure; but how much more worrisome is the grievous ignorance of the populace itself? Polls tell us that the youth demographic gets most of its news from MTV parodies of the news; and though much has been made of the short attention span (now legitimized as a neurological syndrome) that has become normative in America's media-addicted youth, the populace in general acts as if it has forgotten history that was headlines a mere couple of years ago.

A typical example is the public's wholesale amnesia about the deplorable arms-for-hostages plot hatched during the Reagan administration, whereby the CIA hired John Negraponte to sell American guns to Iran—astoundingly, the same Iran that is now being accused by Washington of trying to arm itself—in order to finance the illegal US war in Nicaragua (Negraponte escaped disgrace quite effortlessly; in fact he has since been appointed ambassador to Iraq). In an informed democracy, would it not be expected that the citizenry would notice this outrageous incongruity, and take this opportunity to call the whole unresolved, unprosecuted Iran-Contra scandal into question?

Presidential Conspiracy Theory

The dilemma of the American public lies, as we have seen, in a lack of clean intelligence; that is, an essentially state-run media is distorting millions of Americans' view the world. A citizenry disempowered by epidemic, entrenched ignorance has no hope of deciding issues of national responsibility.

In the years immediately after the 9-11 attacks, every time the American president held one of his doublespeak press conferences the polls reported an increase in the numbers of Americans who believed Saddam Hussein was somehow linked to the World Trade Center bombing. The irony here is that this lie was not just any old lie, it was a *conspiracy theory*—a prime specimen of the very same category of factoid that the president sneeringly dismisses when they are not his own. Indeed, this particular conspiracy theory was the one with by far the most extensive and fatal ramifications of any the culture has seen. But it was believed, by large segments of the public, despite all manner of contravening evidence—because their commander-in-chief said it was so.

Responsible Judgment

Responsible judgment cannot be expected from a court of public opinion whose viewpoint is jerry-rigged. America's institutions have failed to cultivate in its people a working Saturn model—that is, a social structure that could keep them informed enough to hold these same institutions accountable. For a nation to stay on the good side of the god of karma it must act like a group of responsible adults, but an inability to take responsibility informs US culture on every level. Only in America could a customer burn herself with a cup of coffee at McDonald's and then successfully sue the place for selling it to her.

Juvenility has its charms but at issue here are its limits, which reveal themselves every time a Saturn transit hits the American chart. Of particular interest to students of the millennial opposition discussed in the previous chapter was the transit of Saturn opposed to America's Pluto in Capricorn of 2004-05. It featured the same two planets; this time one of them was a natal placement. Here was another of those definitive moments when the planet of karma asked the planet of destruction to account for itself (it should also be considered a precursor to the country's Pluto Return, discussed below).

When this transit was exact to the degree of arc, on October 30th 2004, Osama bin Laden suddenly reappeared on the front page of American newspapers. His new communiqué once again named American foreign policy as the source and raison-d'être of Islamic jihad. Again he drew a parallel between the violence perpetrated by Al Qaeda and the violence perpetrated daily by the American military upon Arab peoples, then and now.

Hurricane Katrina 2005

Planetary stations are astronomical anomalies that occur when a planet appears to stop in the sky, from Earth's vantage point, and gets ready to orbit in the opposite direction it was orbiting in before. Like a photographer saying "Hold still," the cosmos is giving us a chance to look more carefully than usual at the planet's meaning. Pluto stations occur twice a year. During the few days on either side of the station the planet's energy is accentuated, and whatever ongoing themes it has been involved in get a jolt.

There was a direct station of Pluto on September 2, 2005, the day the storm on the Gulf Coast moved in for the kill. The timing and the symbolism were amazingly apt. It would be hard to imagine a more quintessentially Plutonian event: the imagery of floating corpses, wretched survivors stranded in filthy conditions, diaspora and despair were out of a Brueghel painting of the doomed in Hell.

As Pluto got going in direct motion, the staggering social implications of what had happened began to sink into the mass consciousness and the deeper truth of the transit arose. The real shock to the country's system was Katrina's aftermath, a cultural scandal rising from the toxic sludge of a ruined New Orleans.

Collective Taboo

The reader is by now well familiar with Pluto's rulership of breakdown, corruption, mass destruction and toxicity. Post-Katrina New Orleans was horribly emblematic of them all, as the station served to expose the starkly primitive realities hidden beneath America's sophisticated, modern self-image.

After the hurricane, a great many Americans were wrenched into unsavory realizations about the way their country operates, as they witnessed hundreds of thousands of their fellow citizens suffering through conditions that seemed too degraded to be possible in the country they thought they knew. The televised scenes they were watching of the stifling attics, the wretched chaos on the city streets and the sports stadium consigned to shelter the refugees just did not fit the picture.

Racism and Poverty

In Chapter Four, we discussed the Plutonian phenomenon of slavery as a key expression of America's second-house wound. The Civil War which ended the practice was relatively recent, in macro-cyclic terms, and the American psyche has yet to come to grips with it.

This is not the problem—healing is slow and gradual, just as decay is. The problem is that healing cannot even begin where there is mass denial. Unable or unwilling for a century and a half to come to terms with the great historical abomination upon which the national economy got its start, Americans seem not to realize that this legacy is part of their country's reputation: worldwide, US racism is an open secret. A national ethic of disdain towards the poor, which is justified with a fanatical adherence to a capitalism-gone-terribly-wrong (Pluto in the US second house) is another. Katrina revealed both in short order.

With Katrina, the Saturn-Pluto themes introduced by the millennium transit were repeated for the world to see. The hurricane made glaringly evident the criminal (Pluto) negligence (Saturn) of the American government, whose first bright idea in damage control was to send in the guns (Pluto) while scapegoating the victims (Saturn). Stories began emerging of survivors who, after waiting on rooftops for five days, watched helplessly as one after another rescue boat passed them by, manned by rifle-toting National Guardsmen on the lookout for property theft. One family reported being finally rescued by several neighborhood men who'd found a broken-down rowboat, defied shoot-to-kill orders and single-handedly delivered hundreds to safety.

The media did not recognize these unsung community heroes; all the reporters were busy elsewhere looking for looters to put on the evening news. In an ideal society, courageous good Samaritans such as these would have been awarded a medal for valor and service by their government—whose own disaster agencies were caught massively unawares, uncoordinated and barely performing. But as it turned out, these neighborhood men faced more danger from trigger-happy law enforcement than they faced from the pestilent waters. One would not have been surprised to see the president on TV the next day denouncing them as *terr'ist boat-jackers.*

As the days passed, the various officials whom Katrina had caught napping tried to spin the calamitous failure of their rescue operations, with one department head blaming another all along the line of command; but it was too late. The hurricane blew away the trappings that had been covering up a moral bankruptcy in the nation's heart. The Pluto station tells us that the fundamental meaning of the crisis was not telluric; the winds and water were just Nature setting the stage. Katrina was about the rot at the core of the American system—now exposed so that it might be observed, understood and healed.

The 2010 Grand Cross

When we look ahead, we see a stunning series of patterns peaking between 2008-2011. These involve some highly unusual combinations, the most intriguing of which is the Grand Cross in 2010. Seven planets will participate in this configuration—juxtaposed *just so* to form a square in the sky. Mathematicians might calculate the odds of these extraordinary coincidings and infer an abstract layer of meaning from the numbers alone; astrologers see statistical infrequency as an indicator of profundity and infer from crisscrossed orbits like these multiple layers of meaning. This is a historical moment with very important things to say to humanity[7].

Some of the pieces of this assemblage are slow and will endure for several years—like the square (90° angle) between Uranus and Pluto (which becomes a *T-square* when Saturn enters the fray)—and some are quick cycles that will clock in to complete the spectacular array and then move along—like the Sun, which enters Cancer every June and thus will join the configuration for a few days, making the solstice a peak period. When this many planets all come together in a *planetary picture* we expect to see pithy episodes in the external world. In-tune individuals will also feel these geometrical pushes and pulls in their internal world. The wide-ranging symbolism of the various planets converges in a synthesis, and the whole becomes more than the sum of its parts.

Looking for Meaning

What does it mean? Astrologers infer the meaning of a complex package like this by breaking down the whole configuration into its various pieces, considering each piece in depth (*analysis*), and then imagining the significance of their coming together (*synthesis*). We will begin by taking another look at Pluto in Capricorn, the transit that sets the tone for the entire 16-year period (January 2008-2024) during which the Cross appears.

As discussed in Chapter Three, the entry of Pluto into a new sign is one of those every-thirteen-years-or-so *ingresses* that inaugurate a period where the world is broken down in order to be healed in a specific arena. Throughout this book we have looked at the period of Sagittarian decay that is drawing to a close. Now that things are Pluto'd-out in that department, the planet will usher in a period of Capricornian decay: corporations, boundaries, governments and hierarchies will be purged and remodeled. It will be their turn to get radically rearranged.

Pluto in Capricorn

When using astrology to look at the future, it must be remembered that we are accessing a mystical language that works not with specifics but with symbols—which have to be decoded, like a

---

[7] The significance of this Grand Cross extends far beyond the national context. Students of the Mayan calendar may recognize its timing as lining up with the dates singled out at the Harmonic Convergence in 1987 by Jose Arguelles, the most widely discussed of these being 2012. The ancient Mesomericans were among many traditions that saw this period as the end of a great cycle in human evolution and the beginning of another. See http://www.wilsonsalmanac.com/converg.html.

It is noteworthy that 2010-2011 has been cited as the period when world oil production will peak (*S. F. Bay Guardian*, August third, 2006).

dream. The reader will be familiar by now with this astrologer's view: that events are not immutably "written in the stars" or fated to happen in a precise form. Though the great themes of a given epoch are laid out in the sky, the particulars of the future are created at every moment. Anyone trying to make sense of complicated astrological patterns who has sincerely considered the basic symbolism of the planets involved—and then tuned in intuitively—is going to be no less able than a veteran astrologer to envision the meaning of such patterns.

One starts by reviewing the various things Capricorn rules—among them, governments, corporations and all other patriarchal hierarchies; physical structuring devices like mountains and walls and grids; infrastructures, economies and national borders—and then reviewing what Pluto is about: destruction on a mass scale[8] that paves the way for renewal. Next we imagine putting the two together. How might Pluto act upon each of the things Capricorn governs? Each astrologer will come up with different imagery and distinct emphases, though there will tend to be certain common themes.

Capricorn's governance of *governance* is an obvious place to start. This is the sign of the boss, whether expressed on the family level (fathers), the village level (mayors, tribal elders), the company level (CEOs), the national level (presidents)—or the deific level (patriarchal gods like Allah, Yahweh and Jehovah). If Pluto's job is to remove all traces of obsolescence from the things governed by the sign it's in, we would expect any and all of these authority figures to feel it; and the institutions they oversee will "go to hell" in some form. Existing authoritative structures will be pushed into the underworld, to be transformed. Fatherhood, at least the old-fashioned kind, will experience a profound humbling. The expectations in the mass mind around what it means to be a father may change radically, along with the social rituals, agencies and procedures associated with paternity (deadbeat dads; rights of sperm donors; legal authority over wives and offspring, etc.)

Paternalistic governments can be expected to provide a bulls-eye for the transit. Those whose functions have grown stale and useless should be exposed, their bureaucracies streamlined after some kind of purge. We may see many breakdowns of high executive office, especially in countries where the ideals of sound guidance, wise structuring and integrity-in-leadership have been sullied.

Keep in mind that it is the idea of government itself that is the main target of this overhaul, not the individuals who embody it. It may

---

[8] In this discussion we are confining our attention to the collective, but Pluto's destruction-renewal process will also act itself out on an individual scale, in each person's life in a unique way.

very well be that some of the occupants of these offices will serve as sacrificial lambs for the overall process, but it is the idea of paternal authority in general that is the larger focus. Plutonian change is neither about punishing personalities nor about demonstrating right and wrong thinking[9]. The point of a Pluto transit is simply to amputate the gangrenous limb so that the body as a whole can survive.

Thus it wouldn't be surprising if we were to see a sea change in the global acceptance of women in positions of leadership. Nor would we be surprised to see governments that are riddled with rot to fall apart[10]—unless they are flexible enough to change from the very core. If a regime can remain standing while being remodeled, it will survive; if it has to make way for another that can better meet the necessities of the epoch, it will be destroyed.

National Boundaries

The breakdown of the whole notion of national boundaries is already apparent, as the world gets ready to drastically reexamine the phenomenon of nationalism (discussed in Chapter Nine). We have witnessed a new fluidity in national borders in Central Europe since the break-up of the Soviet Union, with small states creating new identities and giving themselves new names. Great Britain, the last global empire to bite the dust, is a Western example of the trend: United no longer though still nominally a kingdom, the UK is feeling the heat from self-determinists in Ireland, Scotland and Wales who want to separate ever further from what was once the Mother state. The same phenomenon can be seen in Spain with the Basques and Catalans, and with Canada and the Quebecois.

The flat-out impossibility of stemming the tide of immigrants into the USA has already begun to make Americans suspect that their borders are not the unifying and immutable identifiers they have seemed to be. Pluto's ingress into the sign of national definition will drive this point home.

The whole notion of federalism may be shaken. An augury of this trend was the sly offer Venezuelan president Hugo Chavez made in 2005 to the state of New Hampshire of heating oil at a discount—an

---

[9] Questions of justice, ideological differences and moral reform belong to Saturn and Jupiter transits, which also have their place. But Pluto doesn't care about those things. Pluto is the blind force of Natural Law that says *You're done; you have to go now.*

[10] Recall that when the Soviet Union—the entity born November 8, 1917—was hit by a Pluto transit to its Sun (a more direct hit than these to the US chart) in 1989, the union broke apart at the seams.

offer he didn't even bother to run by Washington. Also suggestive of this development is the invitation extended in August 2006 to a couple of American anti-war organizations[11] by Al-Maliki, the prime minister of occupied Iraq. In an unprecedented snub to the Bush government, he asked these American civilians to fly to Iraq and help his government resolve the country's violence. Along the same lines, it is noteworthy that organizations such as the Sierra Club are bypassing the federal government by backing fewer candidates for Congress and more at the state and local level. These are hints at the coming challenges to federal primacy that we will probably be seeing on a universal scale.

Uranus in Aries

Pluto will make its entrance into Capricorn in January of 2008 and hang around the early degrees of the sign for a while. Two years later, Uranus, another slow-moving planet, makes a similarly dramatic entry into Aries—where it has not been for 84 years.

Uranus in Aries will give the world a seven-year lesson in new ways to challenge authority: the concept of leadership itself will be revolutionized. Many will feel the impulse to assert (Aries) their vision of democracy (Uranus) rather than just talk and argue about it. Uranus governs literal and figurative revolutions—dramatic, abrupt changes in ideas and practice.

Upon each of their entries into these new signs, Uranus and Pluto will *square* each other: a tense angle that usually forces action (especially in Aries, where Jupiter will be too by that time). This square is the rarest and therefore the most impactful arm of the Grand Cross.

The Sixties Invoked

The best way to understand the Pluto-Uranus square is to back up and look at the dance between these two planets as an unfolding cycle, one that had its beginning forty-odd years ago. Planetary cycles start with conjunctions—two planets exactly overlapping in the sky—and in the mid-1960s, Uranus and Pluto were exactly conjunct. They occupied the same location in the zodiac for a few years, which for astrologers is what made the sixties *The Sixties*. Uranus, planet of revolution, and Pluto, planet of breakdown and renewal, together created a mass consciousness explosion. The counter-culture was born.

From 2010-2015 these two planets will take the next big step in their relationship, by squaring off. Whatever was being seeded back in those heady years of hippies and yippies will pop into a new phase of

---

[11] Code Pink and Global Exchange. See www.codepink4peace.org

development. The flower children's vision will manifest in a sharp new postmillennial way.

Saturn Enters the Fray

By late summer of 2010, Saturn will have entered Libra along with Mars[12] and the Grand Cross energy will reach another of its several peaks. We will be dealing with two square relationships and two oppositions, creating an inter-dynamic tension—the most highly charged configuration in astrology. There's a special buzz in the air when all these cycles come together and face each other down, and clear events tend to manifest in order to express it.

The Grand Cross in cardinal signs[13] will wind down with the calendar year, but its mark will have been made. The post-millennial early teens will arouse America's inherent capacity to create leaders, and global necessity will force a new approach to what leaders do. The country will have plenty of opportunities to try to refurbish its authority in the world.

America's Saturn Return

The Saturn Return is perhaps the best known of all astrological transits, though not the best loved. Saturn returns to its natal position every 29 years, on average; after we have lived three decades of life and are—chronologically at least—ready to face the responsibilities of adulthood. Nation-states, too, cross this important threshold, which is designed to bring the collective consciousness back to the aboriginal promises it made to itself on a soul level: promises to be accountable to itself and others. The USA's Saturn returns in 2011, at the tail end of the long T-square discussed above.

Astrology proposes that each of us has a pre-incarnate soul identity that chooses this incarnation, of which our natal chart is the

---

[12] Saturn-Mars combinations are often difficult for the young and/or psychologically immature, because they call for gradualism, delayed gratification and focus. To the extent that a native resists the necessity to slow down and take stock, this will not be a fun conjunction. But its design is to force concentration, and if approached this way events of late July and August will show us how to handle the Cross productively.

[13] The USA has a predominantly cardinal chart—a Saturn in Libra (cardinal air) and a dominating Sun cluster in Cancer (cardinal water)—and this is the national characteristic that the Grand Cross will provoke and inspire.

Cardinality gets its meaning from the first stage of every life process. Per the archetypal sequencing of all events, a process begins, gets established and then changes. The three *modes* that the twelve signs are divided into—cardinal, fixed and mutable— reflect these three phases. Cardinal signs begin processes, fixed signs establish them, and mutable signs disperse them.

script; and that Saturn is the code within that script which specifies the exact type of responsibilities to be encountered so as to induce a particular type of maturity. We looked in Chapter Six at the USA's karmic responsibilities: to uphold a position of formal authority (the tenth house) in the service of ideals of justice and equality (Libra). We considered the ambivalence (solar square) with which the USA holds its Saturn, comparing the country to a petulant teenager (Jupiter/Sun) who needs but rejects his father (Saturn). We looked at the implications of this Saturn being in the house of governance, proposing that the laws, regulations and injunctions the USA has come up with constitute the very glue that binds the republic together. Come the Saturn Return, whatever institutions America is using to create and execute its laws, such as the legislature, will have to be very strong and very flexible.

All these issues will be brought forth from the background of America's consciousness to the foreground during the several years surrounding the exact Return in 2011. The country will have to confront not only the various systems of law (Libra rules the domestic and international law courts, social justice and equality movements) that already exist but brand new visions of law, that will become necessary to meet the urgency of the times.

America's Pluto Return 2022

Like Saturn, Pluto will soon return to the zodiacal position it was in when the country was born. This will be the first time in its history that America has ever had a Pluto Return, because the country hasn't been in existence for the full time it takes for Pluto to go around the chart. This Return will subject the country's deepest wounds to a kind of cosmic surgery: the most drastic but the most thorough kind of remedy for systemic problems.

The United States will be brought home to the place in its psyche where it harbors irrational fears and manipulative impulses about physical survival. Pluto hitting its own natal position in the second house is a signal that America's territorial drives will have to be transformed and its use of resources completely re-thought. We know this simply from living with our eyes open in today's world, and astrology confirms it. We have looked throughout this book at such second-house crises as globalization and resource depletion. It is clear, for instance, that water will be "the new oil," a shift of meaning that is already underway in most of the world.

As we have seen, the second house indicates the material plane. Planets here designate the relationship between the native and the planet Earth as a physical and biological whole. This transit suggests a confrontation with *materialism* in every sense of the word: both the philosophical assumptions that underlie America's worldview, and the concrete expression of these assumptions as they get acted out in financial life. There will be an irresistible call to overturn the current norms of consumer society, and dissenters may stake out extreme positions as they act as agents of the new anti-materialism. Control over property will be a major focus, as concerns both locations on Earth (personal possessions, real estate and international resources) and sections of extraterrestrial space.

The USA has been heading towards a radical shift in its economic status quo for several years, and the Pluto Return will present a turning point in this arc. At this writing the country is hanging on by a thread to an artificially sustained dollar, a situation too fragile to be tenable for long. We have discussed the fact that America has put all its eggs into one energy basket (as the British once did with coal) while making virtually no investment at all into future energy alternatives—which suggests that when oil is no longer king, America probably won't be either. Moreover, this is the timeframe that will see the baby boomer generation aging en masse, and it is estimated that nearly half of the federal budget will go to seniors if current policies are maintained[14].

Clearly the American system *per se* will not survive without a radical change of economic course.

Global Power Shift

What other aspects of US power might we expect the Pluto Return to challenge?

The 20th was unquestionably The American Century, not only economically but politically, militarily and culturally. For most Americans the thought of the USA being anything other than top dog in the world is probably all but unimaginable—to say nothing of deeply emotionally threatening. But we have seen the augury for such a shift: Pluto's transit over the USA's Ascendant at the millennium. Let us take a step or two back from the subject and look at the country's global status with the dispassion of an outside observer.

On the military front, the same theme the US government encountered in Viet Nam is being repeated in Iraq and Afghanistan (as well as in Palestine and Lebanon, where Israel's battles are waged with American arms and full collusion): the world's most expensive warplanes, gunboats, Blackhawk helicopters and chemical weapons are proving insufficient to eliminate a determined native resistance. Moral

---

[14] Juan Enriquez, *The Untied States of America.*

issues aside, Washington's war planners may have to face the fact that without a ground force, their attempts at conquest will fail in the face of indigenous populations who refuse to give up. (The reinstatement of the American draft would be the wild card in this equation, but domestic politics probably preclude it).

On the geopolitical front, negotiations have become very tricky for Washington. Over the past six years the USA has alienated most of its traditional alliances, vastly expanded and deepened its field of antagonists and squandered any moral currency it might have used to repair burnt bridges. Internationally, America's standing in the U.N. is at this point maintained primarily by threats and bullying. Russia, China and some of the new republics of Central Asia constitute a rising alliance, which (especially if united with India, Pakistan, Mongolia and Iran) already threatens America's hyper-power status. And then there is the volatile potential of the handful of Arab states whose disaffected populations are making their US-friendly dictators very nervous at the moment.

Many international thinkers are talking about China being the next superpower, and some include India in this scenario, though much depends on the course of the AIDS epidemic and the capacity of these nations to cope with enormous systemic problems. The Pluto transit does not augur well for either of these ascendant giants receiving the torch of world power; on the contrary, the notorious corruption of both the Indian and Chinese governments puts them into a perfect position to have a rendezvous of their own with the Dark God as he moves through Capricorn.

Whatever happens, the return of the planet of power to its natal position in the USA chart will be a dramatic teaching. The plutocratic tendencies America has been cultivating over its two centuries of existence will become very easy for its citizens to see, rendered obvious for the sake of hoisting the collective into a new consciousness. The spiritually informed response will be to name, confront and transform these tendencies into a higher level of expression.

All these lessons will have to be either responded to or reacted against. Our intense focus, as individuals, should be on the former. When asked whether I think America is up to the job of renewing after its upcoming rounds with destruction transits, it reminds me that my role as a symbol-reader is different from my role as an American citizen. I have unconditional faith in universal laws—*something* always rises from the ashes—but none at all in this particular system of plutocratic governance—and whether we like it or not, business and government are, at this point in American history, joined at the hip. Unless the country as a whole can rebirth itself completely, not just partially, Americans are in for a wrenching identity crisis.

Responsible Use of Power

The key idea America was given by Saturn and Pluto as it entered the millennium was this: *The responsible use of power.* As the new cycle continues to unfold, each transit to the US chart will ask America to consider[15] this key idea before allowing it entry into its next phase of development. No American will be able to duck this challenge, for as we have seen, an individual's life purpose is tied with that of the group. All who live under the American flag bear the karma of the American chart. All have inherited both its blessings and its afflictions.

But to hold one's group identity mindfully, one has to understand it as part of one's individual identity and not the other way around. When it comes to the true nature of responsibility, astrology holds the same position as mystery schools and religions old and new: the buck stops with the individual. From a cosmic point of view, to use nationalism as the core of one's ego structure is an increasingly bad idea; these transits compel individual citizens to understand their own psyches spiritually and creatively rather than in anachronistic group terms. And one doesn't have to be an astrologer to see that, right now, to blindly identify with the USA is to passively take on some very problematic karma.

Leaders will arise to point the way; they always do. But they will be there to offer inspiration and energy, not to dictate how we should respond. Even the visionary leaders—whose creative solutions inspire us and keep us sane—even they are not there to dictate how we should respond. A true response must be as unique as our own natal chart: symbol of our soul's decision to incarnate into this particular place at this particular time. For those who choose to access them, the planetary symbols in that map can themselves be used as teachers, showing us unique ways to meet the needs of our time.

And so we will turn to the natal chart of individuals in the chapters ahead, to see how to shape a response that is informed by depth, humanity and authenticity.

---

[15] In the etymology of the word *consideration* we find hidden in plain sight a clue about the workings of astrological magic: *con* (with) + *sider* (the stars). The word tells us that profound reflection, far from being an idle mental exercise, aligns us with celestial meaning.

THIRTEEN

Becoming an Agent of Transformation
Pluto Work

We have now completed our astrological delineation of what might be called the *American personality*, in order to understand how the USA fits into the chaotic world scene. We have looked at the key themes presented by the national chart, how recent transits have highlighted them, how global events have expressed them and how they might show up in the years just ahead.

The reader may be forgiven for feeling a tad overwhelmed. At issue is a series of gargantuan problems that directly relate to the group entity of which many of us are members; and once the enormity of these problems is allowed to penetrate our awareness without denial, we may find ourselves facing a crisis of our own. The human mind gets to a point in its information-intake where all seeking leads sooner or later: the philosophical crossroads where we ask, *If this is the way it is, what can I possibly do?* To one side lies hopelessness, and if we stay there, we stay stuck. What is the path that leads off from the other side?

To propose an answer we are going to turn once again to astrology.

We have seen that beneath the Sun-sign shorthand by which astrology is commonly known, there are manifold layers of meaning, compiled into an organized set of esoteric teachings once used by spiritual adepts as guides to mindful living. Just as this numinous system has given us the map to help us see where we are, it can give us the tools to figure out what to do about it.

Every Planet a Wake-Up Call

Every symbol in astrology has its own way of waking us up to ourselves; every transit is there to target whatever part of our psychic musculature needs flexing. The underlying premise behind the whole system is that planetary lessons are generated by the soul-identified Self in order to show something to the ego-identified self, so that we may keep on waking up. When action is called for, the planets indicate what right action would be.

For American seekers in this time of crisis, there are two planets in particular that offer the insight we need: Pluto and Saturn. In an effort to put to use the information we have gathered so far, the rest of this book will address the key messages these two planets are trying to communicate. We will seek to decode their lessons as they apply both to the individual chart and the collective chart—for as we have seen, neither by itself is enough.

We cannot be a fully conscious person without being a fully conscious group member; these two facets of the self mirror each other with our every move. Regardless of their feelings about this country, Americans have been ushered into this field of action for a specific set of karmic reasons. So let's continue with our astrological reconnaissance mission to see if we can do those reasons justice.

Using Pluto to Transform

This chapter will focus on how to use Pluto for transformative work. We will begin with its natal placement in the individual chart,[1] exploring how each of us can work our unique Pluto placements to perform magic on ourselves.

We start with the personal because inner work is where everything begins and ends. Unless we have made an internal commitment to self-awareness, our external strategies will serve no one. Where there is no dedication to the truth of the self, there can be no real dedication to the outer world; even activities that strive to promote the universal good will be polluted with our own confusions.

Conversely, Pluto Work done on the self radiates outwards. When we have achieved a certain degree of self-honesty we become remarkably effective in the world, often without even trying. We find that our energy is even more unique than we always suspected, and that it starts to impact the whole in ways that are sometimes obvious, sometimes subtle and sometimes delightfully unexpected.

---

[1] Readers who have not had their charts done are encouraged to make use of the many online services that offer horoscope downloads. (Astrodienst, for example, has a free service: http://www.astro.com/horoscopes). Knowing the *sign* your Pluto is in tells you about the basic generational lessons you and your peers are meant to learn, as everyone in your generation shares the same Pluto sign. More relevant for the sake of this discussion is knowing what *house* it's in, since this conveys a more specific and individual level of meaning. Once you know the house your natal Pluto is in, you can refer to Appendix II on Page 213 for a brief delineation of what it means.

Personal Pluto Work

Those who use psychology for deep inner work will be familiar with the rewards of rigorous self-honesty. Those who follow a spiritual path will have explored it too, because without it spiritual exercises are just a charade. For such seekers, astrology provides a handy guide to the very areas where we must start digging for the forbidden treasure, ambivalent though we may be about finding it. Though this work is hardly easy, in a sense it is very simple.

The first step is to name our personal taboos.

The second step is to own up to the taboos.

The third step is to release them, which allows their power to be redirected.

In the individual chart, Pluto's placement gives us clues about where our personal taboos reside. Those readers who know their natal charts are invited to ask themselves whether they ever feel simultaneously repelled and fascinated by a certain idea or set of activities related to Pluto's resident house; and whether they invest more time and energy into this department of life than they want others to know about—or, conversely, whether they avoid it like the plague.

As we saw in Chapter Three, natal Pluto indicates where we have been operating undercover—literally undercover, or undercover of our awareness. Even activities that would seem to be as rote and prosaic as commuting or using the telephone (third house) may be associated with feelings of dread or danger when Pluto is resident[2]. This is not because of the activities themselves. It is because for the native, that house's activities channel deeply compelling forces. Unprocessed feelings and urges—perhaps darkened by shame—bubble up from the depths of the unconscious and play themselves out through the department of life in question. Watching for these tendencies in ourselves is part of Pluto Work.

When embarking upon the first step—naming the taboo—we must be realistic about the workings of self-obfuscation. As we saw in Chapter Five, Pluto's operations tend to take place in a separate world from our values and opinions—making it the prickliest area in the chart, squirrelly with feelings that don't fit our picture of ourselves. Like a cult member avoiding questions from skeptical outsiders, we may prepare ruses to throw not only our friends and our therapists but ourselves off

---

[2] It is when natal Pluto is highly aspected by other planets that such feelings tend to be more palpable. If not, the power of the activities in question might remain very unconscious indeed—manifesting as no more than a vague malaise in the background of the native's psyche. When a transit comes around to provoke that natal Pluto, however, its power is likely to arise seemingly out of nowhere, compelling the native's attention.

the scent whenever we get too close to uncovering the taboo. Such might be the case, for example, with a person who has not integrated his tenth-house Pluto and harbors an obsession with social status that he is ashamed to admit because it violates his self-image as a non-competitive guy.

The other thing we must remember is to proceed with a great deal of self-compassion. There is usually sound justification for keeping taboo material tucked away. An issue may be taboo because of a circumstance from the past that was so painful it feels intolerable to revisit it or anything that even vaguely relates to it; or it may stay hidden because our own personal taboo intersects with a family one or a cultural one. The native with Pluto in the eighth house of sexuality may have many reasons—societal, religious, ethical—to deny his own fascination with, for instance, the darker side of erotic imagery. But if our commitment is to really look at what is down in the psychic cellar, we will look, no matter how it got down there. Personal Pluto Work entails changing these dramas from being "taboo" in the modern sense—frightening and forbidden—to *taboo* in the original sense: so powerful that they can transform us from the inside out[3].

Power is tricky stuff, for the wise as well as the foolish; and even the most considered use of Pluto requires caution. This makes for an exploration that is not only intellectually demanding but also somewhat psychologically threatening. For self-investigation of this nature we must summon up emotional courage as well as spiritual maturity. We are grappling with subject matter which dare not speak its name.

Step One: Naming the Taboo

So speaking its name is exactly what we must do. This is the way healing begins; witness the Twelve-Step meeting, where the first step on the road to recovery is to say out loud, "I am an addict." Once named, the issue we've always taken such pains to hide may suddenly seem patently obvious. We may be struck with the realization that other people have always seen this part of us quite clearly (and—surprise, surprise—*without* the harsh judgment we ourselves have applied to it), whereas all the while we'd assumed nobody knew.

---

[3] Stripped of all moral and philosophical evaluations, *taboo* (from the Polynesian word for *sacred*) conveys the idea of dangerous potency. When we approach it dispassionately, without fear and without notions of "good" and "evil," we see that the impulse behind declaring something *taboo* is a respectful one, even a practical one. A taboo is a prohibition intended to forestall prematurity of action and immaturity of spiritual intention. The injunction in some families against mentioning a relative's suicide, for instance, has the same root as the injunction in Bali against leaving the god's mask uncovered overnight.

The reason soul-work facilitators, from shamans to psychologists, emphasize the importance of *giving things a name* is that once named, energies no longer have the same power over us. Remember the story of "Rumpelstiltzkin"? When the heroine (self-awareness) pronounced the secret name of the troll (unintegrated Pluto) who was holding her baby hostage, she acquired all his power. He was suddenly revealed as nothing more than a sputtering little man with control issues.

That said, this naming process is not something one rushes headlong into. Calling the Dark God by name[4] is a ritual properly attended by a sense of awe and respect. As we have seen, it is not for nothing that taboos exist; there is a reason for the sense of danger that surrounds Plutonian themes. So this first step is often the most difficult.

To name our taboos it is helpful to go outside of ourselves for perspective, for what needs to be revealed may be impossible to see alone. The person with Pluto in the fifth house of performance, for instance, may tell herself any number of stories to cover up the troubling feelings she has about exhibiting her creativity, hoping to fashion a cut-and-dried explanation so as to avoid her feelings about it. These stories may have been with her for years, to the point of becoming part of the warp and woof of her life. There is nothing as guardedly subjective as a Plutonian blind spot.

Where does one find a suitably Plutonian guide? Though modern Western culture, as a whole, fails to provide us with the initiation rites that could support soul work such as this, by metaphysical law the individual on the path of transformation will nonetheless attract modern messengers of Pluto's teachings when and if he is ready for them. Respectfully and deliberately invoking these messengers is an integral part of the seeker's practice. Books that trigger revelations, gifted counselors, deep-body workers or spiritual teachers often come forward at the onset of a Pluto transit, as those who have had Pluto cross a personal planet or natal angle will have discovered. Spirit guides or ancestors may come to our aid. At just the right moment, something or someone will appear to provide the perspective we need.

Step Two: Owning the Taboo

The second step in personal Pluto Work involves acknowledging our role in creating the taboo we have just named, despite its

---

[4] To invoke (from Latin, *invocare*) means to call upon divine forces, an act that in every tradition has been seen to properly belong only to those who knew what they were doing. Mickey Mouse found out as much, in The Sorcerer's Apprentice segment of Disney's *Fantasia*.

noxiousness. This step is not for the faint of heart. Plutonian subject matter is very often repulsive, icky, even horrifying. Literally, it is associated with the unsavory releases of decay and bodily detoxification. (At this point, readers may be forgiven for wondering, *Can we please do Venus Work instead?*)

It should go without saying that Pluto work is not for the purpose of corroborating the idea of ourselves that we already hold. A native with Pluto in the second house, for example, may privately feel extremely threatened by having to part with even small amounts of money, despite the fact that her image of herself is not at all one of miserliness. She may be too defensive to look at the feelings that course beneath her financial life because they seem to invalidate her values; she may project these feelings upon other people, which makes her own impulses easier to repudiate (at least in the short term). But to rigorously apply the second step of Pluto Work we need to examine our personal relationship with the taboo, whether it is widely shared or imagined to be unique[5]. This means confronting those psychological nooks and crannies in the psyche where most of us would prefer to let sleeping dogs lie.

There are two good reasons to wake the dogs up. When we raise our taboos to consciousness we are blessed with empowerment; when we keep them unconscious we are cursed with disempowerment. The truth is that if Pluto is not working for us, it is working against us. Ask yourself whether the part of your life indicated by your natal Pluto placement ever feels like an insatiable beast that needs feeding by the hour. We may think we have the beast safely imprisoned, but from an energetic point of view this beast has *us* imprisoned. In this way an unexamined Pluto retains its power, while keeping the chart in stagnation.

How do we get close enough to it to turn the situation around? When exploring these vulnerable places within the self, our goal should be to observe our fear rather than identify with it. This helps a great deal when we feel like we're casting around in the dark, groping for something that could bite our hand off once we find it. The goal here is to keep reminding ourselves that it makes sense to feel fear—and then proceed anyway, armed with a commitment to the promise of Pluto: that profound healing will come of following where this is leading.

Fear is actually quite helpful in this context. Though our intellects are of little use down in Pluto territory, our fear can be used

---

[5] In the example of the money taboo, all Americans share this one, as we have seen, by virtue of Pluto's placement in the second house of the US chart. Thus an individual American with this placement will be working with it from two angles.

like a Geiger counter, telling us we're getting close to the source of power.

Step Three: Releasing the Taboo

It's our approach here that makes all the difference. There are wise ways to release power, and there are some very unwise ways to release it. Think of a pressure cooker, building up steam. When and if the lid comes off—*KABLOOIE!*—we get an explosion of scalding heat. Clearly, it would be in our best interests to carefully harness that energy—to approach the pot with an oven mitt, to adjust the valve deftly and purposefully—rather than letting the steam find its own way out, all at once, involuntarily, via burning and pain.

Approaching Plutonian power unwisely means allowing our life situation to determine what form the energy will take when it is released. This would be like a person yakking away on his cell phone while a pressure cooker rattles and fumes and gets ready to blow right next to him. If we do not own up to our participation in what is trying to happen, there will be no other way for Pluto to perform but to blow up. Those natives who have grappled with an unconscious natal Pluto know that this planet does not fool around. The power of our own taboos is like the contents of that pressure cooker; and if we want to tap it, our approach must be as conscious as we can make it.

If we have done the naming and the acknowledging, we have already disarmed the denial mechanisms that kept us from the knowledge that we have this power inside of us. All that's left to do is to allow the energy to do its work. At this point we will already be quite aware that though we have committed to being in charge, we are not, ultimately, in control here—Pluto is. Step three is not really in our hands.

Allowing Natural Law

To confront and approach one's Pluto issues with care, respect and curiosity is to appeal to Natural Law to take over. We don't have to *do* anything more, except keep from shutting down. The transformation of trapped power into creative power is not an event, per se, but a consciousness shift—symbolized in fairy tales by the ugly frog turning into a prince.

The moment of release is a form of magic[6] that happens within the psyche, and it is usually accompanied by a distinct sense of renewal

---

[6] Those inexplicable forces that humanity has variously chalked up to magic, supernaturalism or divine grace are represented in astrology by the transpersonal planets, which represent a different order of Natural Law than the personal planets. Though we may chart them and discuss their qualities, the purposes and operations of Uranus,

and vitality. It may happen when the native is sitting on the therapist's couch, in a spiritual ceremony where the energy is high and clear, in an unguarded moment out in nature or even in the middle of an emergency situation or health trauma. It could happen at any time or place where we have made that internal commitment to go forward into our deepest truth without fear—or rather, despite our fear—and trust the process.

The impact of this release is often felt in our outside circumstances too. As explained in Appendix I, it is axiomatic in metaphysics that the external and internal realms are not separate spheres: the world of events and the world of the psyche are twin realities. Thus the release of Plutonian power from its prison in the psyche often coincides with remarkable shifts in the native's health, work, home front or relationships. Readers who have done their own version of Pluto work can attest to the fact that when their inner vision breaks through in an area where they had once been blind, things may fall into place in their life situation in an unaccountably fortuitous way. "Coincidences" happen.

This is step three taking care of itself. When we do the work of Pluto, its power suddenly pops out of hiding and is at our disposal.

Pluto Mastery

Personal taboo work is not for everyone. Though the planet resides somewhere in every natal chart, plumbing the Dark Mysteries in a conscious, deliberate way—whether through astrology or some other practice—is a niche specialty. One thing it requires is the willingness to take a leap of faith—something that is viewed by many modern thinkers as a liability rather than a virtue. We have seen that the proud intellect, so championed in our age, cannot help us here.

Natives with Pluto dominant in their birth chart are well-suited to Pluto Work; certainly they would suffer more than the average person if they did *not* do it. But a strong Pluto placement is not in itself a guarantee of mastery. To commit to knowing the facets of the self that one has formerly shunned is a profoundly bold act, and to hold on to that commitment despite the emotions that come up during the search requires a kind of spiritual surrender not allowed by every belief system.

Neptune and Pluto are ultimately unfathomable to the conscious ego and its thinking mind. In order to understand their challenges and access their power we need to shift our conceptual context from the purely psychological to the psycho-spiritual.

In every age, in every tradition, it has been believed that when sincere seekers pursue truth with humility, open eyes and a sense of surrender, they receive the kind of results that we might use the term *miraculous* to describe.

To say that Pluto Work is difficult is both an understatement and an over-simplification. Its difficulty will seem, in the end, irrelevant—the same way a new mother feels about her labor pains once she is cradling her new baby in her arms. A core principle of occult thinking is that to achieve self-understanding, we must face the most insecure parts of ourselves; and the irony is that in doing so, a profound sense of security will arise. Could it be that fear isn't the deal-breaker we always thought it was?

Individuals who make Pluto Work a way of life tend to seek out activities that explicitly act out the regenerative phase of the Pluto cycle. They may be drawn to do midwife-like work in whatever field they are already in—as in the case of a literary consultant who helps birth a book from idea phase through publication; or a business consultant who guides a failing company through a restructuring process. The best therapists and healers who coach the long, hard rebirth of individuals after some kind of breakdown are inevitably those who have gone through Pluto Work themselves.

Collective Pluto Work

We now have a sense of what it means for an individual to do Pluto Work. But what does it mean for a collective entity to do it? What would happen if America did it? How might these ideas get acted out in the external world?

For those of a Plutonian persuasion, here is a chance to apply the much-touted but little-understood theory of synchronicity to the quest for *right use of power*. The Pluto energy expressed in world affairs is the same stuff as the Pluto energy we're trying to access within our psyches. Once we have committed to exploring Pluto's laws, we will want to examine them wherever they reside.

Atomic Power

As Above, So Below has a corollary: As Within, So Without. To see how this axiom applies to Pluto Work let us use the example of atomic power, one of Pluto's mundane associations that trumpets the power of an archetype in the raw. The very concept of the atom is still new and astounding enough to smack of hyperbole: it is humanity's most recent statement of a feature of existence so unvarnished and essential that it feels like it could have been the invention of a science-fiction visionary. This makes the atom the perfect illustration of Plutonian principles and how to use them—and how not to use them.

The atom's secret code—ingeniously hidden by Nature herself—was cracked in 1930: by the Law of Correspondences, this was the year the planet Pluto was first sighted in the sky. Thus began the Atomic Age, whose apocalyptic potential is directly related to humanity's failure to understand Pluto. As myriad peace activists and ecologists have warned for 75 years now, modern culture as a whole has not applied spiritual understanding to its examination of the atom, which is now firmly linked in the human mind to the specter of mass demise.

When we apply the As Within, So Without law to this situation, we see the potential of global wipe-out as a warning about the mortal need for us as individuals to integrate Pluto. We are being cosmically cajoled to apply spiritual awareness when stepping into our own secret nooks and crannies, and we are being given a clear symbol of the destructive potential of letting that power remain separate and hidden.

In our discussion of personal taboo work we have seen that the psycho-spiritual equivalent of atomic power resides within each one of us. This is cosmic mirroring in action: there is a parallelism between the havoc we could wreak within ourselves by misusing our personal Pluto, and the havoc we could wreak on the world by misusing the atom. And the very same equation applies between the rebirth we can choose on a personal level and the rebirth the world could choose via Pluto Work.

Pluto Work and America

The American chart's Pluto, just like our own, reveals the potential for nothing less than total consciousness transformation. Used with awareness, that Pluto could transform the country virtually overnight; and by extension, the world at large.

It is becoming increasingly clear to more and more people that healthy fuel technologies, for example, could be pressed into service in America *next week*—were the powers-that-be not dead set against them. The notion that America's devotion to the internal combustion engine is and always was an indisputable inevitability is shifting. People's understanding changes when they are informed; for example, about the historical reality of General Motors and oil and tire companies buying up streetcar lines around the country in the 1920s in order to create a car culture where one did not exist before. Were this kind of information disseminated in the newspapers as widely as the foreign-enemy stories that are now the staple of the mainstream news, the American public would come to see the mess we are in right now *not* as an unavoidable certitude but as a function of a series of deliberate, counter-intuitive social campaigns imposed upon the country from within, right under the populace's noses[7].

There are many other examples of immediate transformation that would happen with mass consciousness change. For years social visionaries have been making the case that the whole world could be fed, for example, with the amount of food being grown *right now*—were agriculture allowed to fall back into patterns of ownership and distribution informed by justice and local tradition. It has even been argued that the potential exists for the safe and productive use of the atom itself—via fusion instead of fission—and that the only reason the collective is not funneling its resources into that line of inquiry is because it is stuck in another mindset.

We have seen that when Pluto Work gets to the third of its three-step process, the trajectory of destruction makes a spontaneous pivot. A sudden storm of creation is unleashed—a development that the Pluto Worker himself cannot be said to have "caused," for it is just a function of Natural Law. The kind of social and planetary changes that the world would experience once Pluto were used consciously would happen in the same swift, organic, inevitable-seeming sequence.

As to what could occur if America's Pluto continues to be used unconsciously, we already know about that.

Pluto Workers for the Group

As daunting as personal taboo work is, the prospect of investigating a country's collective blindness seems exponentially more so. Yet in every age and in every location we find individuals who take it upon themselves to challenge and redirect the wounds of the whole. Not very many, perhaps—it may be that the statistical incidence of consciousness workers follows a kind of Bell Curve—but as we have seen, such things are not a function of numbers. As Andrew Jackson said, "One man with courage makes a majority."

Metaphysical law tells us that a given culture will give rise to the very souls who are necessary to meet that culture's demands. This is not so very strange; when we think about it, it would be odd if it did *not* work this way. In the natural world, we would be surprised to see a pond,

---

[7] The documentary "Who Killed the Electric Car", released in the summer of 2006, is one of an increasing number of reports about how plutocratic forces in the USA have suppressed policies that could have ended global warming before it began, and could stop it now that it is underway. The film posits that the hydrogen cell, currently being promoted by Washington under the banner of forward-minded planning, has been chosen as a political stump-speech trope because it is decades away; meanwhile the electric car is a practical actuality but one which the fossil fuel industry believes would rob them of twenty years' worth of profits.

for example, that was *not* inhabited by the very marine life exactly suited to its specific temperature, depth and degree of acidity... including just the right types of microflora and fauna to regenerate its detritus, turning dying into rebirth.

Let us consider how we might apply what we have learned about Pluto's operation to the collective American consciousness. This means imagining what it would look like to harness instead of misuse the immense power we have seen represented in the USA chart.

This exercise comes with bonus points. Because inner and outer Pluto Work aid and abet each other, in the process of imagining the group being healed we may discover profound individual capacities that we didn't even know we had.

Naming the Hidden Truths

The 1-2-3 process outlined above suggests that we must first identify the secrets obscured by unconscious natal Pluto within the American mind. In this category we might put any of the instances discussed so far in this book of the discrepancy between the American self-image and the actual expression of its power (e.g. "We're Americans: we don't torture prisoners;" "Nobody starves in the USA.").

Such discrepancies take a terrible toll on the mass mind, for they must be defended behind ever-more-elaborate fortresses of national denial ("Well, maybe there weren't weapons of mass destruction in Iraq, but the world is still better off without Saddam.") Group stories like these are so pervasive it may be impossible to know we are guided by them ("Everybody knows that Fidel Castro is a dictator") unless we deliberately strive for a global perspective, rather than the in-house perspective that is considered normal.

Acknowledging Personal Role

This segues into the next step, which is to acknowledge how we buy into group delusions. To understand our personal role in the maintenance of collective taboos means conceding that we might not know the full truth of what the American government is doing in the world—nor on the domestic front, for that matter. And to set about informing ourselves.

Wherever we engage Pluto we need to be prepared to encounter unsavory material. As we have seen, there is a reason taboo material is taboo; opting out of collective blind spots means opening up to information that is often frightening and upsetting. We expect this with individual blind spots, and it's no less true with the group ones. It is human to want to look away from hearing about the atrocities happening on our watch—about the campaigns of terror being waged against Coca Cola union organizers in Colombia, and against Nigerian farmers who are trying to stop American refineries from being built on their land. It is extremely troubling to think about the Chernobyl-style nuclear reactors being set up by the US nuclear industry in the Third World. But how realistic would it be to expect a nation's dark secrets to be easy to look at?

From the point of view of the soul, there isn't any difference between the difficulty of collective Pluto Work and the difficulty of personal Pluto Work. They both involve fear and feelings of distress. And one either does the work anyway or one doesn't.

Curiosity and Common Sense

We looked in Chapter Seven at how America's natal Mercury, planet of communication and the media, opposes its Pluto. We talked about the country's fated struggle with polluted and manipulative information—how Free Speech vs. Darth Vader is a classic plot line in the American story. We proposed curiosity and common sense as antidotes: curiosity to cut through the denial, and common sense to get the country's feet back on the ground. Together they could be a healing balm, and both are freely available to each of us.

We also spoke of cynicism, the distorted mirror image of curiosity and common sense. Cynicism is what happens when the particularizing perception of Mercury gets cut off from the heart, and the mind loses its sense of the whole. Cynicism is the hope-free zone, and it is more pernicious an energy-sucker than either raving fear or violent rage—which at least have some life in them.

Everything that occurs in our reality—whether we like it or not, whether we understand it or not—is fair game for those committed to Pluto Work. We have proposed that looking at the epoch's current darkness where it exists is the place to start. If American culture is absurd right now, then we must let it be a dark comedy of absurdity, and allow ourselves a laugh or two. In some cases, that may be our only response, but at least it is an appropriate one. If, as is often proposed, it is "a joke" that the government gave the name "The Clean Air Act" to a bill that would allow more pollutants to be spewed into the air, then it makes sense to laugh darkly at it. That doesn't mean we're not taking it seriously; in a way, this is the most serious response of all. If our politicians are absurd, we must remember that they are absurd, think about them as if they are and talk about them as if they are.

The point is that it is not healthy to know that America is crazy and then go about our business as if it weren't. This is ducking the obvious, and it takes a toll on the physical and psychic health, not to mention the self-respect. When our big-city newspaper puts the guy who won the fourth-of-July hot dog eating contest on the front page while elsewhere whole countries are burning to the ground, we know we've entered Crazy Land. If satire is dead because each statistic we hear about American life is more absurd than the last, it is only because the social parodists can't keep up with the insanity of real life.

Our job as millennial realists is to call a spade a spade. If, when we look with full alertness at this country, we find it absurd, then we need to allow that to be our truth—rather than falling into what psychologists call *enabling*: going along with the pretense that it is not absurd. Each of us must decide whether we want to give up our common sense for a badge of normalcy, or whether we want to admit that the world situation is dire—not with resignation and despair but with a knowing that even though we cannot fully understand what it all means, we know it has a meaning.

Astrology is very good at providing clues to that meaning—both about the karma of the group and about how individuals fit into that karma—but the abiding premise that *meaning exists in the first place* is an article of faith that must be continually nurtured by the native.

The chart itself cannot provide that. The chart is just a map.

International Feedback

One way for US residents to keep their wits about them in this period of soul-sickness is to keep abreast of what the rest of the world population thinks of their country and what it is doing. Americans with contacts abroad can cop a perspective this way, as can readers of international publications (the BBC and *The Guardian* of London are examples of English-language outlets that are relatively easily accessible, and the internet has made non-domestic news more available than at any other time in history).

As in individual Pluto Work, allies usually provide, ironically, a less accurate picture than foes do—America's allies being more often than not foreign leaders installed by Washington. In the foe category, we have a news agency like Al-Jazeera, whose trials as the voice of the Middle East—despite censorship and fatal missile strikes by the Pentagon—are portrayed in the 2004 documentary *The Control Room*. Originally an arm of the BBC, Al-Jazeera's clear-eyed, lucid reporting makes it a much more reliable source of information than the US news industry about what is happening in a part of the world whose story line Washington has a vested interest in controlling.

There are also domestic alternative media that manage to operate outside of state control—free speech radio, the alternative press, indy media on the web—whose information the curious can fold into the picture they get from the mainstream media. All incoming information has something to tell us, though we must view it for patterns of meaning. Who is telling the story and why? If a rock concert is sponsored by Reverend Moon, that's a piece of data I want to know when deciding whether to buy a ticket. If National Public Radio gets funding from Lockheed, their reporting about the war industry needs to be assessed accordingly. This is common sense.

Cultural Midwives

As part of the third step of collective Pluto Work, certain citizens might choose to embody the transformation that happens when the burden of denial is set down. We may take up the mantle of the light worker: an individual who dedicates her work explicitly to the healing of the group. Through environmental and political activism, awareness-raising art, nonprofit work, private spiritual ritual that addresses global suffering and myriad other means as wide-ranging as human creativity itself, there are more and more Americans who do collective healing as a main gig. They are the midwives of the new consciousness.

The decision of these Pluto Workers to express their service in the particular way that they do is dictated, once again, not by any prescription to "do good" but by a spontaneous merger of

- their own distinct talents,
- an awareness of the blind spots of the collective, and
- the urgency of the times.

For them donating their gifts to the whole is not merely an exercise to round out their individuality, though it accomplishes that too. They may be naturals for Pluto Work, born into a time when it happens to be the key to global survival. But every one of us has a Pluto by birth right, and its placement points out the ways we can each find our own place in this appalling, astounding, transformative world situation into which we decided to incarnate.

Healing our Relationship to Money

We have said that there is no such thing as an accident of location any more than there could be an accident of birth time. It follows that every one of us who identifies as an American must have karmic lessons to learn as regards the teachings of the second house, where the national Pluto resides. In Chapter Three we proposed that no matter how boldly we may defy consensus thinking, living in a profoundly materialistic culture has an inescapable effect on our personal value system. Americans share the wound of materialism, whether they go blithely along for the ride or resist it tooth and nail; and it is something that those who aspire to Pluto mastery must address.

This means assessing our personal relationship to consumerism, a mass addiction that stands in the way of environmental awareness as well as making America as a whole impervious to global empathy. Whether we notice in our attitudes symptoms of Bourgeois Bag Lady Syndrome or class rage; whether we have inherited the Depression-era paranoia of our forefathers or are struggling to find right livelihood in a world of dwindling resources, Pluto Work necessitates teasing out the imbalances, distortions and dysfunctions that as children we took in with the Captain Crunch and Hostess Twinkies.

A sober, value-neutral approach to this shared money wound will make our self-scrutiny smooth and fruitful. We must not get waylaid by self-condemning; such indulgence is missing the point. When it comes right down to it, all human affliction is just an absence of consciousness: insanities both mild and severe represent natural processes that have gotten stuck, keeping us in a state of artificial puerility. Financial neurosis, like every other kind, is a form of arrested development.

If the culture as a whole is stymied this way, then the neurosis is considered normal—which makes it harder to see, but it does not give it the power to handicap us as individuals. Conventional financial attitudes that the American Pluto Worker finds unhealthy must be identified, isolated and rejected.

Pluto Work in the Service of the Collective

In this chapter we have looked at the lessons of Pluto as they can be applied to our troubled times, and how as individuals we can use these principles to heal our own darkness. We have proposed that our inner and outer selves are flip sides to the same coin; thus there is a parallelism between self-healing and healing society.

Applying the 1-2-3 steps of Pluto healing, we looked at how entrenched neuroses within the self can be transformed by daring to look at what we least want to look at. We considered the idea of acknowledging fear without caving in to it. We saw how by allowing the process of decay/rebirth to work itself out within us, we can free ourselves from our own inner slavery—clues to which are provided by our natal Pluto placement. We revisited some of the issues expressed by the US chart that American Pluto Workers must be particularly alert to— materialism and polluted information—and discussed the perspective that a dispassionate, compassionate citizen might bring to bear upon them.

Once we have committed to personal Pluto Work, we can apply this approach to the group psyche, becoming role models of strong, clear vision. Not only will this make us feel exponentially more alive, but our efforts will be far more useful to our community. They will be fueled by all that power than was once trapped down in that cellar.

FOURTEEN

BEING A GLOBAL GROWN-UP

SATURN WORK

Pluto Work is fierce and unconditional, while essentially internal. With the power it affords us, we may feel as if we are ready for anything. All we need is a sense of commitment and the maturity to show up.

This is where Saturn Work comes in.

Being Grown-up

The key teaching of Saturn is to be a grownup in all areas of life. When Pluto opposed Saturn at the dawning of the millennium, the issue became relevant in a new way: it was suddenly clear that each of us had better get down to the deeper reaches of our maturity. It was no longer enough to just try to act grown-up as a personality. The transit was demanding the kind of maturity that extends into our wider roles in the world.

This is an application of the term *maturity* that is rarely considered in public life and almost never in personal life. Although one sometimes hears professionals described this way (a critic may credit an artist with entering into a *maturity of craft*, for instance) the implications of the idea are seldom explored. Imagine how differently we would play out our adult roles if we gauged our social actions and decisions in terms of their psychological or spiritual maturity, rather than in terms of how high they allowed us to climb professionally or how much money they allowed us to make. Imagine how international relations might be conducted if the success of world leaders were measured by their maturity of mind and character.

Just imagine it.

Pluto-Saturn Hanging in the Air

The transit of Pluto through Capricorn upcoming (2008-23) is a long cosmic echo of the Saturn-Pluto theme, as the sign Capricorn is ruled by Saturn. The sixteen-year transit up ahead (see Chapter Twelve) puts together the same two archetypes as were paired in the seminal opposition. These cosmic signatures spell out an intense need, both individually and collectively, to delve into Saturn's mysteries more profoundly than it has ever occurred to us to do.

What is truly adult behavior as regards membership in the global family? Throughout this book we have explored the woeful lack of maturity of American culture. Where does this leave us as Americans and America-watchers in this new millennial terrain?

An Individual's Responsibility to the Group

We have talked about the relative primacy of Jupiter in the US chart, an archetype that has America incessantly asking itself *What do I believe*? Saturn, not as popular a planet by any means, prompts us to ask something else: *Whatever I believe, am I ready to stand up for it?* Saturn is the one planet in the natal chart that gives us the capacity to take responsibility for who we are; to be accountable for where we find ourselves at this time and place. As we have seen, America as a culture spurns this challenge, which makes it all the more necessary for individual Americans to embrace it.

We have proposed that there is a mysterious relationship between the soul path of the citizens and that of the group soul that encompasses them; and that as the individual grows in consciousness she will be increasingly curious about that relationship. She will start to see the group layer of her identity differently—as something that requires her attention, just as her personality requires it.

Not the same kind of attention, certainly. The collective facet of our identity is an altogether different facet than the individual one, and is not meant to entail responsibilities of the same nature. But as we master Saturn we begin to understand the concept of responsibility in broader and deeper ways. We start to see the impact of our consciousness emanating out from our core self like purposeful concentric circles. And the social whole starts to be seen as one of our lifelong responsibilities: not one that is dictated by some government or agency or ideologue from the outside (although the appearance of such teachers and leaders is also part of the plan), but one that is fashioned from the inside out.

Responsibility is nothing more or less than *the ability to respond* as a unique individual. When Saturn is embraced to this degree, one's responsibilities do not feel like an onerous weight. They feel like an organic outgrowth of selfhood.

Understanding Before Action

The recent specters of global warming, demented militarism and other global disasters—together with the tenure in Washington of a particularly unhinged group of power-mongers—have raised the alarm among many conscientious citizens over the past few years who feel that things have gotten so bad there is no room to sit back on the sidelines anymore: action is crucial. But here's the thing: before we commit to an activity or even a stance, we need to commit to understanding. And we can't just flirt with understanding; we need to commit to it, as a way of life.

Nothing else will lead to righting wrongs. Nothing else will really work. And if we despair over the apparent refusal of many of our compatriots to commit to an understanding beyond the simplistic and inflammatory nonsense they see on television, let us remember first of all that it is not in numbers of people that the power of human understanding is measured. In this department it has never been about quantity; it's about quality. It is through a certain quality of understanding that mass darkness moves into the light.

That said, it should give hope to those Americans pushing for change to realize that even in statistical terms the numbers are on the side of sanity. Since the Spring of 2003, unprecedented numbers of people in cities and towns all over the world have joined American dissenters to protest the current trajectory the world is on. This is important to remember. It is not the electoral process that makes social change happen; elections are a symptom, not a cause. It was not the victory of one political party over another that ended the war in Viet Nam. It was masses of people in the streets, a testament to the radical consciousness shift symbolized by the Uranus-Pluto conjunction of the mid-sixties.

Alliance with the People of the World

Forty years later, the movement is increasingly global. With every month that passes, those watching America from afar become more and more appalled at what Washington is doing. And it is a credit to most of these international observers that they have the political sophistication to focus their antipathy upon the nation's leaders rather than misplacing it upon ordinary citizens. It should humble Americans to recognize that most foreigners are far more astute at drawing this crucial distinction—between the people of a country and the government of that country—than Americans are.

Nonetheless, the fact that the US citizenry has allowed its government to do what it has done in the realm of foreign policy—not just over the past few years but ever since this ambitious young nation was born—reflects a failure of ethical maturity. Since the millennium the American populace has been exposed in a particularly harsh light, as being not just politically and historically ignorant beyond the rest of the worlds' expectation, but far more morally disengaged.

Trans-National Perspective

Our power to heal lies in information and understanding. Both will have the effect of spreading our loyalties outward. Times like these are inspiring many people to mutate from being loyal members of a given political party to being loyal members of the world family. The people of the world are the collective entity Americans need to identify with now[1]. The only reference points that make sense now are trans-national, which means shifting our allegiances from the partisan to the global and finally to the universal—realigning any closer-to-home political and cultural allegiances along the way, if need be. Only by stepping outside of societal group-think can we claim true kindred spirithood with souls anywhere, everywhere, who seek peace and justice. Pluto in Capricorn, as we saw in Chapter Twelve, will assist this process; but as transit-trackers know, it is always wise to position our consciousness one step ahead of world events.

"Think globally, act locally," say the activists. Astrology too subscribes to this maxim, by conferring meaning upon the exact location on Earth occupied by the native whose transits are being calculated. This is astrology's way of saying, *Start where you are.* As the rest of the world watches in dismay from the outside, American truth-seekers must realize that they are on the inside for a reason.

Recent transits echo this point, singling out the principles Americans need to learn right now. Let us make use of them, so that we can get a sense of our place in this stormy sea.

Forbearance

One of Saturn's most beautiful teachings is elegantly simple: that of forbearance. Saturn gives us to understand that Time has certain lessons, and that if we learn them we will mature on the level of body, mind and soul. What is the first thing Saturn counsels us to do in the face of chaos and trauma? To take responsibility—yes; but how about the *very first* thing? It is to do nothing. To watch and take stock. To wait.

---

[1] As *The New York Times* famously proclaimed just before the USA bombed Iraq amidst massive worldwide protests: "…[T]here may still be two superpowers on the planet: the United States and world public opinion." (Feb. 16, 2003).

People power has domestic applications too, as demonstrated by the way millions of immigrants and their supporters pouring into the streets of American cities in April and May of 2006 took by surprise lawmakers and observers on all sides of the political spectrum, and changed the course of the anti-immigrant Stensenbrenner Bill.

Instead of rushing off to lynch somebody after something like 9-11, or following the call of the warmongers to invade Afghanistan, to have sat back for a moment and taken the time to look, listen and learn.

To teach us the lessons of repeated experience, Time imposes postponements and sequencing, forcing us to learn pacing. On the personal level, this understanding becomes a powerful spiritual practice: when we have the presence of mind to forbear from freaking out over each little delay that comes along in the course of a day, we learn something about the natural stops and starts of existence in Time. (When we think about it, it is obvious that stops and starts must be part of human reality no less than of biological and geological reality. But of course, we rarely take the time to think about it.)

We discussed in Chapter Six how the notion of forbearance flies in the face of conventional American mores: not only is patience undervalued, but waiting in general is seen as something done only by losers whose time has no worth (witness the self-aggrandizing professional gambit of keeping the client waiting, or the caller on hold, as a power play).

Humility

In this chapter we are looking at Saturn not merely as a bestower of personality traits but as a consciousness guide—from which point of view America's Saturn-phobia is doubly problematic. Not only does this phobia make us miss out on personal virtues that would help us function more effectively, but it arrests our spiritual development by keeping us from learning humility. And humility is what we have to have if we are going to respond, rather than react, to the world around us.

We see humility shining forth from the great spiritual teachers of history and legend, and from the contemporary leaders the people of the world esteem most highly. In our personal experience, when we think back to a favorite teacher or mentor whom we remember as being not just knowledgeable but wise, we may find that the feature we loved most about them was their humility. And it is humility that is the one feature conspicuously absent in the destructive and self-promoting individuals we see in high office today.

Part of Saturn's teaching is to accept everyday hardships with a quietude that comes of knowing they have a meaning that we cannot immediately see. Thus the Saturn acolyte's task is to see past the skewed associations that have grown up around humility in contemporary culture (self-abnegation, lack of resources, absence of ambition) and to cultivate it as a deeper response to life. The world needs our responsiveness right now. The world needs our humility.

Giving Up Blame

Among those who work with astrology, the big complaint about Saturn is that it imposes limits. People do not like to be curbed and restricted. How can we embrace Saturn when it gives us hurdles? What good is it if it keeps us from fully expressing ourselves? As students of transits know, Saturn usually slows down or stops the trajectory we are on, for reasons that seem either inscrutable or downright contrary: the planet is notorious for standing in the way of what we think we want.

Frustration and inhibition are part of life; the question is, what do we do with them? Those who seek mastery of the Saturn principle make a practice of noticing when they are feeling the urge to blame, and then taking a moment to reconsider. First one identifies the compulsion to blame; then one forbears. Though reacting to grievances with blame is an all-but-universal habit, from a metaphysical point of view it just displays ignorance of Saturnine Law[2].

If one believes that we each have a soul identity that writes the script of all the challenges we will meet in this life, then blaming events and people for things we see as going awry seems a tad unclear-on-the-concept. Plenty of people do not believe in any such script, of course; but in the case of those who do, holding on to blame is a theoretical inconsistency. It would be tantamount to cursing a school-crossing guard who signals us to slow down. Just as the crossing guard may be aware of little kids running around just outside of our field of vision, astrology proposes that Saturn knows something we don't know about the course we are on.

Even astrologers, of course, are apt to identify Saturn—natally and by transit—with the problems it seems to cause; so even when we avoid blaming the external inconvenience, it is possible, using this ruse, to blame Saturn for causing it. But shifting blame from event to planet is a sophistry astrologers should take care to avoid. In fact the assumption that a glitch means *there is something wrong* is itself a judgment call we should question.

---

[2] At this point one might say, "Wait a minute: what if I'm hit by a car that runs a red light? That driver is indisputably to blame. They broke the rules of the road." And this is true; but if one aspires to look at things astrologically, it doesn't go far enough. On the social and legal levels, there are indeed rules where fault is assigned, and it would be irresponsible not to enforce those rules and assign blame accordingly. But on the metaphysical level, blame is not the issue. The issue is whether we can derive a larger meaning from that "accident," in which the innocent driver participated as well. The goal of astrological inquiry is to derive soul meaning from every event in which we participate, for it is axiomatic that our participation had meaning.   ➤

Mistakes and Problems

Granted, the general view of Saturn's hurdles is to see them either as mistakes that we curse ourselves for making, or afflictions that seem to strike us arbitrarily from the outside, such as a head cold that interrupts our work week or a clueless driver on the road who slows us down, or even drives into us and forces us to stop. Or we may dismiss a Saturn glitch with an all-purpose feeling of resentment: a shutting-down-to-the-moment, justified with vague notions about life just being hard. But this is no more than another form of blaming, which fails to lead us to self-understanding and keeps us from integrating Saturnine law. Whether we blame ourselves or other people or a microbe or the planets themselves, blame is not only a big fat waste of energy, it's a distraction from the lesson at hand.

From the perspective of astrology, problems are fungible. If it wasn't one thing going awry under a Saturn transit, it would be another. In a way, the specifics don't even matter. This is a concept with radical implications. Instead of jumping into an obsession over the details, when something goes "wrong" we might try experimenting with the astrological view: accepting that we were just plain fated to experience a blockage or a slowdown of some kind. It was going to happen by hook or by crook. And that the ultimate meaning of the bad/painful/flawed event has less to do with something being wrong than with the nature of blockage. It's not a punishment, it's not a put-down; it's a teaching about an inevitable phenomenon of life. Nothing personal.

Even when it is only partially grasped, this line of thinking takes a good deal of the sting out of the situation we might find ourselves in when, for example, Saturn transits one of our personal planets. We will avoid the paralyzed feeling of having done wrong or having been wronged; we will decide to just not go there. All the energy we would have put into worry, self-abnegation or blame can instead be put into resolving the issue at hand. Instead of shutting down to what happened, calling the event a problem and making it an enemy, we open up to what happened. Then we can take in the lesson the planet is trying to teach. This approach will pay off immediately by making us more effective with trouble-shooting; and it will certainly pay off at the next Saturn transit[3].

---

[3] In particular, the seven-year juncture points of the Saturn transit cycle tend to echo and resolve each other. For example, a lesson unlearned at the Saturn Return is likely to show its face again at the waxing square; if we resist it again we'll get another chance at the opposition; and so on.

But the most sublime result of this practice is that it breaks the conditioned reflex of reactivity, and retrains us to really respond. We open up to the moment. We enter into a state of presence, from which we can access our innate intelligence in its clearest form. This is how we cultivate the kind of responsibility that will engineer a shift in mass consciousness.

Mature Use of Resources

Saturn is the planet of eliminating, solidifying, consolidating and simplifying. Its frustrations always have something to do with nipping in the bud some kind of excess. Absorbing the implications of this teaching on an individual level would radically alter our participation in America's favorite pastime: consuming.

We looked in Chapter One at how the failure to take responsibility fits into the mass conformity-fest that is American shopping, and how this failure is exploited by advertising. Though fashion has been called an organized form of narcissism[4], what makes it such a Saturn-phobic experience is actually its *avoidance* of individual ego concerns. The tongue-in-cheek phrase "fashion victim" is an apposite one, for it refers to the surrender of one's uniqueness to a passing notion of what the wider group seems to want. Trend addiction represents an overdose of Neptune uncorrected by Saturn. An out-of-balance Neptune seduces us into merging with all manner of mass silliness, displacing our authentic soul-prompted values with whatever the group seems to identify as worthwhile.

The antidote to all forms of mass hysteria, from blockbuster movie openings to war fever, is the cautious sobriety of Saturn. It instills in us, ironically enough, a kind of defiance: we defy the collective impulse to align our values with whatever corporations and their ad departments (or governments and their spin departments) appoint as the correct aesthetic decision or political stance. If it keeps us from buying Ikea bedroom sets and skirts with annually-changing hem-lengths, Saturnine defiance will certainly keep us from wasting money. But if it keeps us from merging with violations of standards of human decency, this defiance will take us even further: it will prevent us from getting soul-sick.

Going along with the crowd is usually thought of as a side effect of apathy, and shrugged off as an innocuous human failing. But to live disengaged from one's own hard-wrought values is to turn one's back on

---

[4] Glen Obrien, "If It Makes You Think, is it Fashion?" in the anthology *The Revolution Will Be Accessorized*, Harper Perennial 2006.

Saturn, the planet of karma—which, from the point of view of the soul's evolution, is a very serious matter. Such disengagement keeps us at the level of the child who excuses his petty crimes by saying, "But everyone does it." If untutored by Saturnine Law this kid will grow up to be the cynical senator whose corruption is justified as business as usual; or the immigrant shop owner who hangs an American flag in his window when his adopted country starts a war he knows is wrong; or the corporate polluter who tells himself he's just doing his job as he searches for ever-more-ingenious ways to slip through EPA loopholes.

The area where America needs Saturn's teachings the most is indicated by the national chart's natal Pluto in the second house of resources. Not to put too fine a point on it, the USA's abdication of responsibility with natural resources is imperiling life on Earth, and there is no way to stop the trajectory except through individuals addressing the issue—each in his own way in his own context. Thoughts of driving a hybrid car, starting a community garden, conserving electricity and water, riding a bicycle to work—will, in a very few years, be more than feel-good topics to discuss over Chablis. They will be immediate, hyper-relevant aspects of an urgent national debate. Understanding responsible custodianship in a limited physical world will be flat-out mandatory in the USA, as it is right now in many other places around the globe.

For the sake of our own soul health as well as that of the Earth, the transits have given us the heads-up to consider Saturn's teachings now rather than later.

Leaving the Driving to Daddy

On an individual level, integrating Saturn means taking control of ourselves the way children—psychically and actually—cannot. We have looked at how, in a Saturn-phobic culture, chronological age is no guarantee of psychological maturity; but if we want to use these eternal principles to heal the collective, we need to reject the conventional view and start making our age pay off. This means giving up the vain hope that somebody *out there* should or could take care of us.

Saturn's collective shadow guise is fascism, or the willingness of a people to "scoot over and leave the driving to Daddy.[5]" Through the ages people have given up their own Saturns, as it were, by projecting them outwards onto ill-chosen father figures; thus have oppressed people surrendered their wills throughout patriarchal history to a monarchy, council of mullahs, papacy or government to use for its own ends. In

---

[5] David Kipen in the *San Francisco Chronicle Book Review,* describing the proletarians in George Orwell's *1984.*

Chapter Twelve we looked at how the recent transit of Saturn, the planet of the Father, passing through Cancer, the sign of the Mother, illustrated this theme against the backdrop of the chart of the USA. This period brought up some very primal dynamics from the depths of the group psyche that caused the child/parent drama to be played out en masse, with its attendant themes of helplessness/authority and dependent/protector.

At this writing, these issues are still raging in the national discussion, putting a palpable emotional panic into the debate about executive power and citizen compliancy. Indeed, at this point there seems to be no official crime so outrageous nor any abrogation of human rights so degrading that it cannot be waved aside as a necessary evil of the Daddy-state's "war on terror."[6] If Americans do not choose a different script from the one they are currently following, the drama will continue with the people in the role of the vulnerable child, and a tyrannical government in the role of the oppressive guardian.

The upcoming years of Pluto (power) in Capricorn (government/ corporations) will make the choice very clear. Though the era of the mega-businesses will eventually come to an end just like every other era, until the transit is over we will witness the extreme scenarios that are Pluto's only guarantee. The world stage is set for the continuing consolidation of power into the hands of a smaller and smaller group of international business interests—the Daddies—who feel they have too much at stake to allow the people—the Children—to determine world policies with their cute little elections. To the extent that the dark side of Pluto in Capricorn dominates, mass anxiety will continue to be pressed into service by the powers-that-be to keep the populace childlike.

The good news is this tactic cannot work when people commit to individual responsibility. If moral sanity is to be reclaimed in the years ahead, it must start at the individual level: with every adult citizen acting like an adult. Were enough individuals to commit to the necessary self-reflection, the real promise of the Saturn archetype could be fulfilled: democracies would be run not by false father-figures but by masses of people taking responsibility, which would include holding their public servants accountable.

---

[6] Though the word "terror" has been turned into government-speak for whatever villainy the designated enemy is supposedly doing or could hypothetically do (as opposed to what the government itself is doing), a dispassionate analysis of the mechanics of terror would cut through much of the disempowerment from which the American populace is suffering. Psychological studies have shown that a continuous, nonspecific, low-level anxiety—the kind maintained by incessant but vague references to "bad guys" who could attack at any time and any place—is the most debilitating type of fear.

Becoming Our Own Good Parent

This commitment to individual responsibility is the only way we can know real security. If Saturn could be said to have an intention during these times, it is to coax each of us to develop ways of protecting and nurturing ourselves and our fellows in ever-more-authentic ways— that is, in ways that actually work. There is immense benefit to be gained right now by individuals and society at large from deliberate, engaged self-parenting.

Once the inner child is nourished, there is no need to be enslaved by a false parent in the outside world. This is the key to staying safe and self-responsible at once, and for those who do not submit to collective fear, the opportunities will be there in full force to turn the key in the lock. Once we integrate our Saturn we require no strongman-father to promise not to abandon us, for we are un-abandonable. We are impervious to protectionist blackmail, because we trust ourselves to know how to make our lives safe. We become the wise, careful parent we always wanted to have.

Living Through Our Suns

This is how we arrive at fully-empowered adulthood; and from no other vantage point can we truly live out the potential of our Sun placement: maintaining our singular identity in the face of overwhelming pressure to surrender the self. Once we have accepted the idea that our soul must have had its reasons for incarnating into this particular group, benighted though it may be, we can settle into our purpose and apply our unique skills to the challenge. Centered in our natal Sun—symbol of our life purpose—we can remain detached yet heartily engaged, without being negated, harmed or even held back by the group's incapacities.

Once we're centered in the Sun in our chart, we can meet not only the group's needs, but our own. We can now connect personally (Venus) and tribally (the Moon); we can connect through right action (Mars); we can identify the beliefs that give meaning to our lives (Jupiter). We can work on our very own ways of living responsibly (Saturn). Staying rooted in the singular self (Sun), we can make sense of our nationality, assimilating it without becoming assimilated by it.

Responsibility for Being at War

Before we conclude our discussion of responsibility, let us clarify a confusion that often arises because of the tendency of words to arrive loaded with invisible trappings. When working with the esoteric implications of common terms, we need to allow for these trappings before bandying the terms about.

In popular usage, *responsibility* is associated with fault and guilt: in the American vernacular the word is often used as an outright euphemism for *blame*. This is why the proposal that each American bears *responsibility* for the war their government is waging is likely to provoke the indignant reaction: "I am not responsible for America being at war," which means: *It is not my fault.* We have said that taking responsibility in the archetypal sense means making full use of one's Saturn, symbol of the universal law of karma—a concept in which fault and blame have no place. But when we bring the idea of responsibility into the realm of highly charged situations like war and disaster, we need to be explicit about what we mean or we will elicit negative reactivity.

When the peace activists of *Not in Our Name* chose that phrase for the name of their group, they were drawing on the teachings of Saturn. The phrase implies a fully adult position: that of citizens taking responsibility for what their country is doing. Though their stance is one of emphatic opposition—to the government's actions and to its imperial intentions—it is noteworthy that the emphasis in the chosen phrase is not on *the Other*, but on the self. The words proclaim the right and duty of the individual to resist having his or her decision-making choices taken away.

Not every conscientious American is a political activist, of course, as not every musician is a trumpet player. The good Goddess has endowed each of us with an utterly unique set of skills and sensitivities: every natal chart compels the native to express her heart and mind in definitively distinct ways. In the case at hand, however, the common thread uniting each American is that of membership in a group that is at war—an undeniable similarity of circumstance that, from the soul's point of view, is not an arbitrary one. In the face of this common dilemma, every citizen will have a unique style of responding. What is shared is the necessity to do so.

After reading in the newspaper about a massacre of human beings taking place far away, a musician may be moved to exercise his Saturn by composing a lament. A student may volunteer to collect petitions; his coworker may call up a friend and get a conversation going. Others may read and write, dance, speak, weep or pray. The key is to refuse to shut down: to instead respond. Though we may feel powerless in the face of terrible global events, we are never powerless when we truly respond.

The Saturn Mission, if We Choose to Accept It

In this chapter we have considered how a deep understanding of the Saturn archetype can be our guide in fashioning a response to the critical times we face now and in the years ahead. We have looked at the issue of responsibility metaphysically, proposing that the individual is in some way responsible for the group he inhabits—not in the sense that he is at fault, but in the sense that his membership in that group has a karmic meaning. We have discussed how a vision of true adulthood can become a personal and spiritual practice, capable of rendering us psychologically and effectively secure. We have also discussed how the lack of this vision renders us dangerously insecure; susceptible to being manipulated by destructive cultural forces.

We have proposed that in the face of the soul-sickness of the collective, the first step in taking responsibility is to refrain from reacting. After that, right action includes self-informing and seeking patterns of meaning; and, most important of all, looking within the self in order to discover—there and only there—what response would be just right, for us, in the context at hand.

This is where knowing our own chart comes in very handy: in it we will find a marvelous coded description of this very thing—that distinctly appropriate response. Every one of us has a natal Saturn, whose placement outlines the particular style and circumstances in which we were born to express our adulthood, as well as the unique fears we may face when we do.

Two Levels of Responsibility

So what we are calling *Saturn Work* has, like Pluto Work, two layers to it: a collective one and a personal one. The former is represented by the afflicted Saturn in the USA chart, discussed in Chapter Six; the latter is represented by each individual's own Saturn placement. The intricate relationship between these two layers makes for a fascinating study, a kind of soul-polishing, for those whose understanding of their earthly incarnation extends beyond the personal to the social and universal dimensions of being.

We have discussed at length the collective Estranged Father complex indicated by the US chart and many of the ways it impacts Americans as individuals. We have suggested that to be a responsible citizen, a clear-eyed skepticism needs to be erected towards the faux-parental messages coming from the external: from the public health official who tells us that if we don't get the flu shot we will fall deathly ill, to the military spokesman who would have us buy duct tape to forestall enemy attack. By learning to name these intrusions of wounded

Saturn that come at us from the collective, we call them when we see them and act accordingly. This is the way we begin to disassociate from the puerilism of the mass mind.

Next, the reader is invited to go back to his own natal Saturn, to understand the nature of his own unique path towards maturity. Saturn's sign provides clues as to his immediate sub-generation's issues with growing up; and when thoroughly decoded by sign, house and aspect, this same natal Saturn reveals those maturity-generating activities and contexts that are exclusive to the native and in which he will grow and flourish[7].

Like Pluto Work, this kind of self-study will force us to face our fears: the same ones Peter Pan revealed when he declared he would never grow up. If we are honest about the acute vulnerability of this part of the self, we will know to approach our Saturn with caution and self-forgivingness; for we are stepping into the tender arena of the inner child. We all know how exploitable children are—our fullest compassion comes out whenever we're called upon to protect these defenseless beings—yet how seldom we consider that this part of our own psyche feels equally young, incapable and vulnerable! It is what has made Karl Rove's job so easy.

Everyone who has trembled in their boots but gone ahead and done something anyway knows that facing fear is its own reward. With consummate efficiency, the cosmos has engineered it so that when we truly respond to our culture's suffering, we enact our own soul work. Full-heartedly responding to collective fears means healing the inner child's fears at the same time. Both involve channeling one's natal Saturn. Some people's Saturn gets acted out primarily in the outer world; others act it out in the domestic sphere. Public or private, each Saturn has its preferred setting.

If our efforts are sincere, wherever we act it out we will be developing a rock-solid integrity. By being truly grown-up in our own way, in our own style, at our own pace, we will burn off collective karma at the same time that we keep our inner child safe—something nobody else will do, and nobody else can.

---

[7] Readers who know their own natal charts can refer to the guide on Page 211 to get an idea of the ways Saturn Work may be best applied for them personally.

FIFTEEN

A NEW ERA

When we work on ourselves in a spirit of deep honesty, we start to see responsibility as a prize rather than a curse. Then we quite organically begin to apply this insight to broader and broader scenarios.

It starts to feel like it's not enough to try to act grownup just because we are penalized if we don't—like at work. It feels insufficient to try to be responsible in personal relationships just to avoid conflict; or to vote on election day just to avoid guilt. We start to realize that the act of *responding* confers self-respect, whereas *reacting* takes it away. Gradually, this sense of responsibility starts to feel inner-directed rather than outer-mandated. We begin to conduct our lives as if everything we do matters.

We start to feel as if our own peculiar qualities are necessary to the people in our lives, and that the groups to which we belong require exactly what we have to offer. We start to understand that it's not an accident that we joined them when we did. Our presence in a given country starts to feel meaningful, to the point where we no longer take our society's blessings for granted nor turn a blind eye to its wounds. If we sense soul-sickness all around us, we start to feel a consequent incentive to find out what it means. If we feel, as Americans, that our culture is flailing in pain, we would no more seek to deny this collective distress than we would deny it in our own beings.

Once inspired by curiosity and responsibility, we may start to muse about our membership in humanity as a whole—a massive whole of blessed and afflicted, creative, inter-related beings—a whole of which we are an indispensable member. We may start to think about the human race as if it were a single teeming organism, damaged as well as blessed, going through a dark night of the soul. We may start to see not just the USA but the modern Western mind itself, with its machines and weapons and power games, as having grown distorted to the point of insane. We may find ourselves joining the millions of thinkers from many different worldviews who have proposed that we give up on the dominance/submission gambit, the paradigm that has prevailed for the last five thousand years or so, and look to a new (and very old) one: that of synergistic interconnectedness.

There are spiritual systems everywhere that use this paradigm as their central premise; any of them could serve to wake us up to who we are, where we are, and what is happening around us. Astrology—along with the elegant philosophies of the Far East, the Western mystery schools and the religions of countless indigenous tribes whose names have been lost but whose legends and rites remain ensconced in cellular memory–all are based on the principle of universal interrelatedness. Moreover, many new teachings have come out of depth psychology and the human potential movement that refashion this aboriginal teaching in contemporary terms. Popular interest in such knowledge has burgeoned over the past several decades, even as humanity's upheavals have grown more convulsive.

The American identity shift chronicled in this book is taking place against the backdrop of a world growing out of one era and into another. A mass movement in the realest sense of the term, the human consciousness movement is so big that there are barely words to describe it. Astrological macro-cycles and the Mayan prophecies are two examples of frames of reference big enough to talk about this immense threshold; as is the calendar of ancient India, which called our age the *Kali Yuga*: the Dark Time—a penultimate epoch preparing for a rebirth of global consciousness. There has never been a better time to access the information that has come down to us from these ancients, keeping in mind that it is encoded in the subtle and dispassionate language of symbols—which require a deeper way of seeing than we are used to in this era of instant intel. We need to consider the meaning of the New Age in a way that goes beyond pop cliché. Our goal must be to get in touch, on a gut level, with the fact that the breakdowns we see around us are signals of incipient breakthrough.

Deep within every one of us—imbedded in our animal-body, encapsulated within our birth chart—is the knowledge that we incarnated into this time in order to play a role in this mortal drama. Some of us go through our lives more or less insensible to this knowledge; others quicken to it and let it lead them. The goal of the seeker should be to tune into this role, commit to it, and pump energy into people, ideas and activities that match it. Opportunities to do so are planted here and there, with utterly purposeful serendipity, as we proceed along our path. When we make it our business to keep an eye out for these myriad clues, living in the moment turns into a delightful game—playful and dead-serious at once: a great treasure hunt. The treasure is self-awareness. The hunt is Life itself.

WHAT IS ASTROLOGY?

This Appendix is not an attempt to teach astrology. It is intended as a tool for those unfamiliar with astrology, to help them make sense of this book. For these readers and also for those already conversant, I will first say a few words about the philosophy behind modern astrology and the particular approach this book takes to it, addressing a few widely held misconceptions in the process. Explanations of basic astrological terms used in the book will follow. Those interested in more substantive reading on this vast subject may refer to the Bibliography on Page 216.

What is astrology? Or to put it another way: Why on Earth should we look at the sky to find out about ourselves?

To paraphrase Carl Jung's paraphrasing of ancient wisdom: *Every thing born at a particular time and place bears the qualities of that time and place.* Astrology is predicated on the assumption that the meaning of a life—that of a person, a country, a business, a relationship—can be deduced from the context into which that life arose into being. And to describe that context, we use the sky as a reference point. Why use the sky? Because the interplay of various planetary cycles has been found to have the qualities of a clock: an astoundingly intricate, mysteriously precise clock. Astrology has organized the workings of this clock into symbolic patterns, from which we can infer meanings about "what time it is".

What Astrology Is Not and What It Is

Newcomers are often intrigued by but wary of astrology, seeing it as a spooky hieroglyphic language that is rumored to have an inside scoop—reductionist but somehow magically authoritative—on who they are. There is also a fear that the astrologer will read the future in their chart, and tell them things they don't want to know. It is true that before it was embraced by the human potential movement and returned to its roots as a tool of consciousness, astrology was all about making predictions; and some schools of astrology still make them. But it is this astrologer's view that our chart doesn't tell us what we are going to do; it only tells us why.

Most astrological thinking in the contemporary Western world is strongly influenced by psychology and ancient spiritual philosophies. In this approach, which is shared by the writer, the *native* (the person whose chart is being cast)—not "Fate"—is seen as the star and the director of the show. Interested readers will want to acquaint themselves with the tenets of humanistic astrology as laid out in the writings of Dane Rudhyar[1].

Responsibility Begins and Ends with the Native

Most contemporary astrology places the emphasis not on the external realities that line up with planetary movements, but with the consciousness changes in the native that such movements symbolize. Consciousness changes and external realities, both, are understood to take place because of a teamwork we enter into with the cosmos: if we learn something, it is because we participate as part of that team. Without pro-activity on our part, it won't happen. The gods help those who help themselves, and so do the planets.

We cannot read someone's chart and guarantee that they will understand and benefit from the planetary lesson that is coming their way; and we cannot look at an astrological chart and tell what is going to happen—as if the outside world had it all secretly planned out. It is a given in metaphysics, no less than in the New Physics, that there is no such thing as an objective, absolute truth about anyone or anything. Reality exists only as relative to the observer (called in some divinatory practices the *querent*); and the more fully the observer can take responsibility for the dramas in his life, the faster his consciousness can change.

Though the planets can teach us, they can't make us learn. Celestial cycles don't cause us to do or be or know anything, because they do not have agency. They simply announce themes, which can, if read with discernment, become lessons for individuals and humanity at large; and they specify when those lessons are going to be taught. If astrology disappoints those who expect more than this, call it an occupational hazard. Meanwhile, instead of entertaining ourselves with parlor games or wasting time defending specifics and literalisms astrology is incapable of providing, I propose we make use of what astrology *is* capable of doing: de-coding these themes for those who wish to understand.

---

[1] Dane Rudhyar was the great mind behind this early-20th-century breakthrough in astrology, which took Carl Jung's idea of the shadow, among other new theories, and used it to redeem old fear-based notions that had kept astrology mired in medieval gloom. Rudhyar unbound an earlier astrology from its literalistic straightjacket by means of new insights about the unconscious mind, which he recast in a spiritual perspective. The reader is encouraged to read anything she can get her hands on by this sublime thinker. See the Bibliography.

Using Astrology with Understanding

Let us take a moment to consider a few of the metaphysical premises underlying the astrological approach taken by this book.

There are myriad different ways of using astrology. Both skeptics and masters in the field will readily agree that it is not an exact science; it is a fluid, subtle symbolic system with interpretive results as varied as those who practice it. How does one begin to get a grasp on astrological symbolism? What steps might the serious astro-phile take to begin to understand the goings-on in a chart?

The first step is to realize that we modern thinkers have absorbed certain intellectual and philosophical assumptions through cultural conditioning—a couple of which we will have to question if we want to use the part of our intelligence that can fathom astrological truths.

The Reality of the Non-Physical: One such assumption is that a thing has to be physical to qualify as real. In the modern worldview, especially as espoused in American society, intangible and invisible energies are generally seen to be something other than, and less than, real—figments and fancies. It is believed that something is real only if we can measure it, feel it, see it, taste it, smell it or hear it. In what is called "scientific thought"[2] it is presupposed that the realm of matter has greater validity than the other realms. But this is not the way life has been viewed everywhere and always.

Astrology, like many other ancient philosophies, divides all experience down into four utterly equal parts—matter, thought, emotion and spirit. Only one of them—matter—has anything to do with physicality. In other words, astrologers grant no special credibility to something just because it possesses visibility, weight and three dimensions. Indeed, metaphysicians tend to consider manifested form (earth) to be the Johnny-come-lately of the elemental foursome. Physical things are believed to arise out of ideas (air) and sparks of impulse (fire). And water trumps them all: the water element is the universal solvent, the aboriginal matrix that underlies everything in the universe. Matter (earth) is the last to join the party.

So this is the first conceptual leap. Whether we are looking at a planetary symbol in an individual chart or a group chart, we will not be able to grasp its meaning within the shuttered purview of mechanistic

---

[2] But a remarkable divide has arisen between what most people think of as "scientific thinking," on the one hand, and the theories contemporary scientists are actually coming up with, on the other. As discussed in Chapter Four, though the New Physics has dramatically refuted many of the notions of Newtonian physics, the "modern" world doggedly holds to its assumptions about causality and the objective reality of matter as if they were the latest word on the nature of existence.

materialism. To undertake a meaningful study of that symbol is to challenge every assumption we ever had about the supremacy of physical matter.

Cause and Effect: Cause-and-effect thinking is something else we must temporarily set aside if we want to understand how astrology works. The truth is that events are not *made to happen* because heavenly bodies occupy certain angles and placements in the sky. Difficult as it is for the modern mind to fathom any other mode of operation, celestial influences cannot be explained this way. Nor do planetary transits compel behavior by means of vibrational emanations from the physical rocks and gas balls that orbit the Sun; nor because there are supernatural beings up among the clouds whose job it is to bestow curses and blessings upon us.

Transits affect us because of our own mysterious connection with the cosmic principles that the planets represent. The planets stand for universal laws, which can, if read with discernment, teach us about the true nature of existence. Their transiting placements specify when these teachings are going to be strongest and in what ways they are likely to be expressed.

This is a pivotal point of understanding—one that many aficionados of astrology fail to make, and that even many serious astrologers slip in and out of. But it must be stated up front that without this understanding, it is impossible to pursue astrology with our psychological freedom intact.

As Above, So Below

Those readers who know the work of Carl Jung will find relatively familiar the astrological idea that each of us is born with an "inner sky": an innate template of the various symbols and their meanings. We are, after all, part of the system. Though we tend to forget it, humans are ingredients in the universe; and whether we realize it or not we go by the universe's rules. Somewhere within our beings there is a library that stores astrological laws. The outer sky—the actual solar system—merely mirrors our inner sky back to us[3].

When asked to explain the relationship between *what's going on up there* in the heavens and *what's going on down here* on Earth, most astrologers are tempted to simplify things by talking about the impact the planets have upon human life. But, again, this is misleading. The idea of an *inner* and an *outer sky* in mutual reflection is trickier to grasp, but it's closer to the truth of how astrology works. This dynamic is succinctly

---

[3] See Steven Forrest's classic *The Inner Sky.*

summed up in the ancient maxim *As above, So Below*, sometimes called Hermetic Law or The Law of Correspondences.

The physical planets are no more than markers, like the hands of a clock. We don't impute agency to the clock on our desk *("The clock made me do it!")*; and neither does it make any make sense to impute agency to the clock-like system in the sky—no matter how far away it is, and no matter how subtle and manifold its moving parts.

Inborn Knowing

The Jungian view of the human mind holds that archetypes such as those to which the planets refer are inborn: they are understandings that are universal to human experience. They already reside within us, as spiritual and occult traditions worldwide have iterated since time immemorial. The key is already in our pocket; the ruby slippers are already on our feet; the kingdom of heaven is already within us. In the same way that the act of plucking a guitar string does not create music out of nowhere—the music was already in the strings and is released when we pluck them—the study of astrological symbols is less an acquisition of knowledge than a triggering of something we know on a cellular level.

In attempting to "release the music" of Mars, for example, we can begin by looking up the planet's *mundane rulerships* in an astrology book. These are compiled lists of everyday phenomena that have been assigned to each planet by astrological tradition. We might read, for example, that "Mars *governs* war, iron and the color red." Or that Venus governs honey, the arts and the color pink. Such lists are random samplings, neither exhaustive nor definitive. Yet they serve to point us in the direction of the meaning of a planet, just as metaphors and analogies point us towards meaning in poetry. We may find that reading these planetary associations awakens something in us.

Reading that Saturn governs glue, frames, scaffolding and rocks, for example, may prompt an inner recognition on the visceral level with that unnamed essential *something* that unifies glue, frames, scaffolding and rocks, and of which they are all symptomatic: a truth more meaningful than the sum of the four items themselves. Knowing the mundane rulerships helps us to get in touch with something underneath the words and concepts: to find the common thread, and thereby get a sense of its essence.

ASTROLOGICAL TERMINOLOGY

Although astrologers try their best to avoid simplistic descriptions for the planets and signs—Goddess knows, trying to encapsulate into a few words the meaning of a richly layered archetype is like trying to play Beethoven's Ninth on a toy harmonica—in the interests of practicality, an abbreviated rundown of basic astrological terms is offered below. Hopefully this glimpse will inspire non-astrologers to further research elsewhere. It may also provide a review for longtime students and give them a sense of how certain familiar terms are meant in the context of this book.

ASTRO 101

Let us begin by proposing that the **birth chart** is our life script (the playwright of which is the soul, or the Higher Self). The ten **planets**[1] are the actors in the play, and the **signs** they are in are the roles being played.
Where the birth time is known, the planets are placed against the backdrop of twelve segments of the sky—the **houses**—each of which is a stage of the action. Finally, the **aspects**—key geometrical angles between the planets—can be understood as the main plots and subplots in the script.

The **astrologer**'s job is to discern how these components interact to tell a story, and then to translate that story into communicable terms.

Astrological Charts

An astrological chart (a.k.a. wheel of planets, or *horoscope* [literally, *pointer-to-the-hour*]) is a schematic rendering of the dome of the sky, which shows where the planets were located at a given moment from a specific latitude and longitude. Divided into twelve sections like a pie, the wheel designates the Earth's horizon, the placements of planets above it and below it, the signs they were in and meaningful angular relationships between them. See Page 220 for an example.

---

[1] For horoscope interpretation purposes, these include the two *Lights*: the Sun and the Moon; as well as Pluto—whose recent reclassification is discussed in the footnote on Page 13.

A Natal Chart (a.k.a. birth chart) is a map of an entity's life purpose laid out in coded language. It is derived from the arrangement of planets at the exact time the entity was born or brought into being[2] from the vantage point of the exact place of its birth.

A birth chart reveals the potential genius[3] of the entity born (*native*): its inborn talents and strengths, as well as the areas where its growth trajectory tends to get stuck. In the chart we see what the entity's inner resources are, what it has to work with. We get hints about the nature and direction of its development. From this we infer its soul purpose or *dharma*.

Transit and Progressed Charts: Astrology also addresses the potential unfolding of that life purpose, phase by phase, by drawing up a comparison between the birth chart and the placements of the planets at any given time *after* the birth. These charts of *transits* and *progressions* are based on the natal chart.

In this way astrology reveals not only our life path, but pinpoints where we are upon it. Though the natal chart does not change—which is to say, our potential does not change—our development does. This is reflected in the fact that those planets whose positions are set down at birth do not stay in those same positions up there in the sky: they keep on moving; and as they proceed through their cycles they give clues as to what turning points and growth phases the native will encounter.

Group Charts: As is clear from the subject of this book, non-human entities like countries can have charts too[4]. To the extent that an

---

[2] Much can be gleaned from the date and year, but when we know the hour and minute, too, our interpretation can be all the more precise.

[3] The original meaning of *genius* starts to make sense when we remember that the ancient world believed the unique skills and understandings of human beings to be divinely bestowed, not mere accidents of personality.

[4] In the case of individuals, most Western astrologers use the baby's first breath—its first act of independence from the mother—to mark of the birth moment, but the analogous "first breath" of a nation is a rather more elusive call. There is often extensive debate among practitioners as to what constitutes the historical birth of the country in question.

I use the Sibly version of the USA chart, which is based on July 4th, 1776 5:10 pm* This date finds widespread acceptance among astrologers--no less than among celebrators of America's national holiday--deriving as it does from the national founders' official declaration of independence from its mother-state, England. Still, the issue remains a subject of contention, especially as regards the birth hour (see, for example, *Political Astrology* by Michael O'Reilly).

* The version of the chart used by Dane Rudhyar, upon which he based his seminal study *The Astrology of America's Destiny* (Vintage Books 1974), uses a 5:13 pm birth time.

entity arises into being at a certain place and time, it has a natal chart; and from this an astrologer can infer a life purpose, strengths, challenges and karmic lessons to be learned. Transits and progressions to this chart will indicate trajectories of development that are peculiar to the entity, as they do in the case of an individual. This book focuses on the natal chart and the transits (rather than the progressions) of the chart of the USA.

The Planets

Planetary cycles have been used to mark time ever since humans first looked up into the night sky. The universal archetypes represented by the planets[5] have multiple layers of meaning, the most commonly referenced of which are summarized below.

The Sun is the native's life purpose. In the case of a country's chart, we will consider it as the national spirit: the country's reason for being. Ideally, the Sun is the sovereign of the chart[6] around which everything else in the chart coheres.

The Moon: The Moon in a personal chart represents our feelings and security issues. Traditionally associated with The People of a nation[7], we might call the Moon the emotional tenor of the public; the mass mood.

Mercury is the communicative function. In a group chart it governs the media, the popular intelligence, language issues and ideas in currency.

---

[5] Until very recently in human history, astrological observation of planetary cycles was limited to the seven planets in the solar system that could be seen with the naked eye; the three most distant planets--Uranus, Neptune and Pluto--were integrated only after the invention of telescope. This aligns with the Law of Correspondences, which tells us that when humanity is ready to become conscious of something, the planetary symbol that represents it "appears" in the sky (that is, it is uncovered or "*dis*covered").

That said, it is this astrologer's opinion that the sublime understandings represented by the three outer planets were probably known to shamans and seers in every age, even before the planets were charted; whether through astronomical calculation, such as those of the astoundingly sophisticated MezoAmerican mathematicians, or through psychic vision.

[6] In the days when it was believed that kings were incarnated into position by divine right, the Sun in a country's chart was seen as signifying the actual monarch--a traditionalism that is perhaps not as anachronistic as it might seem, especially in the case of a putative democracy where the executive acts more like a king than a public servant.

[7] Mundane astrology, which focuses on predicting events, assigns specific meanings to the planets, signs and houses which diverge in significant ways from the meanings assigned by popular astrology. Though there is an overlap, the terms in this book do not reflect strict mundane usage.

Venus is the feminine function: the native's relationship life, aesthetics and ways of seeking pleasure. In the national chart it encompasses collective values such as attitudes towards art, marriage and recreation, as well as alliances with other countries.

Mars is the masculine function: our aggressive urges and primal desire nature. Its collective meaning is the self-serving impulses of the group, whose darker face is war.

Jupiter, which rules education, religion and ideologies of all kinds, represents not just knowledge but the impulse to increase and expand. It governs the judicial system and collective ethics.

Saturn represents the structures that limit and enclose an entity: laws, inhibitions, authority figures, boundaries, fear of failure. It governs a country's borders, its executive government and patriarchal figures.

Uranus is the planet of revolution. It governs the urge to individuate, to break rank, to usher in ideas whose time has come. In both individuals and countries, it functions to disrupt the status quo.

Neptune is the planet of the undifferentiated All-That-Is, which exerts a pull from beneath conscious awareness. It has been linked to the dream state, the imagination, the Muse, the sense of higher calling. In the national chart it represents deep collective yearnings, which when misunderstood lead to mass confusion, credulity, and conformity.

Pluto is the planet of breakdown and renewal: recycling in all its forms, including destruction and makeovers. In both individuals and groups, it involves the operation of unseen forces and the expenditure of raw power.

The Twelve Signs

The signs of the tropical zodiac[8] derive from the astronomical relationship between the Sun and the Earth. Each sign is identified by its element (fire, earth, air or water) and mode (cardinal, fixed or mutable).

Aries is the first sign of the zodiac, which is the most telling thing about it. Like an eager newborn, it is the spark of life that sets off the whole cycle of signs. It is *out for number one*: a sharp, vital call to action, direct as a bullet from a gun.

Taurus is grounded and solid, the earth which receives the seed. Its genius is its resourcefulness: it understands and appreciates the physical world and its laws, among them the perceptions of the five senses.

---

[8] The tropical zodiac is the one most widely used in Western astrology, by contrast with the sidereal zodiac--used more widely in India--which retains a direct relationship with the spatial constellations.

Gemini is the quick mental energy that drives thinking and information systems. The twins that symbolize this sign represent multiplicity, making this the sign of variety, diversification, connection-making and changes of opinion.

Cancer is a water sign, sensitive and deeply personal in its frames of reference. Its job is to shelter, protect and nurture itself and its environment; its focus is the establishment of emotional security.

Leo exists to express the self in all its creative singularity. Sunny and intense, it uses the world as a stage for its performance, exuding heat and light and modeling joie-de-vivre for others.

Virgo is a detail-oriented sign whose function is to align that which is in disarray. Careful and acutely perceptive, it strives for accuracy in the ordering of systems through the use of pragmatic analysis.

Libra is the awareness of the Self-Other dynamic, wherever it exists: from personal relationships to social justice issues. Both sides of a given polarity are weighed and compared, and balance is sought.

Scorpio is the urge to merge. Psychologically knowing, it traffics in the unspoken energies that exist between entities that are invisibly bonded. It intuits truths beneath the surface.

Sagittarius is a passionate, restless fire sign whose trajectory is out and up, like an arrow shot through the air. It seeks ever-broader fields of action and ever-more-encompassing truths.

Capricorn is a sober earth sign that understands responsibility and effort. Self-contained and authoritative, it weds practicality to maturity of purpose. Its genius is an understanding of karma.

Aquarius is the sign of the individualized human being who moves the larger group forward into the future, by embodying a unique vision and pledging allegiance to it whether or not it is popular, acceptable or even understandable to the group.

Pisces is the least ego-driven of the signs, encompassing as it does the energies of all the others. The full range of humanity's pooled experience through the ages exists within the Piscean sensibility: a vast reservoir that can be used either to inspire, get lost in or surrender to.

The Twelve Houses

The houses are the twelve slices the chart wheel is divided into, based on the Sun's daily movement. Very broadly speaking, the meanings of the twelve houses link up with the twelve signs; but are not so much elemental energies as situational fields of activity that serve as settings for the planet(s) within them.

The houses derive from the four angles, which can be understood, for the sake of our study, to have the following meanings:

The **Ascendant**, which is established from an exact birth time, is the outer shell of the native. The sign it is in is called the **Rising Sign**.

The **Midheaven** or M.C. (*Median Coli*) denotes the native's position in the outer world; the societal role and reputation.

The **Descendant** refers to the native's relationships, and to the side of the native that comes out in relationships; the way we view peers, friend or foe.

The **Nadir** or I.C. (*Imum Coli*) refers to the foundation of one's life and consciousness; the past; ancestry, home and family.

The **first house** refers to outer-directed self-expression, making the qualities in question particularly obvious (physical appearance, self-image, how the native initially comes across).

The **second house** is concerned with resources, often but not exclusively material ones, teaching lessons of value and ownership (possessions, business and territory).

The **Third house** involves the native in activities that have to do with the intake, processing and output of information (schools, offices, the media).

The **fourth house** encompasses personal and domestic life, early childhood and old age, and issues of roots (real estate, history, tribal and racial genealogy).

Fifth house activities include recreations and artistic expression, as well as gambling and other rituals based on risk (speculation, having children).

The **sixth house** is associated primarily with paid or unpaid work, duties and healing (labor issues, the health and service industries).

The **seventh house** is about the meeting of one entity with another in some kind of team, whether contractual or through unconscious projection (rivalries, agreements, marriage, alter-egos and "evil twins").

The **eighth house** teaches how to use the fruits of some kind of union (sexual, material or corporate mergers; taxes); as well as the suspension of individual consciousness (death, breakdowns).

The **ninth house** has to do with mind expansion, ethics and reform, and the institutions that purport to promote these (higher learning, religion, the justice system, publishing, long-distance travel and foreign entities).

The **tenth house** relates to settings of maximal public visibility and societal role (the official face of a government, the career persona of a person).

The **eleventh house** refers to organizations, clubs and groups of all kinds: individuals operating as members of some larger campaign (social movements; political parties; the human race seen as a species).

The **twelfth house** hints of past deeds to be redeemed and spiritual lessons to be learned (prisons, hospitals, ashrams and retreats, charity work). It has been described as a repository of the accumulated karma of the group: the collective unconscious.

Aspects

Astrological **aspects** are meaningful geometric angels between planets[9] and groups of planets that reveal relationships between the different components of the psyche. We will look at only the most commonly used major aspects here.

The **conjunction** represents an angle of more or less[10] 0 degrees of arc between one planet and another, or a planet and the Ascendant, Midheaven, etc. Planets that were overlapping in the sky at the time of birth will be placed right next to each other in the erected chart. Conjunctions fuse the meaning of the two planets together, pronouncing and strengthening each.

Sextiles are 60-degree angles between planets, denoting the possibility of a productive energy flow.

Squares are 90-degree angles, where the bodies in question are at cross-purposes: a challenging aspect suggestive of the need for adjustment in order to ease the tension.

Trines are 120-degree angles suggestive of harmony and flow. The planets thus connected support one another.

---

[9] This very abbreviated treatment leaves out non-planetary components of an astrological chart such as asteroids, nodes, points and fixed stars.

[10] The orb allowance—that is, by how many degrees a trine, for example, may diverge from exactly 120 degrees and still be called a trine—differs widely, depending on the aspect involved (narrower aspects like sextiles are allowed a smaller orb; oppositions and conjunctions are allowed a larger orb); the planets involved (outer planets are allowed less of an orb—e.g. an aspect between Neptune and a Pluto that was five degrees off would be considered by many astrologers too far apart to qualify; while the Sun, Moon, Ascendant and Midheaven may be given eight to ten degrees); and the presence of mitigating factors (such as other aspects and planetary configurations of which the aspect under consideration can be considered a part). All that taken into consideration, five or six degrees away from exactitude is the general rule.

Oppositions are formed between planets oriented across the chart from one another at more-or-less 180 degrees, like a tug-of-war within the psyche. They involve the native in situations where two extremes are in tense equipoise. Integration and resolution come from the realization that the two poles are both facets of the self.

APPENDIX II

Saturn and Pluto through the Twelve Houses

Using this Appendix

In order to try on for size the ideas proposed in Chapters Thirteen and Fourteen, readers will need to know what particular areas of life showcase their Pluto and Saturn lessons; now that we have looked at these areas in general terms, they will be able to see how they apply to them in their own lives. In order to know this, they will need to know where these planets reside in their own natal charts. At that point they can look up their placements in the following guides. (Those readers who work with transits will find that the following delineations may apply to the current placements of Saturn and Pluto, too, as they move through the chart, specifying where these lessons are being taught right now.) Readers who do not have their natal charts will need to have one cast. A free chart or *horoscope* can be downloaded from the web (e.g. at http://www.astro.com or http://www.alabe.com). Or, even better, they can have one erected by a real astrologer—and receive a full, in-depth interpretation.

A natal chart is not really something you can interpret with books and computer printouts alone; all these can do is describe the pieces that make up the whole. We may start this way, accessing the disparate data, and soon find that the blending of all the pieces into a meaningful whole requires more than patchwork analysis. Astrology begins with geometry and ends up with a kind of magic. A good astrologer will have studied the rules of this marvelously intricate and symmetrical system (and with the kind of rigor that may strain the patience of many in a culture conditioned to instant information), and will then use his intuition to let a holistic meaning come together in front of him–almost as if it were arising from the page.

Readers are encouraged to invite this kind of intuitive process to occur when looking up their planetary placements in the lists below.

SATURN'S NATAL PLACEMENTS

For the sake of brevity and because of the parallelism that exists between the twelve houses and the twelve signs, this appendix has blended the sign/house delineations for Saturn. However, most readers' Saturns will have natal house placements that differ from the corresponding sign; so it is best to know the planet's sign and house placement, both (and, even more ideally, its transiting position too), all of which can then be referenced below.

Saturn spends a couple of years in each *sign*; so everybody born within a two-and-a-half-year-long sub-generation will share, in a general sense, the same set of issues regarding responsibility and maturity. Against the backdrop of this shared theme, the *house* that Saturn is in describes a more precisely individuated layer of the psyche than the sign does, rounding out the picture with information about where the native's specific challenges are likely to take place. Saturn's *transiting* house placement shows in what areas of the native's life certain lessons in responsibility are being imposed for the roughly two-and-a-half-year-long period the native is in right now.

The native with **Saturn in Aries or in the First House** has a particularly direct experience with being a grown-up. In this placement, the persona itself exudes adulthood; and the responsibility of just showing up can feel daunting. One must construct and maintain an identity with which to face the challenges of everyday life, and be a role model for the inescapable truth that life's inherent responsibilities are not to be taken personally—they *just are*.

Saturn in Taurus or in the Second House demonstrates his adulthood through earning—not just money, but in the slow, respectful development of personal values. Getting something for nothing feels like a cheat to this native. By building and maintaining resources like a responsible adult, he cultivates his own character and shows those around him what maturity looks like.

Those with **Saturn in Gemini or in the Third House** may have to work harder where schooling and communication are concerned than others in their educational phase (or so it may seem to these natives), but this work is their training in maturity. These folks are the very ones who may end up with rock-solid reservoirs of information and skills of self-expression, conveying to the rest of us how to say what we mean and back up what we say.

Natives with **Saturn in Cancer or in the Fourth House** know instinctively that accountability is built into every aspect of a parent's role, and into every act of nurturing—even that of keeping a houseplant alive. They take security issues very seriously, so much so that they must learn to distinguish between their fear of abandonment and their appropriate concerns about protection. Once they understand the difference, they become a wise parent figure for others.

Saturn in Leo or in the Fifth House teaches maturity through the experience of going on stage, figuratively speaking—sometimes literally too—as in the case of a dedicated artist who trains hard and long to achieve mastery of performance. For these natives, to take responsibility is to dare to express their unique talents before some kind of audience: to show up, in the moment, and display themselves without withholding.

The native with **Saturn in Virgo or in the Sixth House** learns maturity by mastering his fear of making mistakes, and by patiently learning to align systems that are out of alignment, such as his daily schedule or his own physical body. Dealing with the logistical snafus of life and human error are meant to humble this native's perfectionism while teaching him the importance of craft and technique.

For those with **Saturn in Libra or the Seventh House**, relationships are meant to be entered into with a deliberate sense of commitment. The native may attract mature partners, too, but the core teaching is to cultivate his own mature relating skills. Contracts and agreements of all kinds are taken seriously, for they are the testing ground. The key teachings here are to understand the phenomenon of mirroring, and to transcend blame.

With **Saturn in Scorpio or in the Eighth House** there may be a resistance to intimacy, and other more tangible mergers; a resistance that involves the self or the partner shutting down somehow—signaling the need to plumb a sensitive area which may be taboo (the eighth house is associated with Pluto) not only with the native herself but in the culture at large. The teaching is to watch the impulse and take responsibility for it, per the one-two-three steps of Pluto Work (Chapter Fourteen).

Saturn in Sagittarius or in the Ninth House teaches maturity by forcing the native to undertake his quest for higher learning in a strikingly independent way: there is a good reason why easy answers to the big questions of life are not immediately forthcoming, or are resisted when they are. By trying on a succession of different viewpoints and using only what fits, he becomes a model for others of responsible scholarship and philosophical search.

Saturn in Capricorn or in the Tenth House offers the native a slow, steady trajectory towards achievement, in the course of which her society's notions of success need to be measured against her own inner values. Maturity comes from building a reputation in the group of which she is a part; whether her authority is personified by the native herself or projected upon someone else (as happens when, for example, cultural injunctions keep a woman from public prominence).

Saturn in Aquarius or in the Eleventh House teaches that friendships and working in groups can be difficult, a realization that turns towards mastery when the native realizes that such things are not supposed to be easy. By facing the realities of these interchanges head-on, with patience and authority, he grows into his adulthood and becomes a natural leader.

Saturn in Pisces or in the Twelfth House insists that responsibility be somehow taken for the subtle realm beneath consciousness awareness, whose poignant impulses are tricky to pin to a source. This haunted part of the psyche—the dream state, the past-life reservoir, or call it *the unconscious mind*—is the stage upon which life's sobering duties must be acknowledged, accepted, and worked through.

PLUTO'S HOUSE PLACEMENTS

Pluto by Sign vs. by House

The sign natal Pluto is in has a different significance from its house position, which has more of a personal relevance. Given that this planet takes two-and-a-half centuries on average to pass through all twelve signs, its tenure in each sign tells us more about a whole generation's issues than about the specific ways in which those issues will play out in the life of the native. For the purpose of applying to the reader's own chart the ideas discussed in Chapter Fourteen, Pluto's house placements are listed below. These delineations, like the ones above for Saturn, may also be used by those familiar with their transits to understand the current arenas where Pluto Work is most appropriate.

Pluto in the **first house** is maximally apparent, its intensity often showing up in the native's eyes. Here it is the person's "look" that projects power: there may be immediate evidence in the wardrobe/adornment, or facial scars, of his having gone "through hell and back". The engine of the Pluto Work will be the native's own personality.

Pluto in the **second house** manifests as a need to go to extremes financially, at least in one's attitudes. The native (e.g. the USA itself) understands raw power in terms of resources owned, and can potentially transform itself through the use of territory.

In the **third house**, Pluto puts its make-or-break energy into the act of communication. The pen is far mightier than the sword; the spoken word could be developed to the level of invocation. Pluto here may inspire the native to channel profound social change where education and media are concerned. Siblings and neighbors may be a source of transformation.

A **fourth-house** Pluto often shows up as an intensely complex relationship with the natal family, particularly with one of the parents; by extension, with housemates. Themes of destruction and redemption may play out through tribal and racial identity. The native may be prompted to ask deep questions that may heal generations.

Pluto in the **fifth house** may make children a source of life-and-death teachings. Creative performance of any kind is likely to have an all-or-nothing undercurrent. Romantic liaisons can be possessed of a mythic drama, for such pursuits, as well as any and all recreations, are for this native areas of self-regeneration.

With Pluto in the **sixth house**, the native is driven to dig beneath conventional attitudes towards work and health. There may be an insurrectionary pattern as regards everyday regimens; an instinctive understanding of holistic health; a key role to play in the remodeling of the work environment.

In the **seventh house**, Pluto plays itself out in one-to-one relationships, which may be charged with power plays and characterized by seemingly fated beginnings and/or drastic endings. The drive to transform the self through union ideally leads to conscious merger rather than enmeshment. Teamwork may trigger profound changes in society.

In the **eighth house**, Pluto is at home. Investigations into secrets of all kinds are charged with a drive that may seem extreme from the point of view of societal norms. There may be a fascination with death, sexuality, psychological breakdown and renewal. Cravings that may arise need to be seen within a transpersonal context in order to avoid waxing self-destructive.

A **ninth-house** Pluto intensifies knowledge-seeking, whether it is religious, academic, philosophical or ethical. Beliefs may "die" through a dramatic repudiation, after which the native is reborn ideologically. There may be life-altering experiences with foreign people and places, and deep impulses towards social reform.

In the **tenth house**, Pluto combines behind-the-scenes power with officially-sanctioned authority, as in the case of a psychic healer who goes professional, or a shadowy presidential adviser. The career trajectory may be fraught with themes of dominance and control, or the native may end up working with power quite literally (e.g. for an gas-&-electric company). She may make herself over from scratch professionally at least once in her lifetime.

An **eleventh house** Pluto puts power dynamics into group activities such as friendships and collegial or team relationships. The native may be drawn to organizations on the threshold of decay, therein to play a role in their renaissance. There may be involvement in social movements whose goals are deeply threatening to the culture at large.

The **twelfth** is the most inscrutable house, especially suggestive of motives and drives that cannot be explained by the circumstances of the current lifetime. Prisons, spiritual retreats or hospitals may provide the setting for transformative change; the native's dreams or imaginative life may be rich in underworld symbolism. Powerful unconscious energies are there to be confronted, healed and, ideally, tapped—in ways that reveal the merger of the native's own karma with that of the collective.

Bibliography

Books on Astrology

Beginner and Intermediate:

Alli, A.
   1990. *Astrologik*. Seattle, Washington: Vigilantero Press.

Arroyo, S.
   1975. *Astrology, Psychology and the Four Elements*. Davis, California: CRCS Publications.

Oken, A.
   1980. *Alan Oken's Complete Astrology: The Classic Trilogy*. New York: Bantam Books.

Elwell, D.
   1987. *Cosmic Loom*. London: Unwin Hyman.

Forrest, S.
   1984. *The Inner Sky*, New York: Bantam Books.

Greene, L..
   1976. *Saturn*. New York: Samuel Weiser.
   ---.
   1978. *Relating*. York Beach, Maine: Samuel Weiser
   ---.
   1983. *The Outer Planets & Their Cycles: The Astrology of the Collective*. Davis, California: CRCS Publications.

Hand, R.
   1981.*Horoscope Symbols*. Rockport, Massachusetts: ParaResearch.

Jones, M. E.
   1941 and 1969. *The Guide to Horoscope Interpretation*. Wheaton, Illinois: Quest/Theosophical Publishing House.

Spiller, J.
   1997. *Astrology for the Soul*. New York: Bantam Books.

Wickenburg, J.
   1981. *A Journey Through the Birth Chart*: Search Publications.

Intermediate and Advanced:

Arroyo, S.
   1978. *Astrology, Karma & Transformation*. Davis, California: CRCS.

Arroyo, S. and L. Greene.
   1984. *The Jupiter/Saturn Conference Lectures*. Davis, California:
CRCS.

Meyer, M. R.
   1974. *A Handbook for the Humanistic Astrologer*. Garden City, New
York: Anchor Books.

O'Reilly, M.
   2005. *Political Astrology: How to Make Accurate Forecasts Using the
Scorpio-Rising U.S.Horoscope*. Livermore, California: WingSpan Press.

Rudhyar, D.
   1936. *The Astrology of Personality: A Reinterpretation of Astrological
Concepts and Ideals in Terms of Contemporary Psychology and
Philosophy*. Wassenaar: Netherlands Lucis Publishing; Servire/ 1963
(Doubleday Paperback edition distributed by Shambala Booksellers,
Berkeley, California 1970).
   ---.
   1963. *The Pulse of Life*. The Hague, Netherlands: Servire/ *Astrological
Signs: the pulse of life*.1978. Boulder & London: Shambhala.
   ---.
   1972. *The Astrological Houses*. Sebastopol, California:CRCS.
   ---.
   1975. *The Astrology of America's Destiny*. New York: Vintage Books.
   ---.
   1976 and 1980. *Person Centered Astrology*. New York: Aurora Press.
   ---.
   1978. *The Practice of Astrology*. Boulder & London: Shambhala.
   ---.
   1979. *Astrological Insights into the Spiritual Life*. New York: Aurora
Press.

Tarnas, R.
  1991. *The Passion of the Western Mind*. New York: Harmony Books.
  ---.
  2006. *Cosmos and Psyche: Intimations of a New World*. Viking Press.

PSYCHOLOGICAL AND SPIRITUAL CONSCIOUSNESS:

Eisler, R,
  1987.*The Chalice & The Blade*. San Francisco: HarperCollins.

Harvey, A., M. Matousek.
  1994. *Dialogues with a Modern Mystic*. Wheaton, Illinois: Quest
Books, Theosophical Publishing House.

Hillman, J.
  1977. *Re-visioning Psychology*. New York: Harper & Row.

Jung, C. G.
  1967. *Memories, Dreams and Reflections*. London: Fontana/ Random
House.

Noble, V.
  1991. *Shakti Woman*. San Francisco: HarperCollins.

Tolle, E.
  1999, 2004. *The Power of Now*. Novato, California: Namaste
Publishing.
  ---.
  2005. *A New Earth*. New York: Dutton/Penguin Group/ Namaste
Publishing

GLOBAL CONSCIOUSNESS:

Arendt, H,
  1951. *The Origins of Totalitarianism*.

Carroll, J.
2006. *House of War.* Houghton Mifflin.

Enriquez, J.
2006. *The Untied States of America.* Crown Books.

Heinberg, R.
2003. *The Party's Over: Oil, War, and the Fate of Industrial Societies.* New Society Publishers.

Kinzer, S.
2006. *Overthrow: America's Century of Regime Change From Hawaii to Iraq.* Holt/Times.

Lakoff, G.
1997, 2002. *Moral Politics: How Liberals and Conservatives Think.* University of Chicago Press.

Poole, S.
2006. *Unspeak: How Words Become Weapons, How Weapons Become a Message, and How That Message Becomes Reality.* Grove Press.

Slade, G.
2006. *Made to Break: Technology and Obsolescence in America.* Cambridge, Massachusetts: Harvard University Press.

Rampton, S. and J. Stauber
2003. Weapons of Mass Deception: The Uses of Propaganda in Bush's War on Iraq. *Tarcher/Penguin.*

220

Sibly Chart of the USA

USA -- Sibly Chart

Jul 4 1776   5:10 PM LMT
Philadelphia   Pennsylvania
39N57   75W10
Jul 4 1776   22:10:40 GMT
Tropical   Placidus   True Node

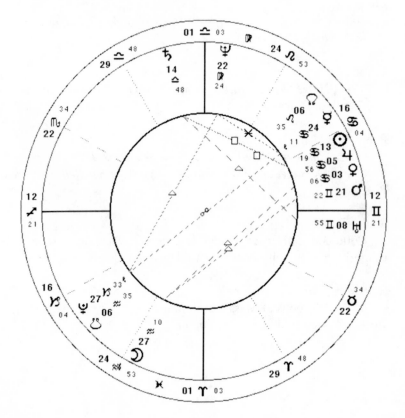

ABOUT THE AUTHOR

Jessica Murray trained as a fine artist before graduating in 1973 from Brown University, where she studied traditional psychology and linguistics. After a stint in political theatre, Jessica began a study of metaphysics and has been practicing and teaching astrology in San Francisco for thirty years.

In addition to her monthly Skywatch column on MotherSky.com, Jessica writes commentary for DayKeeperJournal.com, as well as articles for *The Mountain Astrologer Magazine, Psychic and Spirit Magazine* and other publications. Listen to Jessica's latest interviews with PS-Magazine.com. She is currently working on a book about how to blend spiritual inquiry with social consciousness, using the basic symbols of astrology to respond to what is happening in today's world.

She offers a full range of astrological readings, by appointment on weekdays, in a professional, comfortable setting complete with a pot of fine tea.

Printed in the United States
119250LV00008B/110/P